unto the churches

jesus christ, christianity and the edgar cayce readings

by
Richard H. Drummond, Ph.D.

A.R.E. PRESS • VIRGINIA BEACH • VIRGINIA

ISBN 87604-102-0

Acknowledgements

The articles "Edgar Cayce—Twentieth Century Prophet?" and "Studies in Christian Gnosticism" were previously printed in *Religion In Life*.

Printed in the U.S.A.

CONTENTS

Preface

This book consists of a collection of articles and essays about Edgar Cayce and the material of which he was the channel. The essay on Jesus the Christ, however, so dominates the whole by its length as well as by its intrinsic importance that the title of the book could easily be shortened to *Edgar Cayce on Jesus the Christ*. Indeed, this essay may later appear as a separate publication. Nevertheless, I believe the present collection has a special value in giving both the larger setting and the personal background of the man Edgar Cayce, whereby the primarily contentual material may be the better understood.

Some of the articles have appeared previously in various journals, for which acknowledgment is separately given. The first article, "On Discerning the Times," and the long essay on the Christ were written specifically for this collection. The primary purpose of the whole is to enable the reader to perceive the place and significance of Edgar Cayce in the larger context of his own time (1877-1945) and the present. At the same time, sufficient of the content of the material given through Edgar Cayce is set forth to enable the reader to see the main lines and no little of the details of the world view or religio-cosmic perspectives manifested in this material. The articles entitled "Edgar Cayce, Twentieth-Century Prophet?" and "Edgar Cayce and Divine Providence," as well as the essay on the Christ, are intended to serve this dual purpose. The language of these articles, which were first given as lectures, is retained essentially in the original form.

The article, "Studies in Christian Gnosticism," is a scholarly paper which, of course, needs to be evaluated in terms of its own context and content. It is included in this collection, however, because it represents research in the history of religions which was in a sense "inspired" by the Cayce readings. That is, I made use of certain hints or suggestive comments in the readings which gave me leads to carry through a program of independent research making use of the ordinary procedures of historical-critical or scientific methodology.

Edgar Cayce is widely known for his contributions in the area of medicine and health. The contents of this book, however, refer to such material and activity only in a very brief way. My chief concern has been with the area of philosophy and religion in the widest sense of both words; I use the adjective "wide" in its superlative form because nothing less could do justice to the vast, cosmic ranges of the Cayce materials.

Who and what Edgar Cayce was will appear with sufficient clarity, I believe, in the article "Edgar Cayce, Twentieth-Century Prophet?" Suffice it to say here that he was a spiritual clairvoyant. Some have called him—rightly, I believe—a practical mystic; rightly, because the deep spirituality of this man—in spite of the vast scope of the materials manifested through him—always remained close to the practical, everyday needs of himself and others. In the above-mentioned article I try to define the nature of the man and his role in the history of Judeo-Christian spirituality. I also discuss there various problems related to methodology and credibility.[1] I hope also that something emerges of what Gina Cerminara has called "the warmth, sincerity, generosity, simplicity of heart and mind" of the man. My own conclusion, however, may properly be stated at this point. I do not hesitate to assign to Edgar Cayce a significant role in the long history of Judeo-Christian spirituality. As for this twentieth century, I would rank him among its greatest spiritual figures. I invite my readers carefully to investigate the data herein given in order to draw their own conclusions.

Richard H. Drummond
University of Dubuque
Theological Seminary
Dubuque, Iowa

---

1. It may be helpful to mention at this point that the basic method which Edgar Cayce used throughout his career was suggested to him by "a noted physician of New York" just after the turn of the century. Edgar Cayce himself recounts this point of fact in his brief address entitled "My Life and Work." Edgar Cayce, *What I Believe* (Virginia Beach, Virginia: A.R.E. Press, 1970), p. 8.

PART I

On Discerning the Times

Part I

1

Perhaps nothing is so difficult and at the same time so necessary as to discern, that is, to understand and evaluate properly, the nature and meaning of one's own time. Most liberally educated persons would contend that such understanding is best achieved in the context of perception of time as a part of the wider sweep of human experience that we call history. In spite of counterclaims, such as Henry Ford's famous dictum that "history is bunk," we may reasonably assume with most knowledgeable persons that the place wherein we now stand is in fact a momentarily identifiable location in a long stream of events or activities; or, to change the figure, a point in a strand of an almost infinitely complex web comprising multitudinous strands, strands which are both mobile and conveyors of energy-intelligence in reciprocal action. That is, we do live in a larger structure called history.

The complexity of the whole militates against easy or obvious perception of patterns of order and meaning. The complexity, which is formidable enough even at a particular focus of time, is compounded when seen in the larger context of that focus point in human history, not to mention cosmic dimensions. Hence, we may rightly speak of the difficulty of discerning the times, of understanding one's own time. And yet, the experience of human beings in appreciably large numbers testifies to the fact that we are in some deep way compelled to make the attempt. The quest for meaning—the meaning of human life as a whole, of our own life in particular, of the cosmos itself—seems to be an ineluctable element of what it is to be human. As Colin Wilson has put it, "Man is more deeply moved by meaning than by accident."

Even if earlier modern science could be said to have hated teleology, or the concept of purpose, there is increasing reason to believe that contemporary science is moving from the investigation of fact or event as cosmic accident to a search for the meaning as well as the characteristics of phenomena. Thus David Foster, the cybernetician, has summed up his own conclusions using the imagery of computerized data processing: "One establishes a new picture of the universe as a digitized universe, an information universe, but I think that because of the strong cybernetical influences at work, I prefer to call it The Intelligent Universe."[1]

There is thus increasing perception, or at least intimations, of the meaning of the Whole; but most people, while inclined to posit such larger significance, are generally more concerned with smaller ones—the meaning of their own time and their own life in that time, and of particular events and experiences within that narrower compass. Almost inevitably, to be sure, the quest for and the attribution of significance in this kind of personal context takes on religious connotations, not least because the ascription of some dimension or aspect of meaning is said by many specialists to constitute an integral element of what we call religion. Meaning of any extent can also be said to have cosmic implications, and even though the conclusions of a scientist like David Foster may be cautiously qualified, the positing of cosmic Intelligence and "programming"—therefore, of purpose—can be called, by reason of the nature of the language used, religious perception as much as scientific speculation. There is no need, therefore, to fear the religious aspects of this quest for meaning.

The purpose of these brief prolegomena has been to give some rationale for an attempt to understand our own time, or at least certain aspects of it. If I may speak of my own participation therein in the first person singular, I was born at the end of World War I, have some memories of the so-called "roaring twenties," retain poignant memories of the Great Depression and the late thirties, and experienced my formative years, including both university and graduate studies as well as military service, during the thirties and forties. Not only for myself, but for almost all persons of somewhat comparable age in the industrial countries of the world, both in the East and the West, one of the most astonishing series of events or developments in our time has been what I shall call here a massive, ultimately worldwide and

---

1. Colin Wilson, *The Occult* (New York: Random House, 1971), pp. 26-29.

obvious—at least it later became obvious—shift in consciousness or mentality and consequent change in life style among large sections of our youth. This was a movement which began in the late fifties, reached a kind of crescendo in the late sixties, and has continued on into the mid-seventies with less flamboyance but perhaps no less power than before.

This shift in consciousness and life style had from the beginning certain manifestations that we may call extreme, such as the hippy movement and those of the flower children and beatniks. Religious dimensions, ranging from Americanized ("hippyized") versions of Zen to the later Children of God and Jesus freaks, were present in the larger movement, also apparently from the beginning. More relaxed and indeed looser modes of living, both personally and corporately, made their appearance. Consciousness-altering drugs emerged in the open in a way evidently never before known in American life, constituting what has been called the use and abuse of psychedelic experience. Strangely enough, the development which seemed to express for many in our culture the extreme dimensions of the movement and indeed caused perhaps the greatest resentments in the widest circles was the young people's practice of letting their hair grow long. It mattered not that in the societies concerned, such as the United States and Japan, over long centuries of their previous histories, men had generally worn their hair long, or at least longer than had become common after World War I. Many, if not most, members of the older generation tended to react to this and related developments as if they were under personal and institutional attack.

This reaction of the older generation, while in some individual cases singularly mindless, was in fact not without some basis. It was a reaction to a protest, for the young were increasingly feeling themselves in opposition to the technocratic, industrial societies of the world and the way those societies were marching to affluence through wars, depressions, and heedless, reckless despoilage of human and natural resources. As Theodore Roszak, who in his book *The Making of a Counter Culture* gave perhaps the ablest depiction of the cultural dynamism of American youth in the 1960s, has written, "For better or worse, most of what is presently happening that is new, provocative, and engaging in politics, education, the arts, social relations (love, courtship, family, community), is the creation either of youth who are profoundly, even fanatically, alienated from the parental generation, or of those who address themselves primarily to the

3

young."[2] There was a veritable psychology of alienation from technocratic societies that were seen to degrade art, demean the imagination, and let war govern the nations—societies, in short, that neglected and often trampled upon humane values.

2

It would be a mistake, of course, to overvalue the importance of the so-called counter culture in the narrow or strict sense of the phrase. The youth who belonged to it in that sense were a minority in any society of the West or East. It did not include the more conservative youth, who were offended by the flamboyance of the movement as well as by the politics of Herbert Marcuse and the psychology of Norman O. Brown. The politically more liberal young people, including members of the New Left, were perhaps unable to take the religious dimensions of Alan Watts or Allen Ginsberg. The militant black youth, for quite different reasons emerging out of their own need for ethnic solidarity, did not comparably participate. But it would be an even greater mistake to wipe off the counter culture in the larger sense as of little or merely passing account.

The counter culture can easily and indeed properly be criticized. As Roszak wrote in the first sentence of the preface to his book, "As a subject of study, the counter culture with which this book deals possesses all the liabilities which a decent sense of intellectual caution would persuade one to avoid like the plague."[3] In spite of the high aspirations for love and beauty, for authentic human life, that permeated almost all segments of the movement, perhaps the most persistent critique that could properly be made is moral. Beatnik Zen lacked the serious ethical dimensions underlying Zen at its best in China or Japan. The quest for new life styles to express more adequately truly humane values at times lacked the elemental sense of moral responsibility for self and others without which love and beauty, or true community, cannot exist.

But the counter culture was in one sense only the tip of an iceberg. It was a perhaps bizarre, certainly often offensive, expression of far deeper and more significant realities. Somewhat oddly expressive of the power of these realities is what came to be the almost total permeation of longer hair styles among all ages and levels of the male population. We are, however, dealing with

---

2. Theodore Roszak, *The Making of a Counter Culture* (Garden City, New York: Doubleday & Co., 1968), p.1.
3. *Ibid.,* p. xi.

4

important changes in the mentality of modern man, changes especially noticeable from the middle of the twentieth century, changes away from the thinking that increasingly came to dominate educated men and women from the beginnings of modern science in the sixteenth and seventeenth centuries. Especially following Isaac Newton's mathematical work—the results of which in no wise altered his own profound spiritual perspectives and concerns—the universe came to be seen as "ordered, predictable, built up of tiny billiard-ball atoms which whirled around in the aether according to immutable laws of cause and effect."[4] This world view increasingly came to hold no place for God, revelation or even human freedom. It was a world view that became more and more rigidly materialistic, however sophisticated its rationale, and therefore nonsupportive of, if not actively hostile to, humane values. One is reminded of the strenuous, and in the late nineteenth century apparently hopeless, efforts of Rudolf Steiner in the German-speaking parts of Europe to turn this sweeping tide of materialism with a forthright affirmation of spiritual realities and values in the universe.[5]

Louis Pauwels and Jacques Bergier have admirably summed up the mental climate which permeated every branch of scientific knowledge at the end of the nineteenth and the beginning of the twentieth centuries—the scientific establishment that at first ruthlessly persecuted Albert Einstein! "The limited nature of the physical structure of the Universe; the non-existence of atoms; restricted sources of fundamental energy; the inability of a mathematical formula to yield more than it already contains; the futility of intuition; the narrowness and absolutely mechanical nature of Man's internal world: these were the things the scientist believed in, and this attitude of mind applied to everything."[6] " 'Philosophy is often much embarrassed,' said Kant, on hearing that his brilliant contemporary Swedenborg had mysteriously become aware of a distant fire at the actual time it was burning, 'when she encounters certain facts which she dare not doubt, yet will not believe for fear of ridicule.' "[7]

It is particularly significant that at this time when the great majority of scientifically trained people "found that fear of

4. Rosalind Heywood, "Notes on Changing Mental Climates," in *Science and ESP*, ed. J.R. Smythies (London: Routledge & Kegan Paul, 1967), p. 48.
5. Rudolf Steiner, *The Course of My Life* (New York: Anthroposophic Press, 1951), *passim*.
6. Louis Pauwels and Jacques Bergier, *The Morning of the Magicians* (New York: Stein and Day, 1964), p. 14.
7. Heywood, *op. cit.*, p. 48.

ridicule, plus their own very reasonable recoil from the seemingly irrational, was more powerful than alleged facts which did not fit into the (then generally accepted) scheme of things," a small number of "adventurous-minded scholars and scientists," mostly from Cambridge University in England, were led to ask some probing questions regarding the basic suppositions of contemporary science. As a result, at the very time (1882) that classical Newtonian physics was at the height of its influence, the British Society for Psychical Research was founded.[8] Even though the position of these men by no means represented the views of the scientific establishment of their time, it is more than suggestive to note the consistently high quality, both professional and personal, of the presidents of the Society from its inception to the present time. As Arthur Koestler has pointed out, among them were "three Nobel laureates, ten Fellows of the Royal Society, one Prime Minister and a galaxy of professors, mostly physicists and philosophers."[9]

The first president of the British SPR, Professor Henry Sidgwick, summed up the thought of his colleagues at the time as follows: "Now our own position was this: we believed unreservedly in the methods of modern science, and were prepared submissively to accept her reasoned conclusions, when sustained by the agreement of experts; but we were not prepared to submit with equal docility to the mere prejudices of scientific men. And it appeared to us that there was an important body of evidence—tending *prima facie* to establish the independence of the soul or spirit—which modern science had simply left on one side with ignorant contempt; and that in so leaving it she had been untrue to her professed method and had arrived prematurely at her negative conclusions."[10]

Like Sidgwick, "whose reputation for sanity, truthfulness and fairness was well known to everyone who mattered in England," Sir William Crookes and Sir Oliver Lodge in Great Britain, Mme. Marie Curie in France, Guglielmo Marconi in Italy, Thomas Edison in the United States, and, of course, in his own way, Albert Einstein in Switzerland and Germany were among the brave vanguard of those who pioneered in what has become a veritable revolution in the physical sciences and mathematics. In particular, the revolution in physics, which is still in process, has

---

8. *Ibid.*, pp. 48-49.
9. Arthur Koestler, *The Roots of Coincidence* (New York: Random House, 1972), pp. 31-34.
10. Heywood, *op. cit.*, pp. 52-53.

shown that "the classical notions about the nature of time, space, and matter are not all-embracing when it comes to the realms of the very large and the very small."[11] Or as Louis Pauwels has written about twentieth-century physics, "A new science has been born, less dogmatic than the old one. Doors are opened on to a different *kind* of reality... Doors have been thrown open in almost all the strongholds of science, but that of physics has lost almost all its walls to become a cathedral entirely built of glass wherein can be seen the reflections of another world, infinitely near."[12]

The role of the work of the pioneers in depth psychology, especially Sigmund Freud and Carl Gustav Jung in Europe and William James in America, in the larger scientific revolution during this century is too well known to require retelling. Suffice it here to add that Freud once wrote in a recorded letter that "if he had another life to live he would dedicate it to psychic research." Freud also wrote to his American friend, Dr. Ernest Jones, of his desire to lend the support of the whole movement of psychoanalysis to the work of investigating telepathy, so impressed was he with the long series of telepathic experiments which Professor Gilbert Murray, the famed classicist who was president of the British Society for Psychical Research from 1915 to 1916, had carried out between 1915 and 1929. Jung, in the last years of his life, made two startling contributions to the ongoing scientific revolution of this century. One was the principle that he named synchronicity, which asserts that "events can, so to speak, bunch together in time and space, not because one is *causing* the other but because their *meanings* are linked." The other was the statement in his autobiography that "ESP [extrasensory perception] had been a vital and recurrent factor in his own life and in his relations with his patients."[13]

The revolution in physics, in the life sciences, in psychology and in anthropology has been in process now for over three-quarters of a century. It is, however, still no doubt true that the outlook of the majority of people, even educated ones, has not yet been changed to conform adequately with the new ideas. Time is, of course, needed for these to permeate and modify the thinking of all of us who have been educated in the context of the older

11. *Ibid.*, p. 60.
12. Pauwels and Bergier, *op. cit.*, p. 16.
13. Heywood, *op.cit.*, pp. 55, 60. Cf. C.G. Jung, *Memories, Dreams, Reflections*, ed. Aniela Jaffé (New York: Random House, 1963), pp. 146-169, 170-222, 289-354; Aniela Jaffé, *Apparitions and Precognition* (New Hyde Park, New York: University Books, 1963), *passim.*

presuppositions. As has been said, "The most fundamental change of all—to a concept of 'solid' matter as being convertible into elusive 'intangible' energy—is only now beginning to exert its influence in the outside world."[14]

In this context or climate of thought, the relatively new science of parapsychology—actually a direct heir of the older activities in psychical research—has gained an unexpected respectability. A brief summation of some of the factors behind this development will serve also, I believe, as a summation of the process or processes which I have tried to delineate up to this point.

The ecological anxiety and the dissatisfaction with the materialistic world which characterized the counter culture of the sixties increasingly came to seep into the outlook of the larger population of industrialized nations in the world. The moon flights, with their dependence upon the most sophisticated scientific knowledge and technological skills and apparatus, did something to all of us at another level of our awareness. The spiritual conversion experienced by astronaut Edgar Mitchell, lunar module commander of Apollo 14, on his journey to the moon seems to represent a kind of focus of a far wider change in the thinking of his contemporaries. He is reported as having gained, in reflecting on his experience, "a sense of being totally insignificant yet highly significant, and insight into the great pattern of control and divinity in the universe. It was a sense of the earth being in critical condition, a recognition of the massive insanity which had led man into deeper and deeper crises on the planet... above all, I felt the need for a radical change in our culture. I knew we were replete with untapped intuitive and psychic forces which we must utilize if we are to survive, forces that Western society had programmed us to disregard..."[15]

These perceptions, particularly to a man of scientific and technological training like Edgar Mitchell, were of course rendered both intellectually and psychologically more plausible, indeed more cogent, by what has been called "the dematerialized character of contemporary physics." Francine du Plessix Gray has summed up the significance of this development in physics in the following way: "A science filled with such bizarre components as advance potential (waves of electrons perceived before they are generated), tunneling effects (electrons penetrating barriers diagnosed as impenetrable by laws of probability) and tachyons

14. Heywood, op. cit., p. 60.
15. Francine du Plessix Gray, "Parapsychology and Beyond," The New York Times Magazine, August 11, 1974, p. 13.

(particles traveling faster than light, which would imply the possibility of a backward flow of time) no longer offers a secure rationale for the denial of any paranormal event."[16] Astrophysicists, such as John Wheeler of Princeton, have come to ponder such questions as whether other universes are possible, universes which may serve as the source of the brilliant quasars in distant space, into which material in the form of energy is pouring from "somewhere else."[17]

A highly significant survey of key developments in the life sciences is found in the paper presented by John Poynton at the Parapsychology Foundation Conference held in August of 1972 in Amsterdam, Holland.[18] Poynton is a member of the faculty of the Biological Science Department, University of Natal, Durban, South Africa. He forthrightly criticizes the position, as typified by Bernhard Rensch in *Biophilosophy*, that views the universe of our physical existence as a closed causal system and leaves no room for causal action deriving from some other system. Over against this view, Poynton posits an interacting cosmic dualism or pluralism. Charging most biologists and psychologists as "still almost aggressively trying to conform to outdated world-views that in some way constitute their idea of 'physics,'" he takes his stand with the physicists who share the Copenhagen interpretation of quantum theory, a circle which includes such men as Niels Bohr, Werner Heisenberg, Wolfgang Pauli and Janos von Neumann. This interpretation holds that virtual particles and other such features in a world as perceived, or rather constructed, by the physicist are not as such to be taken as constituents of physical reality. At most, they represent what Werner Heisenberg has described as "a world of potentialities or possibilities rather than one of things or facts." The experiments and reflections of physicists over recent decades have led them, as Henry Margenau has put it, "to doubt such fundamental propositions as the principle of the conservation of energy, the principle of causality, and many other commitments which were held to be unshakeable and firm in the past."[19]

These developments encouraged Poynton and many of his

16. *Ibid.*, p. 78.
17. Walter Sullivan, "A Hole in the Sky," *The New York Times Magazine*, July 14, 1974, p. 35.
18. John Poynton, "Parapsychology and the Life Sciences," *Parapsychology Review*, March-April, 1973, pp. 10-26.
19. Henry Margenau, "ESP in the Framework of Modern Science," in *Science and ESP*, p. 213. We should note that the concept of acausality and that of synchronicity as advanced by Carl Jung do not posit a total absence of causal factors within the cosmos;

colleagues to reject the completely mechanistic view of man and his evolution, which perhaps a majority of biologists still hold and which, one may add, has been largely responsible for the predominantly behavioristic trend in psychology during the twentieth century. Poynton contends that we now possess appreciable evidence of a physical-nonphysical interaction in the cosmos. He shares with J.L. Randall the conviction that "the physical universe is showing the characteristics of an open system" and with Sir Cyril Burt and Michael Whiteman the conclusion that "all perception has a clairvoyant character." Poynton contends that biologists working in Africa tend to have a "feel" for such things as psi (personal factors or processes which are nonphysical in nature). He also affirms that there is a wide acceptance of parapsychology in South Africa, especially among younger biologists.

Current studies in psychology focusing on altered states of consciousness, of which Robert Ornstein's books are significant examples, have served to create a friendly environment among younger scientists for areas of research that border on or plunge into the psychic or paranormal.[20] Hence the phrase, "Parapsychology is an idea whose time has come."[21] Elmer Green at the Menninger Foundation in Topeka, Kansas, has used highly sophisticated devices known as biofeedback equipment to measure the brain waves, heartbeat and other vital functions of persons in deep meditation, especially of those with long experience in the practice, such as Zen monks or Hindu yogis. Similar work has been done at the Langley-Porter Institute in San Francisco.

Recent work in anthropology has also contributed to the new climate of opinion. Anthropological studies have in general led to and come to be based on the presupposition of a kind of cultural relativity. This development, of course, needs to be seen in the context of changes in the consciousness of Western peoples *vis-à-vis* the other cultures of the world, especially the older cultures of Asia, but in some ways including the more "primitive" cultures of Africa and its neighboring islands. The experience of two world

rather, they relate to the lack or imperception of cause at the level of reality at which natural science works.
20. Robert E. Ornstein, *On the Experience of Time* (Baltimore, Maryland: Penguin Books, 1969); with Claudio Naranjo, *On the Psychology of Meditation* (New York: Viking Press, 1971); *The Psychology of Consciousness* (San Francisco: W.H. Freeman, 1972); *The Nature of Human Consciousness* (New York: Viking Press, 1973).
21. Cf. Paul Chance, "Parapsychology Is an Idea Whose Time Has Come," *Psychology Today*, October, 1973, pp. 105-120.

wars focused in the West has led to an astonishing diminution, if not loss, of the former Western attitude of cultural superiority and arrogance toward "the lesser breeds without the law." Specifically, Western concepts of space, time, causality and mind-body relationships, long held to be immutable laws of the cosmos, have come to be seen as cultural constructs needing appreciable modification, modification which at times can be made with the help of the perceptions of other cultures. A very significant indication of this development is the recent book by Fritjof Capra, *The Tao of Physics*, which gives the results of a trained physicist's exploration of the parallels between modern physics and Eastern mysticism.[22]

Finally, but of course by no means last or least in importance, there are the recent developments in religious thought and theology. Sensitive readers of this article will have perceived the religious implications of almost all the developments heretofore related, whether in the physical and life sciences or in psychology and anthropology. A survey of the development of religious thought during the twentieth century would, of course, take us far beyond the purview of this article. Suffice it to say that in spite of many exceptions, as well as what may be called retrogressions, a new climate has appeared in Christian and Jewish theology; this new outlook is characterized by an openness that is more sophisticated and knowledgeable, as well as more spiritual, than the older theological liberalism. I trust my readers will forgive me if I direct them to the last chapter of my book on the Buddha for a somewhat lengthy survey of recent developments in Christian theology, particularly with reference to evaluation of other religious traditions in the world.[23]

In this larger climate of understanding and thought that has emerged in the second half of the twentieth century, the two great clairvoyant figures of the century, Edgar Cayce and Rudolf Steiner—so very different in their cultural and educational backgrounds and yet so similar in their spirituality and world views—appear as singularly appropriate contributors to their times and places.

3

What of the Church, the Christian Church, in all this? Rosalind Heywood, in describing the mental climate in England during the

22. Fritjof Capra, *The Tao of Physics* (Berkeley, California: Shambhala Publications, 1975), *passim.*
23. Richard H. Drummond, *Gautama the Buddha* (Grand Rapids, Michigan: Wm. B. Eerdmans Publishing Co., 1974), pp. 153-208.

early years of psychical research there, wryly notes that in spite of many accounts in the Bible of what would, in contemporary language, be denoted as ESP or psychic phenomena, "the Church was still too convinced of its diabolical nature to see a possible ally [against the sweeping tide of nineteenth-century materialism] in psychical research."[24] It is widely known that psychic experiences were largely driven underground by the Church under pain of the sanctions which from the time of Constantine (A.D. 280-337) she was able to use with such compelling effect.[25] The condemnation and burning at the stake of Jeanne d'Arc is, of course, a dramatic example of a procedure that was usually employed less drastically but with no less telling effect. And yet in the case of Jeanne, the ecclesiastical tribunal was a tool of the English and the Burgundians; the Church in the rest of France did not concur, and the judgment of 1431 was officially annulled as early as 1456.

Such developments demonstrate that before trying to characterize the attitude of the Church in any matter, we must confront the more basic question, "What is the Church?" For nearly a millennium and a half the Christian Church in Europe was almost completely synonymous with the total community of the areas into which she had gone; for this reason it is often difficult to isolate and identify the action of the Church—which can be perceived as bearer of the tradition and sharer in the life of God communicated through the spirit of Jesus Christ—and to distinguish her actions from those of the larger community or, in particular, the ruling classes in state and Church. The Roman Catholic Church has traditionally identified the essence of the Church with the leadership, technically termed the hierarchy, of the organization; and she has ascribed to teachings of the hierarchy, specifically those teachings that originate in the papal office and relate to matters of faith and morals, an infallible character. But, in fact, this theory has had to be modified and qualified. In the late nineteenth century John Henry Newman brought forth his famous concept of the development of doctrine, which actually presupposes changes in the otherwise unchangeable, and this concept has become the generally accepted basis of interpretation in twentieth-century Roman

24. Heywood, *op. cit.*, p. 53.
25. There are important qualifications to be made to this statement. As Richard Woods has pointed out, the higher clergy and the ruling classes in the Middle Ages and into modern times often made use of psychic instrumentalities at the very time they forbade them to the common man. Richard Woods, *The Occult Revolution: A Christian Meditation* (New York: Seabury Press, 1971), p. 48.

Catholic theology. The current dispute over the issue of papal infallibility, especially as seen in the work of the great protagonists Karl Rahner and Hans Küng, actually presupposes important modifications of any strict interpretation of the doctrine.

A question that has an important relationship to any discussion of the nature of the Church is that of the quality of her life as well as of her teaching. The most convinced and loyal churchman is all too aware of the lights and shadows, even the black darkness, to be seen in the history of the Church. What or who, for example, is most representative of the Church? In Spain, should we single out the great Carmelite mystic and monastic organizer, St. John of the Cross, or the Dominican inquisitor-general, Thomas Torquemada? Or, to complicate the picture further, we might consider the case of John Calvin, the powerful leader of the Reformation in French-speaking Geneva; was Calvin more representative of the Church when he was writing his commentaries on the Psalms or when he was active in securing the condemnation and execution of Michael Servetus for having differing views on the Divine Trinity? Who was right, in terms of perceptions of the deepest levels of Christian faith, Meister Eckhart or the organs of the Church which accused him of heresy? These are admittedly extreme cases, and my rhetorical questions hardly need answers. But the issue, I believe, is clear. It is not at all easy to determine precisely and concretely what is the Church, nor even what is Christianity.

Those who consider themselves members of the conservative wing of the Protestant tradition, including those called Fundamentalists, focus upon the written Bible as their source of religious truth, regarding the book as divinely—and in not a few cases inerrantly—inspired. At first glance, this posture appears greatly to simplify the problem of what is truth and even what is the Church. But upon closer examination, one perceives that people of this persuasion practice a highly selective use of the Bible, of the New Testament as well as the Old. On the basis of presuppositions usually not openly acknowledged, often perhaps not even perceived, they assign priority to some passages over others; in so doing, they at times end up with interpretations, beliefs and practices that in spirit are essentially akin to the historic Church at her condemnatory worst and in other cases are alien to the faith and understanding of the bulk of historic Christendom over long centuries. We shall consider specifics along this line a bit later.

13

The reason for this brief discussion of the nature of the Church lies in the fact that in this twentieth century we are experiencing developments in both science and religion that are in fact not entirely new, but somewhat altered reformulations of more ancient perceptions. These developments actually constitute critiques or protests against distortions and reductions of originally legitimate concepts and activities. Many writers who have considered the philosophical implications of natural or physical science since the 1920s have made sharp, indeed increasingly sharp, strictures of the pride and arrogance of the late nineteenth-and early twentieth-century scientists in claiming universal validity for their formulations. To be sure, this older spirit is still not dead in the sciences, as is evidenced by Bernhard Rensch's statement in his 1971 work, *Biophilosophy,* that "everything goes to show that biological rules or laws, like all chemical and almost all physical and astronomical ones, fall within the scope of a *universal causal law acting without any interruption.*" [his italics][26] Rensch's position actually runs quite counter to trends in biology that reject completely the older "mechanistic, materialistic, behavioristic approach." One example of the more modern outlook is the general systems theory, which is characterized by "an approach to open systems that feed on negative entropy and seem to go counter to the second law of thermodynamics." Among younger biologists, there is wide discontent with the claim of orthodox Darwinism or neo-Darwinism that random mutations coupled with natural selection explain everything in the process of evolution.[27]

Some of the most recent scientific discoveries or formulations of perceptions seem to have been prefigured or even specifically known in earlier periods. At this point we enter a highly controversial area of contemporary thought, but the issue deserves careful consideration, at least to give historical perspective to our contemporary *locus,* and certainly to help us transcend the myth of universal or inevitable progress that dominated the thought of the late nineteenth and early twentieth centuries. In the area of preclassical, ancient history, the recent publications of Cyrus Gordon and Charles Hapgood have by no means gained universal assent, but they are carefully documented and serve to give scholars and intelligent laymen a new respect for times once thought entirely primitive.[28]

---

26. Quoted in Poynton, *op. cit.,* p. 10.
27. Cf. Arthur Koestler, "The Perversity of Physics," *Parapsychology Review*, May-June, 1973, p. 3.

In some ways, the life of Isaac Newton has long been both an enigma and an embarrassment to his biographers. During the very years in which he was doing the basic work which resulted in his formulations of laws governing the physical universe, and which later led scientists to exclusively materialistic concepts of the universe as a closed system, Newton himself practiced a life of religious faith that had dimensions some have called occult. But concretely, with reference to his precursors in science, Newton believed in the existence of a chain of initiates, who were both religious and scientific in their concerns, reaching back to ancient times. Newton evidently believed that these initiates, whom we may largely identify with the alchemical and mystical tradition, understood and in some cases made use of the secrets of the transmutation of matter, now known in atomic theory and construction. Newton's famous statement, "If I have seen further, it is by standing on the shoulders of giants," is actually a concrete expression of his very great respect for his precursors, who in Newton's view, as reported by Francis Atterbury, his contemporary, not only were "men of genius and superior intelligence," but had "carried their discoveries in every field much further than we today suspect, judging from what remains of their writings."[29] Actually our present scientific knowledge of the world has benefited greatly from the tradition of alchemy, from Albert de Grand and Raymond Lull in the thirteenth century through Paracelsus (Theophrastus von Hohenheim) and della Porta in the sixteenth, and so to the time of Newton. Newton himself did his scientific work in the context of deep respect for the Hermetic writings.[30]

The perception of the dimension of the unconscious in the human psyche—commonly thought to be a quite new discovery, deriving from the twentieth-century work of Sigmund Freud—has roots which go back, if not to the *memoria* of Augustine, at least to the *sensus naturae* of William of Conches (1080-1154), a Platonic scholastic philosopher. This *sensus naturae* was an "unconscious, instinctive, supernatural knowledge" which animals as well as human beings were believed to possess. This perception as formulated by Avicenna (the Muslim Ibn Sina, 980-

28. Cf. Cyrus Gordon, *Before Columbus: Links between the Old World and Ancient America* (New York: Crown Publishers, 1971); Charles H. Hapgood, *Maps of the Ancient Sea Kings: Evidence of Advanced Civilization in the Ice Age* (Philadelphia: Chilton Books, 1966).
29. Pauwels and Bergier, *op. cit.*, p. 70.
30. *Ibid.*, pp. 67-70.

1037) was taken to explain the gift of prophecy and telepathic capacities in human beings. Significantly, this *sensus naturae* (called *lumen naturae,* or the "light of nature," by Paracelsus) came to be associated with the work of the Holy Spirit by some of the greatest Christian philosopher-theologians of the Middle Ages, beginning with William of Conches himself and including Abelard, Guillaume de Paris, Albertus Magnus and, later, most Western alchemists.[31] This tradition, in fact, constitutes a very proper context for discussion of what are now called psychic phenomena, for it was clearly in the mainstream of faith-understanding in the Christian Church.

Part II

Just as twentieth-century science constitutes both a critique and a reformulation of earlier scientific perceptions, not a little of the creative religious activity of the twentieth century has done the work of critique and reformulation. It is not always known among Christian laymen in the United States how sharp and deep-going are the criticisms—especially among the educated classes of Europe—not only of institutional Christianity but also of orthodox formulations of Christian doctrine. As one perceptive English observer who is at the same time friendly to religious faith and activity as such has put it, the decline in the credibility of "orthodox religious philosophy" is proceeding with galloping speed and is cutting off the power and influence which the churches once had.

One reason for this decline is perennial and inevitable in the case of established religious institutions. In most human societies, there is a distinct tension between the roles of prophet and priest; this tension emerges with particular clarity in the history of Israel before the coming of the Christ, as can be seen in the sharp critiques of cultic religion made by the great prophetic figures of the Bible, such as Amos, Hosea, Isaiah and, with inner psychological traumas so akin to modern experience, Jeremiah. The priest or minister is usually, in his primary function, the guardian of existing or traditional ritual and doctrine. The prophet and, to use the term generally assigned to creative religious persons in "primitive" societies, the shaman draw primarily not upon the existing religious traditions of their culture—although they relate to them and generally prefer to

31. Cf. Marie-Louise von Franz, *C.G. Jung, His Myth in Our Time* (New York: G.P. Putnam's Sons, 1975), pp. 31-32.

conform to them as much as possible—but upon what Carl Jung called the primordial experience, which is the ultimate source of these traditions. This is to give a certain, although qualified, priority to personal experience of spiritual reality and the spiritual world. This is what, in the context of the Christian tradition, impelled the Scottish historian and essayist Thomas Carlyle to urge a divinity-school student of his time to come to know God firsthand, through personal experience, and not just secondhand, through the books and lectures of others. The fact that this kind of experience is not sufficiently common among ministers and priests of the established religious institutions of the world (this problem is not confined to Christianity; it exists to at least comparable extent in Buddhism, Islam, Judaism and less sophisticated traditions) has been a significant factor in lessening contemporary credibility in these religious institutions and their leadership. A related problem of great significance is the fact that leaders of religious institutions who do not share comparably in the "primordial" experience or experiences tend to be defensive, if not downright hostile, toward people of their own time who do, especially if these people do not function professionally within the established leaders' own institutions, and sometimes even if they do so function.

Some understanding of these phenomena is vitally necessary for an adequate comprehension of the history of Western civilization, in particular of the Christian Church, although, as I have suggested above, the phenomena are of worldwide occurrence. Of particular significance is the fact that we are here dealing with the manfiestations and responses of generally the most creative persons and activities in human history. We are talking about a pattern which is discernible in Francis of Assisi, in the mystics of the Rhine Valley during the fourteenth and fifteenth centuries, in Martin Luther, in St. John of the Cross and Teresa of Avila, in Ignatius Loyola and Francis Xavier, in Jakob Boehme, in George Fox and John Wesley of England, in Johann Arndt and Philipp Jakob Spener of Germany. The last four, it may be noted, were key personages in the development of two intimately related massive movements for the revival of practical and devout Christianity so pregnant with new life for countless people in both Europe and the Americas, one the great evangelical revival in English-speaking lands, the other the vastly influential activity in Germany and Scandinavia called Pietism. In the case of every person here listed, we find an example, with many variations, of original religious experience, tension—

17

sometimes severe—with established institutions and their leaders, and the end result of enormously creative activity. These persons were all what are currently called "facilitators of change," change that was influential to a massive degree and at almost every level of human life and awareness. To their number I do not hesitate to add Edgar Cayce and Rudolf Steiner, twentieth-century participants in the "primordial experience," or, in other words, in historic Christian spirituality.[32]

Criticism of creative religious persons by representatives of traditional institutions is often made on the basis of doctrine, even though the doctrines of great institutions may differ sharply among themselves at some points. I would hereupon submit the thesis that more important than single points of doctrine are what I wish to call whole constellations of understanding. From this perspective, particular doctrinal criticisms often appear no more than trivial, or even diversionary. As a particularly significant example of the loss of a whole constellation of understanding, I would cite what has been termed the reductionism of modern Protestantism in western Europe and the Americas.

The early Protestant Reformers protested against a number of real perversions of Christian faith and practice which had developed over the Middle Ages in Europe. Their objections included not only the perennial protests against immorality and venality among the clergy, both high and low, against their ignorance and generally low level of spiritual understanding. There were also practices that tended to undermine the very basis of Christian morality in a proper relationship to God; one such activity was Johann Tetzel's sale of indulgences—documents assuring divine forgiveness of sins by the authority of the Church—not only for sins one had committed but also for those which one intended to commit. Objections were made to popular veneration of saints and angels, in which, at times, sight of the priority and unity of the Godhead was evidently lost. The doctrine of the transubstantiation of the elements in the Lord's Supper, particularly as popularly understood, tended to express a covert materialism and to limit, in human minds, the presence and work of the Spirit of God to the physical confines of the sanctuary. These are objections which are now almost universally regarded as valid; the high respect for Martin Luther as an authentic Christian prophetic figure which has emerged in

---

32. We have been reminded that this kind of personal religious experience was retained in the tradition of alchemy in western Europe at the very time it was discouraged in official church circles. von Franz, *ibid.*, p. 105.

Roman Catholic historical and theological scholarship within the past generation is a significant example of this fact.

Legitimate objections or complaints, however, have a way of creating a momentum of their own which may become negative or even destructive if strenuous efforts are not made to keep them essentially or primarily constructive. I shall not speak here of what Jaroslav Pelikan has called the "tragic necessity" of the Reformation itself. But within Protestantism, resistance to improper veneration of the saints and angels gradually led to a relative downgrading of their spiritual significance not only for believers on earth but within the entire cosmos. The process was indeed gradual and at times almost halted by the great movements of spiritual revival, but under the influence of the development of modern science and especially of nineteenth-century materialism, the downgrading became a disbelief in any effective spiritual influence of the saints above and in the very existence of angels; in spite of the writings of Karl Barth and the recent work of Billy Graham, this attitude seems to characterize the bulk of educated Protestants in the world today. This, in turn, has led to a kind of denuding of the spiritual world in popular consciousness, so as to make it bare of all real existence except God and His Christ. A logical development of this trend was the "God is dead" theology of a few years ago, which denied all reality to a spiritual dimension in the universe and proclaimed God dead (nonexistent) and Jesus only an influence on the historical plane.

"God is dead" theology has been largely rejected in Western Protestantism, but the "reductionist" trend is still a reality in our midst. Another example of this is the deemphasizing of the role of dreams. Dreams play a vital role as a mode of divine revelation in the Judeo-Christian Scriptures. The importance of dreams in the patriarchal period is clear; with the exception of "visions," they are actually the only mode we can positively identify in the psychology of perception of divine revelation among the Hebrew prophets. The place of dreams in the perception of divine guidance for the protection of the Christ Child during His early years is particularly significant.[33] The religious importance of dreams over long centuries of the history of the Christian Church is well attested.[34] But, as Morton Kelsey has put it, there is a "long jump" between the understanding-practice of the early Church Fathers and modern Christian attitudes toward dreams as well as

---

33. Matthew 1:20-25; 2:1-23; Luke 1:5-80; 2:22-38. Cf. Matthew 27:19; Acts 9:12.
34. Cf. Morton T. Kelsey, *Dreams: The Dark Speech of the Spirit* (Garden City, New York: Doubleday & Co., 1968), pp. 102-163. Now titled *God, Dreams, and Revelation.*

visions. To be sure, and properly, from an early period important qualifications were made and cautions given about the meaning of dreams, but as recently as the eighteenth century dreams were apparently still considered seriously by leading figures in the Church.

Modern public reticence and shyness about discussions of dreams, indeed the profession of disbelief in their having any real significance, especially among well-educated people, are well known. The origin of this development is somewhat obscure, but it is no doubt largely due to the emergence of modern science and especially to nineteenth-century scientific materialism, even though partial causes can be traced much further back in Western history.[35] It is probably true that even educated persons often take their dreams, at least some dreams, much more seriously than they would care to admit in public. Yet the shamefacedness persists, actually a phenomenon hard to understand in light of the fact that twentieth-century depth psychology, especially in the hands of Freud and Jung, depended for the bulk of its primary data upon the interpretation of the dreams of both patient and therapist.

As a final example, I should like to adduce the prevalent Western attitude toward reincarnation, or the possibility of a series of human lives on earth experienced by the same soul or continuing "personal" focus of consciousness.[36] Most modern Christians of every major tradition tend to think of this concept as an Oriental import, having no place whatsoever in the historic life or teaching of the Church. Actually, this is another area wherein the process of "reductionism" can be seen at work. The concept of reincarnation has been held as an element of faith by many Christians from the earliest periods of the Church. It is clear from various passages in the New Testament that some form of a concept of reincarnation was widely held by Jews, including Palestinian Jews of more than one sect, at the time of Jesus (see Matthew 17:9-13 [cf. Malachi 4:5-6]; Luke 9:8; John 9:1-12; James 3:6 [note the original Greek]; Rev. 3:12 [again note the Greek]). The most natural interpretation of several passages in the works of the Alexandrian Jew Flavius Josephus, roughly a contemporary of Jesus, indicates that the Pharisees believed good

---

35. *Ibid.*, pp. 164-192.
36. In discussing reincarnation, scholars often use the Greek word *metempsychosis*. Both terms are generally confined to the sense of the rebirth of human beings in different human bodies. The term *transmigration* is now used to denote the concept that human beings may be born again in the bodies of various animal species. This latter concept is particularly found within popular Hinduism and Buddhism.

souls return to earth in new bodies.[37] The so-called Pseudo-Clementine writings of the second century are generally classed as forms of "a primary witness to Jewish Christianity," and these materials reveal clearly the presence of belief among Jewish Christians in a series of reincarnations of Jesus Himself prior to His manifestation as the Christ in Palestine at the beginning of our era.[38]

There is a long tradition in mystical Judaism of belief in reincarnation, which can be traced with relative clarity to the earliest periods of this era. We find the belief appearing in the Jewish Karaite movement of the seventh century, in the Kabbalah and in the Hasidim, the great mystical movement among modern Jews, which has continued into our own time. Rabbi Herbert Weiner reports the presence in contemporary Israel of reincarnation as a "commonly held folk belief," especially among the more conservative Sephardic Jews, who came from such areas as Iraq, Yemen, North Africa and India. Weiner writes that, like reincarnation *(Gilgul Nephashot),* the cult of saints plays an important role in the religious life of Jews from North African communities, as does the interpretation of dreams in religious contexts in the larger conservative Jewish tradition. Belief in reincarnation became the basis of a popular form of spiritual therapy which Weiner asserts is reminiscent of Jungian psychology. By various means, rabbis would identify a disciple's prior incarnation and thereby present him a "kind of archetype which could make sense out of his travails or problems." Upon this basis, specific advice and other help could be given. This kind of therapy has very ancient roots and reached a special height of popularity in the seventeenth century with the school of Rabbi Isaac Luria.[39]

It is clear from one of the letters of Jerome (ca. 340-420), the famous translator of the Bible into the Latin Vulgate, that the concept of reincarnation was widely held by Christians, especially in the churches of the Greek-speaking areas bordering on the eastern Mediterranean. This section of the world was, of course,

37. Flavius Josephus, *Jewish War* III, 374; *Against Apion* II, 218; *Jewish Antiquities* XVIII, 15 (3).
38. *Clementine Homilies; Clementine Recognitions; The Ante-Nicene Fathers,* revised by A. Cleveland Coxe (New York: Charles Scribner's Sons, 1926), vol. VIII, pp. 73-346.
39. Herbert Weiner, "Report from Israel," *Parapsychology Review,* March-April, 1973, pp. 13-16. Cf. Jean Daniélou, *The Theology of Jewish Christianity* (Chicago: The Henry Regnery Co., 1964), p. 85; Henri-Charles Puech, "Gnosis and Time," in *Man and Time,* Bollingen Series XXX, vol. 3 (New York: Pantheon Books, 1957), p. 65; Samuel J. Fox, *Hell in Jewish Literature* (Northbrook, Illinois: Whitehall Co., 1972), pp. 129-146.

where the great bulk of Christians resided at the time of Jerome.[40] There are weighty reasons to believe that both of the great Alexandrian theologians, Clement (ca. 150-215) and Origen (ca. 182-251), believed in reincarnation.

According to the English patristic scholar Henry Chadwick, Origen taught reincarnation as a "very plausible opinion."[41] Origen, who was certainly the greatest Christian Biblical scholar and one of the most influential theologians during the first six centuries of the Church, taught reincarnation as a significant element within his understanding of divine providence, which in fact formed the central theme of his whole theological system. To Origen, the providence of God was primarily "educative," in the deepest spiritual and moral sense of the term, and directed to the salvation of the whole person. Origen, like most Christians in the early centuries of the Church, viewed salvation not as an instantaneous event (as distinguished from conversion or modes of liberation, whether physical or mental), but as a process leading toward the total transformation of human character as well as the restoration of the entire cosmos according to the plan of God. This was regarded as a process involving divine action—in which the saving work of Jesus the Christ through the cross and His resurrection was the central and supreme element—and human response, which from the human perspective could be perceived as moral and spiritual growth. In this context of understanding, Origen saw reincarnation as offering the best explanation of the inequalities and apparent injustices of present human life on earth. He held that souls pre-exist and receive bodies and external circumstances in this life such as are appropriate to their former lives on earth. But Origen saw divine providence as not merely karmic or punitive in its action. In one sense, the bodies and circumstances of persons can be called karmically appropriate; but in the providence of God, whose mercy transcends His justice, the very structures of human heredity and environment that are so often felt by human beings to be unduly or even unfairly restrictive are impregnated with, or actually constitute, those spiritually and morally educative opportunities which enable divine action and human response to

40. Jerome, *Letters* CXXX (*Epistula ad Demetriadem* 16).
41. Henry Chadwick, *Early Christian Thought and the Classical Tradition* (Oxford: Oxford University Press, 1966), pp. 88-89, 114-116. With regard to the problem of interpretation of the extant materials of Origen, Chadwick warns against the admitted editoralizing by Rufinus, Origen's Latin translator, to make the material palatable to the Latin orthodoxy of his time.

effect the kind of transformation of character conducive to God's final purposes.[42]

The fact that appreciable numbers of people in the history of the Christian Church, including not a few important personages, believed in reincarnation does not in itself constitute proof of the truth of this concept; that is another issue to be considered, using a variety of methodologies. Its significant presence, however, in the history of the Church does make it, so to speak, a viable issue in the faith and life and theology of Christians. It is also remarkable how the belief continued to reappear over the later centuries, not only in outstanding individuals, but also in weighty Christian movements. I refer particularly to the Paulicians, or Bogomils, who were first heard of in the seventh century on the eastern borders of the Roman Empire and who later spread throughout most of the Balkan Peninsula; gaining tens and even hundreds of thousands of adherents, they flourished for centuries. A related movement was that of the Albigensians, or Cathari, in northern Italy, southern France, northern Spain and even parts of Flanders in the twelfth and thirteenth centuries— that is, in the culturally and materially most highly advanced portions of western Europe at the time. These movements were reformatory, zealous for a purification and ennoblement of Christian faith and life; and, like the later Protestantism, they were vigorously, even fanatically, persecuted by the institutional churches of both East and West. The available evidence suggests that most, if not all, of the Paulicians and Albigensians believed in reincarnation. For this and other disputed points of doctrine they were regarded as heretical, but, as we need to remind ourselves, so was the whole of Protestantism for most of the past four-and-a-half centuries.[43]

From the time of the early Renaissance, belief in reincarnation has continued to reappear, especially among the well-educated in western Europe and the Americas. Among its adherents can be listed many of the most gifted scholars, poets, artists, philosophers and scientists of modern times.[44] The fact, then, that the same concept appears again in the work of the great spiritual figures of the twentieth century, Edgar Cayce and Rudolf Steiner,

42. Origen, *Contra Celsum* VII, 50; *De Principiis* I, 7, 4; I, 8,1; I, 8, 4; III, 3, 5; III, 5, 5.
43. Cf. Kenneth Scott Latourette, *A History of Christianity* (New York: Harper and Brothers, 1953), pp. 299-300, 449-458; Arthur Guirdham, *The Cathars and Reincarnation* (London: Neville Spearman, 1970), *passim.*
44. Cf. Joseph Head and S.L. Cranston, *Reincarnation in World Thought* (New York: The Julian Press, 1971), pp. 230-243, 244-442.

is hardly cause for surprise when viewed from the perspective of the history of Western culture.[45] The same fact, however, can also be considered, in the context of Christian faith, from the standpoint of divine providence at work within that same culture. Hasty or ill-considered criticism of either Cayce or Steiner for such belief is certainly inappropriate from Protestant Christians who participate in the "reductionism" of the main-line Protestant churches. By "reductionism," again, I mean the process, long extended, of losing touch with a whole constellation of understanding that belonged to the Christian Church of the first centuries of her history. The time has surely come for Christians to understand and evaluate the personages and events of their own time, as of other times, by the primary criterion given them by their Lord: "You will know them by their fruits." (Matthew 7:16)[46]

---

45. It may be appropriate to note that toward the end of his life C.G. Jung came to a belief in at least the real possibility and reasonableness of reincarnation. Jung's personal religious faith, however, was not as "Christocentric" as that of Cayce and Steiner. Cf. Jung, *op. cit.*, pp. 316-320.

46. Matthew 7:15-23; 12:33; Luke 6:43-45. Cf. Matthew 25:31-46; John 14:11; I John 2:29.

Knowledgeable readers may be aware that with reference to evaluative criteria I have taken a different position from that adopted by Robert S. Ellwood, Jr., in *Religious and Spiritual Groups in Modern America* (Englewood Cliffs, New Jersey: Prentice-Hall, 1973), pp. xii-xvi, 1-5. In his treatment of the groups under purview Ellwood is both sensitive and open, even sympathetic, indeed to a surprising degree. He regards any of the groups he discusses as potentially able to cast light on at least some facet of truth, whether such truths have current widespread social approval or not. The basic flaw, however, which I find in Ellwood's methodology is his definition of what he calls "normatively Judeo-Christian." To Ellwood, the normatively Judeo-Christian is "what is considered normal in the church or synagogue down the street" in the contemporary United States. I contend that this is a quite unacceptable criterion for "normative" Christianity or Judaism. It was clearly not the understanding from which Francis of Assisi, Martin Luther, Israel Ben Eliezer, John Wesley, Hans Nielsen Hauge of Norway, or any of the other creative reformatory figures in the history of our Christian and Jewish traditions operated. To my mind, it is still appropriate to ask what is authentic Christianity or Judaism. To fail to ask this question is to fall prey to either the Scylla of uncritically affirming the modes of faith and life of contemporary main-line denominations, or the Charybdis of despair of finding any standard or measurement by which ameliorative change can be effected.

24

Edgar Cayce—
Twentieth-Century Prophet?

The name of Edgar Cayce has increasingly in recent years captured the attention of the general public in the United States. Perhaps not so well known is the respect his life and work have begun to command among serious thinkers in the academic community. Best known as a clairvoyant, reckoned by some as the psychically most gifted person in American history, Cayce is gradually winning the right to be heard for the moral and spiritual quality of the content of his communications, as much as for the quality of his person and life.

The distinguished Princeton Seminary professor of theology and personality, Seward Hiltner, in an article in *Religion in Life*, threw down the gauntlet to the entire theological establishment with a forthright challenge that they take seriously for the work of theology the phenomena and the data provided by men like Edgar Cayce. Hiltner quoted his former teacher Anton Boisen, American pioneer in chaplaincy programs in mental hospitals and in clinical education of the clergy. Like other intelligent students of mysticism in both Christian and non-Christian religious traditions, Boisen preferred to evaluate the phenomena by the criterion of their moral and spiritual fruits. Even in the case of a hospital patient hearing what might be called hallucinatory voices, Boisen insisted that the crux of the problem is not whether the patient hears voices or not, but what the voices say. Boisen believed that if the message of the voices led in the direction of wholesome self-criticism and balanced appreciation of both self and others, it could "in a way" be considered the voice of God.[1]

1. Seward Hiltner, "Comment on the God of Ambrose Worrall and of Edgar Cayce," *Religion in Life*, Autumn, 1972, pp. 410-414. Cf. Walther Eichrodt, *Theology of the Old Testament* (Philadelphia: Westminster Press, 1961), vol. I, pp. 289-391.

This approach enables us to grapple directly with a central, recurring problem-need of human life: the necessity to make qualitative evaluations, even daily, of persons and events. Evaluation, of course, is not to judge in the sense of condemnation. To condemn is to wipe off a person's future, to assume that he cannot change, that there is no hope for him. In the deepest sense this is to disbelieve in the mercy, good intent, and power of God. But to live wisely we must and do evaluate individuals and things, even hourly.

A primary issue in any human attempt at evaluation is the question of the criteria, the standards by which we may make our judgments of value or quality. Jesus is recorded as having taught His disciples to evaluate religious teachers by their fruits of conduct. By this means they were to test the religious authenticity of persons; names and professions of faith were not allowed to have a primary significance in the process.[2] We may note that this same criterion was one which Jeremiah employed as primary in his need to evaluate the contemporary "false prophets" in Judah, who outnumbered him, had superior social status and acceptance, and were in the formal sense as much "Hebrew of the Hebrews" as he was.[3]

It is not without significance that the Buddha is recorded as offering a similar criterion in answer to a question as to how to distinguish between true and false religious teachers. His reply was in effect that persons should judge for themselves, and their criterion of judgment should be whether the teachings "when performed and undertaken" lead to moral loss and sorrow or the reverse, to the ethical disintegration of a human being or to his moral and spiritual development. The criterion of religious authenticity for the Buddha was the quality of the ethical content of teachings and their fruit in life.[4]

The problem of distinguishing between authentic and unauthentic religious teachers, of discerning whether the dominant quality of a person's character—or, as the New Testament writers saw the problem, the regnant spirit in one—was of God or not, appears distinctly in the frequent apostolic injunctions to discern the spirits.[5] This process was therefore one which

2. Matthew 7:15-23; 12:33-35; Luke 6:43-45. Cf. Matthew 25:31-46; John 14:11; I John 2:29.
3. Jer. 23:14-22. Cf. Alfred Guillaume, *Prophecy and Divination* (New York: Harper, 1938), pp. 349, 353; John Skinner, *Prophecy and Religion* (Cambridge: The University Press, 1922), pp. 185-200.
4. *Anguttara-Nikaya* I, 187-192 [*The Book of the Gradual Sayings*], trans. F.L. Woodward (London: Luzac, 1951), vol. I, pp. 170-175.

operated throughout the "prophetic period" in the history of Israel and in the early Christian church. The final evaluation of a prophet's authenticity before God and man was made on the basis of the moral quality, as well as the essential fidelity to the tradition, of his teaching and of his life. A prophet's capacity to perform miracles or to manifest what we now call psychic gifts was secondary to this primary test.

Yet we must recognize that these admittedly secondary qualities were considered significant elements of the prophetic character. Indeed, we may say that there is no prophet in the Old Testament who was not a foreteller of the future as well as a forthteller of the word of God. It would seem that for Second Isaiah a distinguishing mark of an authentic prophet was this ability to foretell the future; it was the basis of his claim to speak with the authority of Yahweh, who alone knows the future but reveals it to those whom He chooses.[6] Indeed, all prophets from Balaam on were characterized by what we may call supernormal insight. Elisha's gift of clairvoyance was perhaps more strongly developed than any other's, but all the Hebrew prophets subsequently recognized as authentic by the collective judgment of their nation shared in this gift to a significant degree.[7] Not only the early so-called ecstatic prophets but also the later literary prophets of Israel were essentially alike in this respect. Characteristic of First Isaiah was his consciousness of knowing the will and plan of God in quite specific terms; he was, in the words of Alfred Guillaume, "The supreme vindicator of predictive prophecy."[8] Jeremiah claimed intimate personal knowledge of the God of his people's faith.[9] Ezekiel was highly sensitive to the reality of the unseen world; possessing psychic powers of clairvoyance and clairaudience to an extraordinary degree, he was able to see in visions events which were occurring hundreds of miles away.[10] Vision had marked and molded the personal lives as well as prophetic careers of Amos, Hosea, and other so-called minor prophets.[11]

---

5. I Cor. 2:14; 12:10; I Thess. 5:19-22; I John 4:1. Cf. Matthew 16:3; I Cor. 11:29; *Didache* 11:8-12, in *The Apostolic Fathers,* trans. Kirsopp Lake (Cambridge: Harvard University Press, 1945), p. 327.
6. Is. 41:21-23; 42:9. Cf. Guillaume, *op. cit.,* pp. 111, 152-154.
7. E.g., II Kings 3:15-20; 4:1-9:3. Cf. Guillaume, *op. cit.,* p. 198.
8. Is. 6:1-13; 37:7, 33. Cf. Guillaume, *op. cit.,* p. 153.
9. Jer. 23:18, 22. The implications of this passage would clearly seem to be that, unlike the "false prophets," Jeremiah did stand "in the council of the Lord."
10. Ezek. 1:1-28; 8:1-11:25.
11. Amos 1:1; 7:1, 4, 7; 9:1; Hos. 1:2; 3:1; Joel 2:28-29; Obad. 1; Mic. 1:1; Nah. 1:1; Hab. 1:1; Zech. 1:7-21. The prophets are frequently recorded as "seeing" the word of God.

We perceive, furthermore, that Old Testament prophecy came to life again in the New Testament figures of Zechariah, Elizabeth, Simeon, and Anna, not to mention Christ Himself. The role of dreams in the ordering of the early life of the Christ Child is particularly significant in the context of the Old Testament tradition; there is reason to believe that many of the Biblically recorded revelations must have come to men and women through dreams.[12]

This is not the place for an in-depth consideration of Hebrew prophecy, but some reference to the phenomena associated therewith and to the problems of evaluation felt by the prophets personally, as by their contemporaries, is necessary, I believe, to a responsible consideration of the spiritual and moral authenticity of a man like Edgar Cayce. As I shall endeavor to show, the life and work of this man are indeed such as to warrant, in the wider sense of the term, the descriptive adjective "prophetic."

As we shall see, throughout the more than forty years of the use of his psychic gifts, Cayce never, or almost never, prefaced his statements in trance or out with the words, "Thus says the Lord." We know that the Hebrew prophets, in their sayings as recorded in the Old Testament, often used this phrase to communicate the fact that they believed their message to be the veritable word of God. Their acceptance as authentic prophets both by their immediate disciples and ultimately by the nation as a whole was predicated upon acceptance of this claim. Cayce, however, did not advance the claim to be a spokesman of the word of God in this way. To the contrary, a distinct modesty and reserve characterized his self-awareness at this point. Yet, if we are permitted to use the term "prophetic" for a contemporary figure, as I believe we are, the appropriateness of the term would surely lie not in any formal claim to prophetic status, but in the proper meeting of the criteria which, as we have seen, operated rigorously within the prophetic period of Israel and the early church and, admittedly with some variations, over the subsequent centuries of the history of the church.[13] Certainly, essential conformity to these criteria is a necessary condition for the bestowal of the term "prophetic" as this term has been known and used within the Judeo-Christian tradition in its historically and ecumenically inclusive sense.

---

12. Luke 1:5-80; 2:26-38; Matthew 1:20-25; 2:1-23. Cf. Matthew 27:19; Acts 9:12 (shared dream experience).
13. Cf. Richard H. Drummond, "Authority in the Church: An Ecumenical Inquiry," *Journal of Bible and Religion,* October, 1966, pp. 329-345.

The presumption is that we are dealing with a contemporary figure who makes the kind of "authoritative moral and religious utterance" that a substantial number of people believe to fit their particular condition and need. The question is then whether the ethical quality of this person's life and the religio-theological content of his teaching are in essential conformity to the wider Judeo-Christian tradition. If they are—even if not perfectly nor infallibly so—we may properly affirm, I believe, that such a person can rightly be considered prophetic in the authentic sense of our tradition. He may also be held to speak the word of God to us in our time, even though we may feel impelled to scrutinize his message with care so as to determine whether this part or that may be more authentically and correctly the word of God for us.[14] Let us inquire as to whether Edgar Cayce meets this kind of test.

1

It has been difficult for many people, especially for members of the academic and religious establishment of this country, to take Edgar Cayce with adequate seriousness until very recently. Edgar Cayce in many ways was as American as apple pie. Born in 1877 in the small Kentucky town of Hopkinsville, of French Huguenot and British extraction, in a family originally stemming from Virginia, he was raised in a typically middle-American environment of the time. His receiving no more than eight years of formal schooling also made him one with the vast majority of his contemporaries in the United States. This relative (by present standards) lack of formal schooling has led some interpreters to speak of Cayce as semiliterate, but, in my judgment, this term represents a radical misreading of the evidence. Cayce was not an academically learned man, but by Lincoln-like daily reading of the Bible and by careful perusal and reflection upon the materials received through his readings over the years, he showed himself by the end of his life to be possessed of a high order of mind— subtle, perceptive, wide-ranging, comprehensive—as well as extraordinarily deep and sensitive spiritual insight.

But Edgar Cayce is now beginning to be regarded with increasing respect, even by those who work in the context and by the standards of the academic world. An M.A. student in a theological seminary related to my own is currently, with the approval of the dean and faculty of his school, writing a

14. Cf. W. Sibley Towner, "On Calling People 'Prophets' in 1970," *Interpretation*, October, 1970, pp. 492-509.

dissertation on a comparison of the thought of Pierre Teilhard de Chardin and Edgar Cayce. Specialists in patristic studies have recognized that the Christology of Cayce's materials is at some points similar to that of Paul of Samosata. His understanding of the relationship between Adam and the Christ is like that of the Ebionite Christians, an early Jewish Christian community. Most significantly, not only his Christology but his larger world view are remarkably similar to those of Origen, universally considered one of the greatest scholars and noblest spirits of the ancient church. We shall consider this point in more detail later.

Edgar Cayce first came to the attention of his contemporaries as an unusually gifted clairvoyant. I need not detail these gifts, but a word or two of explanation may be in order. In light of the fact that apart from the particular instance of dreams we have almost no knowledge of the specific nature of the internal or psychological phenomena involved in Hebrew prophecy, the experiences of Edgar Cayce are, at least potentially, of more than passing significance for students in this field.[15] In his early years Cayce had a number of what appeared to be strikingly significant dreams and visions, experiences which recurred at critical points in his later life. We note, however, that his earlier experiences evidently received specific recognition and approval from no less a person than Dwight L. Moody. Indeed, the interview extending over two separate mornings between Moody when he was at the height of his fame and powers and the teen-age Cayce not only is a remarkable piece of Americana but sheds important light on the inner as well as the public life of Moody himself.[16]

Edgar Cayce found in his early twenties that by putting himself into a light sleep, a kind of self-induced hypnosis, he was able to diagnose physical illnesses, his own as well as others', in response to questions put to him by another person while he was in this condition. This gift was first discovered in connection with a physical need of his own, and it soon extended to others.[17] To be properly understood, however, the disclosure of this gift must be seen in the context of the youthful Cayce's sustained aspiration and prayers that his life be helpful to others, especially to sick children.[18] Out of this background of concern came the practice

---

15. We can say, of course, that insofar as we are able, in the context of religious faith, to accept the concept of divine revelation to men, this revelation is transmitted through, and interpreted by, the mind of man. If, however, we use the term "mind of man," we are also able, on the basis of twentieth-century studies in depth psychology, to conceive of the instrumental process as including more than what we generally term the conscious mind.
16. Thomas Sugrue, *There Is a River* (New York: Dell, 1967), pp. 64-69.
17. *Ibid.*, pp. 49-51.

whereby each day Cayce gave himself to two or more sessions in which he answered specific questions regarding the physical condition of other persons near or far. Very shortly after the first attempts he insisted that the responsible person asking the questions be a member of his family, generally his wife, Gertrude, or his older son, Hugh Lynn. In his lifetime there was a total of 8,976 physical readings of this kind.[19] Studies show that—apart from the accuracy of diagnosis, which according to some estimates was over 90 percent—the treatments prescribed by Cayce produced favorable results in approximately 85 percent of the cases in which follow-up reports were obtained.[20]

Something of the astonishing accuracy of many of these readings is revealed in the instance of the "clary water" prescribed in a reading for the managing director of a small Eastern railroad, a man named P.A. Andrews. Andrews was unable to locate the item even though he inquired at all the leading drug houses in New York City and then advertised in medical journals. He wrote again to Edgar Cayce asking if he would take another reading to see if he could thereby learn the specific ingredients of the prescription. Several physicians were present at the time this second reading was given, and, when the formula for the tonic was revealed, they acknowledged that while strong, it would not hurt the patient. Subsequently another letter came from Andrews in New York. He had received a letter from a man in Paris, France. This man had read the advertisement in a medical journal asking for clary water and wrote to say that this was a product which his father had developed and marketed but had ceased to make fifty years before. He enclosed with the letter a copy of his father's formula. It was precisely identical with the ingredients given by Cayce in the second reading.[21]

On this occasion the presence of physicians and their favorable evaluation of the prescription eased Edgar Cayce's mind. But his deep and continuing anxiety lest the materials coming through him in light trance be in error and people be hurt in any way, physically or mentally, remained with him. An equally abiding question was, of course, that of the final source of the materials. One of the earliest terms used to describe the phenomenon was a

18. *Ibid.*, p. 45.
19. Edgar Evans Cayce and Hugh Lynn Cayce, *The Outer Limits of Edgar Cayce's Power* (New York: Harper, 1971), p. 13.
20. *Ibid.*, pp. 23-24. Cf. Sherwood Eddy, *You Will Survive after Death* (New York: Holt, Rinehart, 1959), pp. 91-101.
21. Joseph Millard, *Edgar Cayce, Mystery Man of Miracles* (New York: Fawcett, 1956), p. 80. Cf. Sugrue, *op. cit.*, pp. 25, 120, 126, 129.

"self-imposed hypnotic trance which induces clairvoyance."[22] But later the readings themselves communicated the fact that Edgar Cayce's subconscious mind was the key instrument, able upon suggestion from another person to communicate verbally and audibly its knowledge, and, even more significantly, that of the subconscious minds of others, drawing upon what Cayce called the "soul memory" of persons.[23]

2

This, however, was not the whole story. While Cayce's own subconscious mind remained the instrument, contact was made with more universal sources of information sometimes called "akashic records." More significantly, what Harmon Bro has termed "some kind of swift intelligence" seemed to preside and to move through "space and history and realms of present knowledge," giving scientific, medical, moral, political, economic and religio-theological data of macrocosmic as well as microcosmic scope. All this information was given with seeming awareness of just what and how much of the material could be properly communicated to the person or persons requesting the reading: technical data was relayed to the technically knowledgeable, and moral and religious material was geared to both the need and the understanding of those seeking. Some of the material, distinctly the smaller part, was predictive— predictive, however, in the sense of Old Testament prophecy. That is, the predictions were not declarative of absolutely predetermined events but, in the case of warnings, open-ended statements of trends which were expected to develop in such and such a way unless the person concerned changed his mind and ways. Other predictions were very positive and hopeful. On some occasions the material came through in a style at once "more stately and more urgent," reflecting the veritable ethos of a Biblical prophet. On more rare occasions the "elevated material" emerged "in a style of severe warning and call to righteousness, as stern as some archangel of old." There were also those few times when the voice of the sleeping Cayce stated in hushed tones that "the Master passes by" or gave some words of encouragement "as from the Master." The rarity, however, of this mode of speech

---

22. Sugrue, *op. cit.*, p. 111.
23. Hugh Lynn Cayce, *Venture Inward* (New York: Paperback Library, 1969), p. 74. Cf. Harmon H. Bro, *Edgar Cayce on Religion and Psychic Experience* (Paperback Library, 1970), p. 21.

highlights the predominant modesty and reserve of the entranced Cayce with regard to his ultimate sources or the religious authority with which he communicated his materials.[24]

Edgar Cayce himself throughout his conscious life was a profoundly religious man, for many years a Sunday school teacher and Christian Endeavor leader. He continued throughout his life to have notable visions and dreams, the former definitely occurring while he was fully conscious. The doubts and the questionings, however, to which he continued to subject himself and his pscyhic act:vities reveal him precisely in this light, as a man searchingly concerned, before God, to be morally responsible for his life and actions. "The language of morals" was natural both to Cayce and to his family in their inner wrestlings. Since he had no formal training in medicine, was he not in perpetual danger of giving incorrect and harmful medical advice to others? And when, from the year 1923, the range of the materials expanded to include what were called "life readings" and began to encompass topics of vast cosmic as well as religious scope, was he not in danger of communicating material that could seriously hurt or endanger the spiritual and ethical growth of others? Perhaps more than any other one thing—comparable in this respect was Cayce's lifelong refusal to commercialize his gifts, in spite of innumerable offers—this concern, even anxiety, for the effect of his psychic gifts upon other persons marks the quality of the man. Indeed, I do not think that it would be an overstatement to say that the nature of this concern over long years was such that we may legitimately compare Edgar Cayce with the prophet Jeremiah at this as indeed at other points.[25]

In his earliest questionings Cayce was helped by his mother's evaluation that if his gift was of God, it would do only good. From this perspective and standard he ruthlessly scrutinized the data which came through him and carefully followed up the later reports of patients and other inquirers as they sent them to him. As a part of his concern for accuracy, from 1923 until his death in 1945 Cayce employed a stenographer, Gladys Davis, who transcribed the readings verbatim by shorthand. He quickly learned that his talent functioned best when he remained true to the highest moral and religious standards of his own conscious life—when he remained personally incorruptible and gave readings only in the context of prayer for divine guidance and

24. Bro, *ibid.*, pp. 26-30.
25. Sugrue, *op. cit.,* pp. 110-111, 124-129, 156-159, 209-216, 271-272. Cf. Guillaume, *op. cit.*, pp. 334-336.

help. He had to be consciously allied with the forces of good for good and consistent results to issue from his subconscious.[26] One of the most moving accounts in the story of his life is that of his walking the streets of Dayton, Ohio, through a long night in 1923, as he prayed and tested the materials that had come through him in response to questions put by the intellectually sophisticated Arthur Lammers.[27] And on the few occasions in his early life— before he came to establish his later unvarying rule to conduct no reading without his wife or son present—when his gift was used by others to extract information for selfish purposes, such as data on a forthcoming horse race, he invariably suffered physical ill himself, particularly in the form of severe headaches.[28]

3

Of equal importance in evaluating what we may call the prophetic significance of Edgar Cayce is, of course, the content of the material itself. A point of primary importance therein is its internal consistency. A total of 14,256 readings was given, from the earliest dated reading in 1909 until Cayce's death in January of 1945. An appreciable number of people received more than one reading, sometimes with an interval of ten years or more between one discourse and the next. And yet, the historical, cosmological and ethico-religious material given on these occasions—often in very different contexts and years apart—shows such a rigorous consistency, even if not perfect, as to stagger the imagination. This characteristic is also evident when readings given for different people are compared.[29] But of even more importance than logical or factual consistency is the internal religious and moral quality of the materials.

If we may take up again Harmon Bro's thesis of a "swift intelligence" presiding and moving in the functioning of Edgar Cayce's readings, we have sufficient material—indeed an abundance of material, perhaps a larger quantity than that produced by any figure of religious significance in the whole of known human history—to evaluate with no little precision the quality of spirit of this "intelligence" working through Cayce's subconscious mind. Gina Cerminara has preferred to identify this "intelligence" with the superconscious mind of Cayce. Whether

26. Cf. Bro, *op. cit.*, p. 20; Sugrue, *op. cit.*, pp. 157, 209-210.
27. Sugrue, *op. cit.*, pp. 211-216.
28. *Ibid.*, pp. 171-172; Millard, *op. cit.*, pp. 113-116.
29. Cayce and Cayce, *op. cit.*, pp. 13-17, *passim*.

this is an apt identification I shall leave to another time and perhaps to another person to investigate. But in our present context of thought I should like to quote Dr. Cerminara's beautiful description of her impressions of the qualities which seem to characterize this "intelligence":

"Paramount...is the sense that one is in the presence of a master physician. This is true not only of the physical readings, but equally as much, or more so, in the case of the life readings. In general, he seems to speak with the benign, infinitely patient words of a doctor who is also a friend. The tempo of his speech is unhurried; yet one senses a certain urgency beneath the words. It is the compassionate urgency of one who sees the infinite sufferings of the world and who yearns with every instinct of his being to relieve them. Like a surgeon in a battle-front hospital, he is sober and terse...

"As a doctor to suffering souls as well as suffering bodies, this physican is supremely practical. But he has the long-sighted practicality that knows life to be essentially a spiritual experience in a spiritual universe. He sees it as a continuous thing, proceeding through various planes of matter and operating under certain definite laws of action and reaction, cause and effect. Whenever he has time to do so, and whenever he thinks the patient will understand, he stops to explain the truths of reality and of man's relationship to the universe which apply to the case in question. Philosophy and metaphysics might seem to be remote from the practical reality of pain, but this master physician knows that they are, on the contrary, very close."[30]

Dr. Cerminara describes the physician as "sober and terse." This is indeed an apt phrase, fitting many of the readings, but not all. She herself has pointed out that not a few readings emphasize the value and importance of humor.[31] People are specifically told in some readings to "Cultivate the ability to see the ridiculous, and to retain the ability to laugh. For, know—only in those that God hath favored is the ability to laugh, even when clouds of doubt arise, or when every form of disturbance arises. For, remember, the Master smiled—and laughed oft..." (2984-1) "Hold, then, to that ability to be witty... Quit being too serious. Laugh it off. He did..." (3685-1)[32]

---

30. Gina Cerminara, "The Forgotten Virtue," *The Searchlight,* June, 1954, p. 2.
31. *Ibid.*, pp. 1-2.
32. Cf. Josephus, *Wars of the Jews* II, 8, 10.

The prophetic significance of Edgar Cayce for twentieth-century man emerges with particular clarity and force in the many, many directions for living the religious life given to individuals and groups in the readings. By the term "religious life" the whole gamut of individual and corporate living is meant, all dimensions of life, including the inner and the outer, the conscious and the subconscious, the personal and the social, the economic and the political—all subsumed within a profoundly religious view of the cosmos. Repeated emphasis is placed upon the oneness of God, a central tenet of the teachings, even as at the same time the richness of the Godhead is suggested by the occasional use of the plural number—similar to "Elohim" in the Hebrew Old Testament—in terms like "Creative Forces." (1152-11; 1219-1; 254-87; 3155-1)

The readings also exhibit a radical Christocentricity. In stressing the universality of divine concern and providential order, the readings are one with the Fathers of the early church. The Father's revealing and saving grace as well as His providential care through His Spirit extend, and always have extended, to all men (2402-2; 2072-15; 254-92). "There is only *one* Spirit—of Truth." (262-87) "Is He not God and Lord of the Catholic as well as of the Protestant and of the Jew? Did He not make them all? Does He not love one the same as another? Know ye not that He is not a respecter of persons?" (2783-1) There is not only a generous acknowledgment of the work of God among all men in all times and places, but a specific recognition of the religious authenticity, the meaningful role in the divine plan and working, of certain teachers outside the Judeo-Christian tradition, e.g., the Buddha, Confucius, Muhammad. They were spokesmen to their ages, called to the purpose of manifesting the One Truth-Reality; in all was the "same impelling spirit." (364-9) But this understanding is focused in a remarkable exaltation of the divine significance and role of Jesus the Christ, an exaltation that yet allows contemporary as well as past Jewry a high place in God's work in the world. Edgar Cayce was early informed that the work would succeed when there was a Jew involved in it; subsequently a number of distinguished American Jews became intimately associated with him: David and Lucille Kahn, Morton and Edwin Blumenthal, etc.[33]

---

33. Sugrue, *op. cit.*, p. 183. Cf. David E. Kahn, *My Life with Edgar Cayce* (Greenwich, Conn.: Fawcett World Library, 1971), *passim*.

All the great figures of man's religious pilgrimage, the readings say, whether Abraham or Moses, whether the Buddha, Confucius or Muhammad, have been but stepping-stones to the higher knowledge of the Son of God in the lives of men. In the Christ is found the supreme advocate with the Father (262-14). After the manner of the theology of Origen, a distinction is made between Jesus of Nazareth and the Christ or Christ Consciousness, but Jesus was the Christ manifested, the Son of Man, the Son of the Maker of heaven and earth, the Savior of the world, the example (991-1; 1152-12; 1089-2; 254-92; 826-4; 900-17). In answer to the question, "Who was 'the greatest philosopher of life and love that has ever been known to the earth plane'?" the Cayce source responded, "The Master" (288-27), Jesus the Christ. "In Jesus we find the answer." (900-17) " . . . that light which was the light of the world from the beginning is crystallized in the entity known as Jesus of Nazareth, who passeth by today for thee, and unless ye take hold upon Him, ye must falter." (5265-1) The cross is the "culmination of God's approach to man in his phase of unfoldment in the earth." (3054-4) For "the Resurrection [of the Christ] brought to the consciousness of man that power that God hath given to man, that may reconstruct, resuscitate, even every atom of a physically sick body, that may resurrect even every atom of a sin-sick soul. . . " (1158-5) " . . . even in Elijah or John we find the faltering, the doubting. We find no faltering, no doubting, no putting aside of the purpose in the Master Jesus." (3054-4) "These others are only as lights along the way. The truth is *only* in Him, Jesus the Christ!" (3004-1) "There's only one Master." (3545-1) *But* "God calls on man everywhere to seek His face, through that channel that may be blessed by the Spirit of the Son—in whatsoever sphere this may take its form." (364-9) " . . . *faithful is* he that keeps . . . in the way that leads to *more* light, *more* understanding." (340-15) This is to say that every man in every place has ongoing access to spiritual channels that may be used and blessed by the Spirit of the Christ, by the Holy Spirit, whether these channels bear the name Christian or not.

In the context of current interests and forms of spirituality in the United States, as throughout the Western world and beyond, the guidance given in the Cayce readings seems both relevant and practical. The readings see man as "made that he might become the companion of the Creative Forces . . . " (1456-1) The goal of each entity (a term used to give equal value and significance in God's order to both male and female) is "to become one with, yet aware of its *own* identity *in,* the Creative Force." (261-15) "For the entrance of an entity, a soul, into the earth's experience is to fit the soul for companionship with Creative Forces or God. And if these experiences are made for self-indulgence, self-aggrandizement first, then there are set up in the experience of the soul false gods." (1219-1) Then, while the strongest emphasis is placed upon the significance for spiritual growth of the ethical quality of our relationships with our fellow men, we are directed to find God within as well as without.

Repeatedly the message was "in thy mental meditation, seek the Lord while He may be found. Put Him not away from thee, but seek *only* in the *name* of the *Christ,* the *Lord,* the *Son of man!* the *Savior of the world!*" (1089-2) Even as each soul's primary purpose in life is to manifest "the love of the Savior, Jesus the Christ, for the children of men" (1152-12), we are directed again and again to the "light that comes from within." (877-27) Our dependence is *not* upon the powers without. "A particular church organization is well. For it centers the mind" (3350-1), but "...Christ ye serve and not a church!" (2823-3) We are our brother's keeper, but we must first know ourselves and "Hold to that which the God within directs..." (1158-12) Even as the warning is given that in our time the theological and the spiritual dimensions "have grown and are growing farther and farther apart in the affairs of man as a whole..." this is seen as "a fault—a failure of man to grasp the *one* thought, the *one* ideal..." (1473-1) indeed, the oneness of God, for the readings frequently emphasize Jesus' summation of the commandments in the words, "Thou shalt love the Lord, thy God, with all thy heart, thy mind, thy body; and thy neighbor as thyself." (1401-1)

With regard to the Bible, we are told that indeed "This has passed through many hands" (262-60), but "if ye will get the spirit of that written there ye may find it will lead thee to the gates of heaven. For, it tells of God, of your home, of His dealings with His peoples in many environs, in many lands. Read it to be wise. Study it to understand. *Live* it to know that the Christ walks through same with thee." (262-60)

Men and women are told in the readings to give meditation an important place in their devotional lives. "Speak oft to thy Maker and in Him ye [all] may find the light within." (5265-1) "...that which is helpful, the more oft, is in the still small voice within." (2051-5) "Through meditation may the greater help be gained." (987-2) "For *truth* is a *growing* thing!" (282-4) in the experience of men; therefore we are to turn to the temple within, for there He has promised to meet us ever. In this way we are to obey the law, which is "Seek and ye shall find! *Knock* and it shall be opened unto you!" (262-89) God is good, and is one; "*Love,* then, *Divine;* as was manifested in Jesus of Nazareth, must be the rule—yea, the measuring stick—the rod, by which ye [each] shall judge thy motives, thy impulses, thy associations." (1497-1) In language akin to that of Shakespeare, whom Cayce evidently had not read in his conscious life, we are told to "be true, to thine self—and it *cannot* be thou wilt be false to any." (2135-1)[34] The Biblical principle of proportionate responsibility is forthrightly taught in the words: " ... the greater the ability, the greater is that required or demanded not only of and by self, but [in] self's relationships to Creative Forces as may manifest in a material world." (1341-1) It is repeated in the warning: " ... 'What ye sow, ye reap' is the unchangeable, the irrefutable law; and you are constantly meeting yourself! For with what measure you mete it is measured to you again. If you would have friends, then be *friendly!* If you would know God, then *be merciful* unto others!" (1568-3) "It is not the knowledge, not the power or might, but the simplicity of application that is the wisdom of the sages... " (1318-1)

But above the law of sowing and reaping, which Orientals call the law of karma, reigns the law of grace. We are told to make our will one with God's and then not be afraid. We live in the divine order where the Lord God "hath not tempted any soul, He hath not given any soul that [which] it may not meet. And He hath prepared a way of escape for each soul if it will but harken to that voice deep *within!...* that which is the prompting of the inner conscience." (417-8) "The mere purpose of trying was counted as righteousness." (1968-5)[35] But in all our need we are to remember the Christ, for we were "bought with a price, even that of passing through flesh as thou that He might experience and know all thy thoughts, thy fears, thy shortcomings, thy desires, the dictates of the physical consciousness, the longings of the physical body. Yet He is at the right hand, *is* the right hand, *is* the intercessor for ye all. Hence thy destinies lie in Him... if thou wilt call—His promise has been, 'Though ye wander far afield, though ye be forsaken, though ye be misunderstood, if ye will call *I* will hear!' And if ye be on the Lord's side, *who* can be against you?" (696-3)

We find in the readings ever a creative tension between the call to personal and social righteousness, a keen sense of the working of karmic law, on the one hand, and, on the other, an understanding of God as merciful and compassionate love, ever

---

34. Cf. Shakespeare, *Hamlet* I, 3, 78.
35. Cf. Worth Kidd, *A Way to Fulfillment* (Virginia Beach: A.R.E. Press, 1973), pp. 22-36.

ready to give man the opportunity to turn, to reorient his life-center, from self to God. "What is truth? Law! What is law? Love. What is love? God. What is God? Law and love. These are as the cycle of truth itself. And wherever ye are, in whatever the clime, it's ever the same. For, as it is said of Him, He is the same yesterday, today and forever—unalterable!" (3574-2)

The primary focus of the Cayce readings with regard to human life is on the day-to-day living of ordinary men, women, and children. "As a soul or entity seeks to become a channel of blessing to its fellow man, there are the guiding steps [given] step by step; and doing that which is known in self to be the correct, the right relationships in any given determination fits the body from day to day for that development... Day by day is there shown the way. He that faints not finds the way." (423-2) "... enter into the holy of holies, within thine own consciousness; turn within; see what has prompted thee. And He has promised to meet thee there. And there *shall* it be *told* thee from within the steps thou shouldst take day by day, step by step. Not that some great exploit, some great manner of change should come within thine body, thine mind, but line upon line, precept upon precept, here a little, there a little... for lo, He is within thine own self—yet without, that He may guide, *guard,* direct thy ways day by day!" (922-1; cf. Isaiah 28:10, 13)

5

Edgar Cayce was the man through whom these teachings came, teachings whose abundant richness, subtlety, almost infinite complexity and range, whose compassionate concern and tender love, are but hinted at in this brief sketch. He is the man of whom near the end of his life the source from which he drew asked a group of his associates, "What will ye do with this man?"[36] About this man who came from the heart of America's heartland, as American as apple pie, we consider once again the question, What should we make of him? Measuring my words, and thinking of Karl Barth, Dietrich Bonhoeffer, Toyohiko Kagawa, Karl Rahner, Sundar Singh, and again using the term in its wider sense, I am prepared to call him one of the great prophetic figures of the twentieth century. His work and his words, I believe, fully qualify him to be placed alongside the men whom I have named.

Richard R. Niebuhr and James M. Gustafson are currently asserting the need for American theology to overcome its

36. Bro, *op. cit.*, p. 30.

excessive dependence upon the "maternal theology" of Europe. They ask us to "discover and exploit in greater self-reliance the experiential sources of a 'native' theology."[37] Closeness to the experiential sources of religion has clearly been part of the American religious tradition from Jonathan Edwards through the great revivals and down to the present day. I submit that the life and work of Edgar Cayce constitute one of the most authentic and richest of these experiential sources. Understanding of the nature of the Judeo-Christian prophetic tradition as well as intellectual honesty compel us, I believe, to make an adequate examination of this man and his work.[38]

37. Cf. Richard R. Niebuhr, *Experiential Religion* (New York: Harper, 1972); Morton Kelsey, *Encounter with God* (Minneapolis: Bethany Fellowship, 1972).
38. It may be helpful to relate that the Dominican scholar Richard Woods recently commented in my hearing that Edgar Cayce is properly to be placed in the category of Jonathan Edwards rather than Jeane Dixon.

Edgar Cayce and
Divine Providence

Perhaps the primary reason why I have deep respect for Edgar Cayce, the man and his work, is that he speaks to my own life condition with a correctness of diagnosis and prescription as few men in the twentieth century have been able to do. That is, the clairvoyant readings of which Edgar Cayce was the human instrument, although originally addressed to other persons, become surprisingly accurate instruments for my own moral and spiritual self-knowledge. They also prescribe directions for the cure, for the transformation and development of my character, that my best self recognizes as both fitting and good. I find the Cayce readings to be helpful, in the deepest sense of the word, to me personally and to the wider world of which I am a part.

It is in this context of understanding that I wish to consider some of the Cayce readings which I believe to be vital to the religious life of all persons. I refer to those parts of the readings which deal with our *Weltanschauung*, or world view; in particular, the faith-understanding we have of the framework or structural conditions of our lives.

Perhaps we do not always realize how much certain assumptions, which are in fact part of our basic world view, govern or at least appreciably affect the way we react to persons and events. These reactions may contribute to our life-effectiveness and happiness or the reverse. Let me illustrate. Most people set themselves honorable goals and try to develop and carry out responsible plans to attain those goals. But much of the difficulty we experience in the course of their execution comes from the so-called "interruptions," small or large, which indeed daily "interfere" with our plans. How we understand and cope with these "interruptions" or "interferences" plays a large role in our personal effectiveness and happiness. But how we understand and then cope is very much influenced by the basic assumptions of the world view through which we interpret the experiences. Let us look briefly at some fairly widespread and influential alternative ways of looking at the structures of human life.

We obviously do not have the space to discuss the characteristics and developments of the major world views that have competed for the allegiance of Western man from the time of classical antiquity. Let us therefore limit ourselves to those movements which still contribute to the thought of modern man in the Western world. One of the most germinal of these has been that wide-ranging stream of cultural activity which we call the Renaissance. One dimension characterizing its world view almost from its beginnings in fourteenth-century Italy was a strong affirmation of the almost limitless possibilities of human existence. This meant possibilities for the development of both personal selfhood or character and its cultural expression.

The hopeful, expansive perspectives characteristic of the great personages of the Renaissance—we may cite Dante, Petrarch, Nicholas of Cusa, Pico della Mirandola and Giordano Bruno as outstanding literary figures—can be specifically contrasted with the more limited or constricted expectations of medieval scholastics. Some of these men, such as Mirandola and Bruno, assumed that more than one life might be necessary to complete the process of fulfillment of human life on earth; i.e., they espoused the concept of reincarnation.[1] This larger hope was not merely the result of the fresh study of classical antiquity. This belief was in considerable measure derived from Biblical and early Christian aspirations towards personal sanctification and development. These aspirations in turn had been revived, especially in the Franciscan movement of the thirteenth century. The fourteenth century, which was the focal point of the early Renaissance, was also one of the greatest periods of Western spirituality. The European humanist movement at its best was specifically related to the renewed concerns for the inner life of man and for the spiritual experience which characterized that century.[2]

The movement for religious reform which we call the Reformation was in some ways an aspect of the Renaissance. In

---

1. Cf. Joseph Head and S.L. Cranston, *Reincarnation in World Thought* (New York: The Julian Press, 1971), pp. 230-242.
2. Cf. Christopher Dawson, *The Dynamics of World History* (New York: The New American Library, 1962), pp. 241-242.

its early period there were as many leading figures concerned for religious reform in Italy and Spain, in France and Austria, as in the more northerly areas which later separated from the Roman church and became Protestant states. But the Reformation in its narrower sense distinctly emerged as a kind of qualifying counter-movement to the humanist Renaissance. The major reformers, especially Martin Luther and John Calvin, emphasized that sin and evil persist even in the lives of the redeemed, the committed believers. The Reformers were certainly hopeful—at least for some persons—because they realized in a fresh way that through Iesus the Christ divine mercy had made possible both the initiation and the continuation of the Christian life. In general, however, they rejected what they considered the excessive optimism regarding the possibilities of human life held by the leading figures of the Renaissance.

My reason for bringing these movements to your attention is their important contribution to later and indeed contemporary ways of looking at the world. On the whole, we may say that the relatively optimistic world view of the Renaissance has been the more influential, especially upon later secular forms of thought. It was a unifying principle in the rationalism of Descartes and the French Enlightenment. It has been an underlying assumption of both the liberal idea of progress and the Marxist dialectical view of history. It lay behind the perfectionist hopes of Protestant sectarians as much as it stimulated the utopian dreams of secular social planners in Europe and North America. The more somber Reformation view lived on in English-speaking Puritanism and Continental European Pietism. But even in the churches, especially in the twentieth century, more optimistic views of the world have tended to prevail.[3]

For many reasons the relative dominance, at least among the middle classes, of this more optimistic world view is cause, I believe, for gratitude. This is especially so when we recall that both Luther and Calvin—Calvin more explicitly—taught a double divine predestination of persons. That is, all men, women and children, by God's eternal decree, formed before the creation of the world, are predestined to either salvation or damnation, utterly apart from any merit or desert of their own. This view of God and the world was first brought to full theological formulation by the North African Latin-speaking theologian Augustine between the years 410 and 430. It was, however, a

3. Cf. Reinhold Niebuhr, *The Nature and Destiny of Man* (New York: Charles Scribner's Sons, 1949), vol. II, pp. 157-212.

distinct perversion of the early Christian view of divine providence, which assumed authentic and responsible human freedom, in both will and act, within certain limits.[4]

The Augustinian, Calvinistic view was evidently conceived by both Augustine and Calvin in primarily a positive way, that is, as a source of security and comfort for Christians in a time when long-established political, cultural and religious institutions were in the process of rapid change. But it is really a theologized version of cosmic fatalism which makes God an arbitrary and therefore immoral despot. Human life on earth in its cultural as well as personal dimensions ceases to have, I feel, any ultimate significance. On the other hand, the popularized or secularized versions of Renaissance optimism regarding the possibilities of human life have not been without serious problems. Let me give you a concrete example.

I read in the June 22, 1973, issue of the *National Review*, which you may recall as the magazine edited by William F. Buckley, Jr., a report of an interview with Walter Lippmann. This had been given to Ronald Steel and was published in the *Washington Post* before the Watergate scandals broke into the news. Lippmann, one of the most perceptive and respected American journalists of relatively liberal persuasion during the past generation and more, was discussing recent events in American political life. He felt that some of these events specifically revealed the repudiation by a substantial majority of the American people "of the Jacobin or Rousseauistic philosophy... that man is essentially good and can be made perfect by making the environment perfect, and that the environment can be made perfect by taxing the mass of the people to spend money for improving it." Lippmann went on to say that "we have been in the grip of this general view of the nature of society at least since Woodrow Wilson."

As you can imagine, William Buckley was very pleased with Lippmann's critique of a widely held assumption of American liberal political thought. But the world view of which this assumption is a particular political expression manifests itself also in the economic, social and cultural dimensions of our individual and corporate lives. This popularized, indeed distorted, form of early Renaissance optimism regarding the nature of man and society informs much of our modern thinking about education as well as social reform. Perhaps the emphasis has been more commonly on the malleability than on the

4. Cf. Justin Martyr, *The First Apology* 28, 43-44; Athenagoras, *A Plea Regarding Christians* 24.

goodness of man. In either case, the basic assumption has widely obtained that man, indeed all of human life, is primarily to be changed and molded by his environment, by external circumstances and stimuli. Hence the assumption of much political thinking that the primary foci of desirable change are the structures, the institutions of human society.

There is, I believe, not a little elitism in this way of thinking. If man is infinitely malleable, or nearly so, and can be altered and molded primarily by his circumstances and external stimuli, such as education or training, the media, etc., then man, or the bulk of men, may be manipulated and controlled by a knowledgeable elite. This can be a political elite like the Communist or Nazi parties. It can be a cultural elite such as B.F. Skinner and other exponents of behaviorist psychology.[5]

This is to say, of course, that a wide-open view of the malleability of man does not necessarily result in humane consequences. Our twentieth-century experience with large-scale social experiments—Communist, Fascist, German National Socialist—along with recent events in liberal-democratic societies, has also shown us with abundant examples that human nature is not so malleable, indeed is far more intractable than many have thought. Sensitive thinkers are realizing anew that human beings are in fact born into this world not only with differing talents or abilities, but also with varying predispositions of character and personality. These latter manifest themselves often at a very early age—one thinks at once of infant prodigies like Mozart and John Stuart Mill—and are by no means easily traceable merely to hereditary and environmental influences. I personally feel that one reason for the repressive and terrorist measures employed by both Communist and Fascist dictatorships in the twentieth century has been the frustration of political leaders who believed that men could be molded to suit their, the leaders', goals and plans. They found that human beings just would not, or could not, respond as desired by the planners.

To bring this all to a focus, I find that neither the early Renaissance nor the Reformation world view in their pristine or pure form has captured the allegiance of large numbers of people over long periods. The bulk of mankind seems rather to oscillate between popularized extremist versions of both. During some periods, men have adopted a distorted view of the Renaissance tradition and consequently have tended to believe that anything

---

5. Cf. B.F. Skinner, *Beyond Freedom and Dignity* (New York: Knopf, 1971), pp. 201-202.

or everything in human beings and their environment is susceptible to change, even radical and quick change. Such optimism tends to characterize the early stages of a revolution, whether conservative or radical.

Following the tradition of the Reformation and at times distorting it, others have sunk into total fatalism. Ascribing all events to the "will of God," they have in fact believed that little or no change is possible, either in man or in his society. I believe that we in the United States are at present in such a period of discouragement following the heady optimism and then the relatively ineffective results of the political activism of the 1960s.[6]

The world view underlying secular expressions of optimism has often seen human life as so open that it is presumed to participate in no cosmic order, moral or otherwise. A corollary of this understanding is to see life as but a vast conglomeration of "happenstance," of chance events lacking order, pattern, direction or meaning. This way of thinking is surprisingly common among many of the intellectuals of our society. But the same persons can become frustrated and discouraged and therefore fearful and rigid. The corollary of this mood is to presume that man is the complete prisoner of his circumstances. Here, too, we find no understanding of a true cosmic order at work, only rigidities that lack meaning or moral purpose. In other words, we find persons alternating between views of total freedom and total fatalism, between joy in freedom looking toward vast changes, especially in others, and despair of freedom because all is rigid and resistant and meaningless.

I do not hesitate to draw the conclusion that many of our intellectual and spiritual leaders have not understood aright the real meaning or mode of functioning of the historical process.[7] Therefore at this point of historic need I venture to suggest that the readings of Edgar Cayce offer a way of understanding the historical, indeed cosmic, process, a view of human life and history that is faithful to the basic faith-understanding of both the Bible and the early Christian church. It is also in accord, I believe, with the best insights of the most creative personages of the

---

6. This kind of oscillation is not limited to Western societies. The relative open-endedness and optimism of primitive Islam developed into the fatalism of later Muslim orthodoxy. The profound hopefulness for man characteristic of the teaching of the Buddha was altered off and on in the history of Buddhism into rigid views of the operation of the law of karma. Similarly, in popular Hinduism, rigid interpretations of karma left little hope for the mass of mankind.

7. Cf. Trevor Ravenscroft, *The Spear of Destiny* (New York: G.P. Putman's Sons, 1973), p. 203.

Hindu, Buddhist and Muslim traditions. This is a world view that affirms authentic freedom for man, both to will and to act, in the context of a cosmic order that is morally conditioned. This is an order, divinely purposed and structured, which specifically provides opportunity for the responsible participation of human beings in their own destiny, in their own change and growth. "Our will is a Divine attribute; how we use it determines our destiny."[8]

The cosmic order which emerges with remarkable clarity and consistency from the Cayce readings affirms not only the responsibilities but also the opportunities afforded man. That is, the responsibility we are given to cope with our past and our present, with ourselves and our circumstances, becomes, by the grace of God, our opportunity to turn these realities into stepping-stones rather than stumbling blocks. Theologically put, this world view affirms the Biblical paradox of divine mercy and divine judgment. Neither aspect can be neglected without faulting the other. I feel that with regard to this dimension of our faith Edgar Cayce has appeared in our midst like a veritable prophet of the early Church. Like the writers of the New Testament and the early Fathers, he proclaims the gospel of God's forgiveness and human liberation uniquely effected by the cross and resurrection of Jesus the Christ. Also like them, he insists that this liberation is wrought in the context of the ongoing operation of the law of compensation, of sowing and reaping, of the karmic law, if you please.[9] Let me illustrate.

The Cayce readings begin theologically with the affirmation that God, the Creative Force or Forces (a plural form denotative of the multidimensional aspect of the divine personhood), the First Cause, is. "First we begin with the fact that God *is*... He, God, *is!*" (1567-2) He is "the all-wise, all-merciful Father, the First Cause, the Mother-God, the Father-God..." (945-1) The Lord is good (1215-4), is *mindful* of the entity, of every human being (3188-1; cf. 1747-5). "He cares!" (1567-2) "...the opportunities that are offered to each soul in its search, in its journey through materiality" are a manifestation of the love of God our Father (1842-1). God, the Universal Consciousness (5343-1), the divine Oneness, is gracious (1158-5). Therefore— and here we have a Pauline phrase which occurs frequently with minor variations in the Cayce readings—"God hath not willed

8. *A Search for God* (Virginia Beach, Virginia: A.R.E. Press, 1970), vol. II, p. 63.
9. Cf. Gal. 6:7-8; I Cor. 9:21; Matthew 7:1-2; Job 4:8; I Clement 13:2. The sentences illustrative of this principle which are attributed by Clement to Jesus suggest that Clement drew upon an extra-canonical collection of Jesus' sayings.

that any soul should perish but hath with every temptation, every trial, every disappointment made a way of escape or for correcting same." (1567-2) "... God hath not desired that any soul should perish, but constantly gives opportunities... that it may find itself." (1460-2)[10]

In the Cayce readings the mercy of the all-wise Creative Force is consistently coupled with His justice. We shall consider later how His mercy functions in giving men the opportunities and power to cope with or transcend the strict processes of justice. But first let us observe how in the Cayce readings the justice of God works to effect a cosmic order that is just and fair, yet open-ended. "For, the entrance into the earth's plane of the entity is not by chance. Neither is it destined as to what the end will be, but the opportunities are ever present." (3129-1) The readings in fact proclaim an open-ended universe and an open-hearted God.

The principle of divine justice is again and again expressed in the readings by the Biblical image of sowing and reaping. "God is not mocked, and whatsoever a soul soweth, that must it somewhere, sometime reap." (3660-1; cf. 5343-1) Like many early Christians, such as the Jewish Christian sects of the Ebionites, the Elkasites, the Nasoraeans, etc., and like the Alexandrian theologians Clement and Origen, the readings see the operation of this just principle of sowing and reaping as entailing what we call metempsychosis or reincarnation (but not transmigration!)[11] This understanding not only posits the return of the soul to the

---

10. Cf. I Cor. 10:13; II Peter 3:9. This excerpt is an example of the relatively frequent instances in the Cayce readings where a verse or passage from the Bible is quoted in such a way as to give at the same time an explication or interpretation of its meaning. For example, this Pauline verse is quoted with a variety of concluding variations or qualifications: "God does not allow us to be tempted beyond that we are able to bear and comprehend, if we will but make our wills one with His." (900-44) "For, He hath not willed that any soul should perish, but has with each temptation, each trial, prepared a way of understanding or escape." (2081-1) "He hath not willed that any soul should perish, but hath with each temptation prepared a manner in which each soul may meet itself..." (1663-2) "For He hath not willed that any soul should perish, and thus again and again comes that opportunity." (3581-1) "For, the Father has not willed that any soul should perish, and is thus mindful that each soul has again and again—and yet again—the opportunity for making its path straight." (2021-1) "For when the souls of men had wandered away, He—not willing that any soul should perish—has prepared a way through which, by which, they each may find their way again to that companionship, that relationship with the Creative Forces." (1458-1) "For, He hath not willed that any soul should perish, but hath with each temptation prepared a way, a manner through which each soul may become aware of its faults, its virtues; magnifying the virtues, minimizing the faults—that one may come to the perfect knowledge of one's relationships to the Creative Influences—called God." (2397-1) "Know first, the Lord thy God hath not tempted any soul, He hath not given any soul that it may not meet. And He hath prepared a way of escape for each soul if it will but harken to that voice deep *within*." (417-8)

11. See Ernst Benz, *Indische Einflüsse auf die frühchristliche Theologie* (Wiesbaden:

earth to be reborn in the flesh again and again according to its need, but also assumes sojourns in other realms as a part of the same larger educative purpose.

The readings emphasize that the experiences or sojourns in the earth—or elsewhere—are not by chance (2271-1; 5343-1) but are the expression of a continuity of divine pattern or purpose (3128-1). They affirm that as a manifestation of the principle of sowing and reaping the soul ever meets itself, "For each soul, each entity, *constantly* meets self. And if each soul would but understand, those hardships which are accredited much to others are caused most by self. *Know* that in those [experiences] you are meeting *thyself!*" (845-4) This means that "each entity in the earth is what it is because of what it has been!" (2823-3) "... what we are—in any given experience, or time—is the combined results of what we have done about the ideals that we have set!" (1549-1) "And each moment is dependent upon another moment." (2823-3)[12]

Clearly we are dealing here with an awesome, indeed disconcerting, world view. It takes away the basis of those most common of human pastimes, complaint and criticism of others. Not that we must approve of all that happens about us or in others; the Cayce readings never say that every event is in accord with the will of God. In this view of the cosmos, we cannot blame our circumstances or even the extent of our talents on others (cf. 3671-1; 3138-1; 1302-2). We can no longer claim that someone or something "out there" did us wrong. We cannot assert, like the Marxists, that the "enemy" is the capitalist class, nor imply, as Freudian psychologists, that our parents are chiefly responsible for our mental condition and its effects.

In our initial confrontation with this world view what appear as punitive aspects may loom large, yet the process is more properly to be seen as educative, in the deepest sense of the word and in the context of divine concern. The Lord God loves those whom He has made, and "whom the Lord loveth He cherisheth, whom the Lord loveth He raiseth up to opportunities." (1463-2) "... it was

Verlag der Akademie der Wissenschaften und der Literatur in Mainz, 1951), pp. 185-190. Benz has brought together a number of passages from Origen in the original Greek or in Latin translation which reveal Origen's forthright rejection of any notion of the transmigration of human souls into animal bodies. But cf. G.W. Butterworth, ed., *Origen on First Principles* (Gloucester, Mass.: Peter Smith, 1973), pp. 70-75 (*De Principiis* I, 8, 4).
12. This understanding is remarkably similar to the thought of Rudolf Steiner and his followers. Walter Johannes Stein, one of those closest to Steiner, believed that "History was something the living themselves had helped to create in their former lives on earth. They bore the whole responsibility for what the world was, what it is and what it will become." Ravenscroft, *op. cit.*, p. 203.

selfishness that separated the souls from the Spirit of life and light..." (987-4) Hence we, too, are to learn obedience through suffering (1463-2); the experiences we meet are "necessary for the tempering of the soul for greater service and activity..." (1981-1) "All must pass under the rod, but He has tempered it with mercy and judgment."[13] This means that the process is neither cold nor impersonal, and we do not walk alone. We are told to "Realize, then, that *self* cannot bear the burdens alone, ever; only by the whole trust in Him who is the way, the truth and the light" (2061-1), in "the Father, who has not left His children alone but ever seeks that they should know that the Redeemer liveth." (479-1)

The educative nature and purposes of the human experience are frequently stressed in the Cayce readings. "... each sojourn or indwelling may be compared to... a lesson, as a schooling for the purposes for which each soul-entity enters an earth experience..." (1158-5) "Our entrance into the earth plane at any time is for the purpose that another lesson may be gained, another opportunity for soul expression may be had."[14] The varied experiences in or out of this material realm "are as periods of lessons, in which an entity uses that in hand. And that to which the entity attains is governed according to the use of the opportunities presented." (2283-1) This understanding, we may note, is similar to that of the great Alexandrian theologian Origen (ca. 182-251), who is universally regarded as the greatest scholar of the ancient church. Origen believed this material world to be beautiful and good, the creation of a beneficent God. "But it is not comfortable and is not intended to be." Man is placed here for ultimately spiritual purposes; that is, he is given educational opportunities that he may return to fellowship with his Maker. Origen also taught reincarnation as a "very plausible opinion." He felt that the inequalities and apparent injustices of life on earth could be rightly understood only on the assumption that souls pre-exist and are given bodies and circumstances in consequence of the actions of their previous lives. He held this concept to be "absolutely necessary to any persuasive theodicy."[15]

Similarly, the Cayce readings reveal human life on earth to be set in a framework inherently purposeful, a manifestation of the

13. *A Search for God*, vol. II, p. 59.
14. *Ibid.*, vol. II, p. 65.
15. Henry Chadwick, *Early Christian Thought and the Classical Tradition* (Oxford: Oxford University Press, 1966), pp. 88-89, 114-116. Cf. Origen, *Contra Celsum* VII, 50; *De Principiis* I, 7, 4; I, 8, 1; I, 8, 4; III, 3, 5; III, 5, 5. It is clear from one of Jerome's letters (CXXX, *Epistula ad Demetriadem* 16) that this view (reincarnation) was widely held, especially in the churches of the Greek-speaking East.

divine purpose, which is both good and just. The ultimate purpose is that the soul may find "closer relationships to the Creative Forces" (1460-2), "a cooperative, coordinating activity with the Creative Force..."[16] The affirmation is that "In the beginning, when there was the creating, or the calling of individual entities into being, we were made to be companions with the Father-God." (1567-2) This understanding is beautifully personalized in the statement of "the desire of the Father that each soul shall continue to have *its* thread of gold that runs through each conscious force for its companionship with Him." (805-4)

This God-oriented life purpose is accordingly not to be self-centered. Rather, each entity finds itself and exalts itself in the service of others. The readings repeatedly emphasize that "the whole Gospel of Jesus Christ [as, indeed, the essence of the message of the entire Bible] is: 'Thou shalt love the Lord thy God with all thy mind, thy heart and thy body; and thy neighbor as thyself.'" (2072-14) "The purpose in life, then, is not the gratifying of appetites nor of any selfish desires, but it is that the entity, the soul, may make the earth, where the entity finds its consciousness, a better place in which to live." (4047-2) Or, to express this purpose in a relational way, "each soul's expression in the earth is to be a channel through which Creative Forces or God may be made the greater [or more] manifest in the experience... in the lives of individuals as they deal with their associations." (1206-3)

We note the further, perhaps surprising, affirmation with regard to the divine purpose and mode of operation that "thy Father-God hath need of thy service in the earth..." (5177-1) "...He, thy God, thy Christ, is conscious of and hath need of thee..." (5064-1) "...the Lord hath need of thee with thy faults, with thy virtues." (3685-1) The Lord therefore accepts us as we are, starts with us at our present point of growth and need. But this divine patience works to the end that each soul may become a greater and better manifestation of the love of the Father (1842-1). Our entrance into this material world is not for self-indulgence, "but to beautify, to make the world a better place because you have lived in it" (5392-1), to be "as a light to others." (641-6)

This is all to say that we live in an ordered universe created by a good and loving God, that the purposes for which we have been placed on this earth are not primarily punitive but educative and

---

16. *A Search for God*, vol. II, p. 59.

diaconal. We are intended to serve divine purposes that are both aesthetic and ethical in the highest degree, purposes that are motivated and effected—on the divine plane—in the spirit of pure and unselfish love. However, unlike a certain amount of learned as well as popular Christian thought from the time of Augustine, the Cayce readings repeatedly affirm that man is endowed with free will and is placed in a cosmos whose divinely providential ordering is neither arbitrary nor predetermined in a fatalistic sense (815-7; 1458-1; 1567-2). It is the expression of wise and loving concern and provides precisely those structures or environments of experience that are our best opportunities for spiritual and moral growth, including improvement of the quality of our relationships with others. We should add, however, that our own choices and practices contribute to the building of these structures.[17]

This is a grand picture, but I do not want to hide from myself nor from you that it is certainly not always easy to believe. I want to believe it, I try to apply and practice it, but there are problems. Let us consider some of them. For one thing, how is it cosmically possible for a just God concerned for order and due moral compensation to give opportunities to man that seem specifically better than he deserves? This is an ancient theological problem which has exercised thoughtful minds from Paul to Irenaeus, from Anselm to Mackintosh and Barth. As we might expect, the Cayce readings grapple with the problem directly and from various perspectives. Let us briefly note the following.

In one passage the paradox inherent in the problem is expressed by the juxtaposition of the apparently contradictory terms *karma* and *grace.* But the individual addressed in this reading is forthrightly told, "No longer is the entity then under the law of cause and effect, or karma, but rather in grace it may go on to the higher calling as set in Him." (2800-2) The reading says that this opportunity is offered to any entity as it "sets itself to do or to accomplish that which is of a creative influence or force." How such offering of opportunity is cosmically possible lies in the final analysis in the mystery of the workings of divine love. But the Cayce readings do inform us that the person and work of Jesus the Christ are the culminating element-reality in the effecting of this cosmic possibility. We have been "bought with a price..."

17. Cf. *ibid.*, vol. II, p. 46: "We should remember that our choice, our wills add to the pattern we are building. This pattern destines that we will pass through experiences that are necessary to give us greater opportunities to become one with that purpose for which we came into being."

(696-3) The cross of Christ is the "culmination of God's approach to man in his phase of unfoldment in the earth." (3054-4) And "the Resurrection [of the Christ] brought to the consciousness of man that power that God hath given to man, that may reconstruct, resuscitate, every atom of a physically sick body, that may resurrect even every atom of a sin-sick soul ... " (1158-5)

In conclusion I should like to focus on the understanding which the Cayce readings give us of how the divine providential order functions in our daily lives, in the small as well as the larger events of our experience. In one sense this is to take up another of the "problems" which the world view of the readings poses; in another it is to come to the very heart of their meaning and value, i.e., their practical applicability. In this day when many of us, including even some of the leaders of our society, feel that we are at the mercy of "uncontrollable forces at work on the earth, and also in ourselves,"[18] this understanding constitutes, I believe, one of the most potentially helpful contributions to the fulfillment of contemporary need.

We have seen that life is measured back to us structurally as we have measured unto others (3213-1). But at the same time, these structures or environments of experience are divinely provided opportunities to serve the glory of God and our own good (1204-3). Indeed, "In whatever state the self is found to be, *that* may be *used* as a stepping-stone to greater opportunities and to greater successes—if the laws that pertain to spiritual forces, in expression in a mental and material world, are kept in sight." (1113-1) The emphasis is always upon the here and now, upon what appears to be the small event as much as upon the great. "For each experience, each day, each thought, *offers* an entity an opportunity for development or for retardment. For it ever remains the same, this day—*now*—there is set before thee good and evil. Choose thou." (1913-1)[19] Furthermore, we are told, "Let us look upon every experience as a necessary element in our own development."[20] The lessons of life are properly applied as each person "uses that in hand." We are to start where we are, with what we are and with what we have. "And, that to which the entity attains is governed according to the use of the opportunities presented." (2283-1)

I know that some will take bitter exception to the world view that I have just depicted. Especially will objection be made by

---

18. Shana Alexander, "A Lust for Leadership," *Newsweek*, January 7, 1974, p. 29.
19. Cf. Deut. 30:15-20; Josh. 24:14-15.
20. *A Search for God,* vol. II, p. 58.

those who, like me, have for long years been deeply empathetic with the goals and often the methods of political and social liberalism. We have been deeply concerned for justice in our own and other societies. Some of these people will say that I am implicitly approving and supinely accepting the political, economic and social *status quo* of our societies.

My response is to say forthrightly that such an interpretation radically misreads the meaning and intent of the Cayce readings. After all, the real issue is how desirable change is to be brought about. The readings always assume that there is a long way to go, much to be done, exteriorly as well as interiorly. With special emphasis they look toward change in areas or dimensions of human life often neglected by most pundits of our culture, viz., the attitudinal and motivational. "Change is the activity of knowledge from within." (900-465) Very much like Jesus' own emphasis upon the "morality of intention," the readings insist that man can use his mind to change his surroundings. "Man can only begin...within himself. And as he applies that he knows, that he understands of God, in his daily life, so may there be given him the next step to make." (3976-23) In this context of understanding we are told to "*give God a chance...*" (3976-23) "In thy purposes, in thy desires to know His ways, look ever within. For there has He promised to meet with thee. And if ye will by thy purpose, by thy desire, but seek Him—He will come and sup with thee." (254-101)[21]

Furthermore, even though I have long been generally identified with the traditional liberal position, I submit that this position tends to be elitist. More commonly than not, it speaks of what needs to be done *for* the poor and disadvantaged of the earth—to be sure, a very valid point when directly addressed to the powerful and wealthy of our societies. But Jesus proclaimed good news *to* the poor (Luke 4:18). Do we liberals—religious or otherwise—have anything to say *to* the needy of the world? Can we live and work *with* them? There are times when our pity drops from authentic sympathy into maudlin despair and serves merely to unnerve those whom we would help.

The Cayce readings, on the other hand, affirm that history as a whole, and each individual human life in particular, while participant in divinely structured order, is open-ended. Every person—man, woman or child—is so positioned as to have the opportunity to relate constructively to precisely the situation he

21. Cf. Rev. 3:20.

finds himself in, regardless of how hopelessly dead-ended it may appear from another social, economic or cultural standpoint. We are specifically told, "... do not count any condition lost. Rather make each the stepping-stone to higher things, remembering that God does not allow us to be tempted beyond that we are able to bear and comprehend, if we will but make our wills one with His." (900-44) "May we never think that the opportunity has passed; for God's mercy is without limit ... *Today* is the acceptable day of the Lord! It is never too late for us to begin ... "[22] "There are *always* opportunities! Opportunities are *never* withdrawn." (333-6)

We of the middle classes tend to think that human life has real meaning only when we have some big deal going. The Cayce readings, however, tell us that "it isn't the individual that plans for some great deed to be accomplished that accomplishes the most. It is the one that meets those opportunities and privileges which are accorded it day by day! And as such are used, through the channels and in the manners indicated for this entity, there are better ways opened." (1152-9)

This is, therefore, a profoundly hopeful as well as a majestic view of human life. It is hopeful because no one is excluded for external reasons. We are told, "... only [thou] thyself may separate thee from the love of God. No power in heaven or hell may separate thee save thyself." (3660-1) "No soul has been left without access to the throne of mercy and grace."[23]

It is as practical as it is hopeful. We have noted that we are told to accept, before God, ourselves and our circumstances as they are, and then move on from there. Indeed, we may well ask, where else can we start? But our acceptance is not to be grudging or resentful; it is not to issue in spineless inactivity. We are told, "Learn again patience, yet persistent patience, active patience— not merely passive. Patience does not mean merely waiting ... So with patience, comply with patience's laws, working together with love, purpose, faith, hope, charity ... " (1968-5) Indeed, "if the problems of the experience today, now, are taken as an expectancy for the unusual and [for] that which is to be creative and hopeful and helpful, life becomes rather the creative song of the joyous worker." (1968-5) "Keep creative ever in the activities. This, too. Be *glad* you have the opportunity to be alive at this time, and to be a part of that preparation for the coming influences of a spiritual nature that *must* rule the world ... Be

---

22. *A Search for God*, vol. II, p. 56.
23. *Ibid.*, vol. II, p. 65.

happy of it, and give thanks daily for it." (2376-3) "In whatever way we prepare ourself, then, the time and place to use that prepared will come."[24]

Thus expectancy is the term which properly characterizes this high view of the nature and destiny of man. "For he that expects nothing shall not be disappointed, but he that expects much—if he lives and uses that in hand day by day—shall be *full* to running over." (557-3) This is a vision of human life as an upward climb, a vision much like that of the apostle Paul as he wrote to the church in Philippi toward the end of his life, "I press on toward the goal for the prize of the upward call of God in Christ Jesus."[25] The Cayce readings frequently describe the spiritual growth of man in terms of steps to be taken, "day by day, step by step." "As we apply that which we know, we are given the next step."[26] In this context of meaning, the Biblical verse from Isaiah (28:13) is often quoted, "Precept upon precept, precept upon precept, line upon line, line upon line, here a little, there a little." (922-1; 3416-1; 262-12)

This world view clearly envisages the moral and spiritual growth of man as normally long-range and gradual. This is in accord with the ancient tradition of the Holy Grail, for the term Grail is an anglicized form of the late Latin word *gradālis*, step by step, a metaphor for the "gradual" spiritual development of man.[27] The Cayce readings tell us flatly that "there is no shortcut...save in correct living." (1901-1) We know, however, that repeated efforts have been made in the history of the church to change Christian faith into various kinds of shortcuts to blessedness. Instant religion, zip-zap, salvation without effort, experience without responsibility—we are all tempted along these lines.

The readings say, "Don't be weary in well-doing. If it requires years, give years—but give a service and a praise continually to God, if ye would have life." (3684-1) Let the Light "take its time with thee." (2072-4) Even though we be separated from our loved ones, "we learn more and more that separations are only walking through the rooms as it were of God's house..." (1391-1) Death is but "God's other door." (5749-3) "For it is not all of life to live, nor all of death to die; for one is the birth of the other when viewed from the whole or center." (369-3)

---

24. *Ibid.*, vol. II, p. 58.
25. Phil. 3:14.
26. *A Search for God*, vol. II, p. 48.
27. Cf. Walter Johannes Stein, *Weltgeschichte im Lichte des Heiligen Gral, Das neunte*

Once again, though the way be long, we walk not alone. As the readings say, "Ye cannot bear the burden alone, but He has promised, and He is faithful, 'If ye put thy yoke upon me, *I* will guide you.'" (262-77) "For, as He hath given, which is the greater promise from the foundation of the world, 'If ye call, I will hear, and answer speedily—though ye be far away, I will hear—I will answer.'" (1747-5) "His abiding presence is in and with us."[28] There is no reason even to fear the "last enemy," which man calls death, "when the trust of the soul and heart of the man is in the Lord, who doeth all things well." (5195-1)[29]

I think that you know now why I say that Edgar Cayce speaks to my condition. This man was indeed an authentic channel of divine truth and light in our midst. Surely we can say that he spoke as moved by the Holy Spirit. What astonishes me perhaps more than anything else is that he has shared with us the heights and depths and breadths of the faith-understanding of the great figures of the early church in a way beyond any religious leader of the twentieth century. He deserves our closest attention and deepest respect.

Let me conclude with a quotation from a reading given to a woman in July of 1932, a passage which in brief compass sums up very well, I believe, the understanding of the whole of the preceding material.

In the attitudes as may be had by the body, these—as respecting mental and material conditions—*are* those things, those elements, that the body must face with that knowledge that there is an all-wise providence, and that with the keeping in self of an ideal there is strength, comfort, understanding, that enables the body to meet the conditions which arise from day to day with the knowledge that He doeth all things well.

In that manner of mental outlook will the body find those abilities growing in self, for the steps are to be taken day by day, and sufficient unto today be that grace, that fortitude, that understanding, that will enable the mental forces to keep that balance that makes not afraid. Rather let those conditions come, then, as they may, knowing that He will give within self that knowledge of the Right to be done at the right time.   5678-1

Jahrhundert (Stuttgart: J. Ch. Mellinger Verlag, 1966), pp. 5-8.
28. *A Search for God*, vol. II, p. 60.
29. Cf. P. Franklin Chambers, *Juliana of Norwich* (New York: Harper & Brothers, 1955), p. 114.

Studies in
Christian Gnosticism

I should like to begin this consideration of Christian Gnosticism with a brief statement from one of the Cayce readings. This excerpt is from a reading given at the request of Thomas Sugrue in preparation for his now famous book, *There Is a River*. The question was put by Sugrue, the answer given by Cayce.

Q-21. The...problem concerns a parallel with Christianity. Is Gnosticism the closest type of Christianity to that which is given through this source?

A-21. This is a parallel, and was the commonly accepted one until ... there were the attempts to take shortcuts. And there are none in Christianity! 5749-14

Sugrue's question was not as precisely phrased as could be desired. We shall see that the term "Gnosticism" as commonly used includes a wide variety of both views and practices, but Cayce's answer is intriguing, to say the least. In fact, it would be more accurate to say that his answer could be called disconcerting, at least to most contemporary Christian ministers. The reason, I believe, lies in the connotation which the words "Gnostic" and "Gnosticism" have had for most theologically trained ministers of the past two generations and more.

To be sure, knowledgeable people are aware that the great Swiss psychologist and psychotherapist, Carl Gustav Jung, expressed profound sympathy for historic Gnosticism at its best. Indeed, we may say that his more than ten years (1916-1926) of in-depth studies of the then available Gnostic materials, coupled with a later comparably deep study of medieval and early modern alchemy, gave him what he said was the needed "historical prefiguration of my inner experiences."[1] Jung perceived that the Gnostics and alchemists, like himself, had been confronted with "the primal world of the unconscious and had dealt with its contents."[2] Furthermore, they were primarily concerned, he sensed, with the spiritual or psychic transformation of man. It was only after these studies that Jung was able to arrive at the central concept of his psychology, which he called the process of individuation. This phrase meant for Jung the process whereby "the psyche is transformed or developed by the relationship of the ego to the contents of the unconscious."[3] The goal of individuation is thus a psychic transformation of man wherein the ego recedes in favor of the totality of the integrated self. Jung stressed the fact that the transformation involves a process and stages of development, and only upon the basis of his studies in Gnosticism and alchemy was he able to realize that he was dealing with a process reality.[4]

Another appreciative, although discriminating, evaluation of the larger movement which may be called Gnosticism was made by Rudolf Steiner, the Austrian philosopher, Goethe scholar and pioneer in new methodologies of education, the arts, medicine and bio-dynamic agriculture. Steiner believed that "we may class as Gnostics all the writers of the first Christian centuries who sought for a deeper spiritual sense in Christian teachings." He saw these writers as focusing theologically on the problem of the relationship between the historical Jesus and the pre-existent Logos. He recognized also their concern at the time to relate the historical Jesus, as known from both the written and the unwritten traditions of the church, to their own awareness or apprehension of the Christ in personal, contemporary experience. This was to ascribe a legitimate, even though not solely normative, role to what Steiner called spiritual clairvoyance.[5]

1

Given, then, this largely appreciative evaluation of the Gnostic

1. C.G. Jung, *Memories, Dreams, Reflections*, ed. Aniela Jaffé (New York: Random House, 1963), pp. 189, 199.
2. *Ibid.*, p. 200.
3. *Ibid.*, p. 209.
4. Aniela Jaffé, *From the Life and Work of C.G. Jung* (New York: Harper & Row, 1971), pp. 51, 57-58.
5. Rudolf Steiner, *Christianity as Mystical Fact* (Blauvelt, New York: Rudolf Steiner Publications, 1961), pp. 181-183. Cf. A.P. Shepherd, *A Scientist of the Invisible* (London: Hodder and Stoughton, 1971), pp. 168-169.

tradition by Carl Jung and Rudolf Steiner, why, we may ask, do I have reason to suggest a possible widespread resistance to acceptance of Edgar Cayce's similarly favorable response? The reason is not far to seek; it lies in the weighty and sustained negative critique of Gnosticism made by continental European, especially German Protestant, historical scholarship from the beginning of the century. A wide consensus then developed which essentially agreed with Adolf von Harnack's definition of *gnōsis* as a "radical Hellenization of Christianity."[6] A large number of scholars came to see Gnosticism as constituting a dissolution into metaphysical speculation of the reality and religious significance of the historical events from which authentic Christianity derives its existence. Indeed, the approval of Gnosticism by Carl Jung, with his apparent preoccupation with archetypal images and symbols, may have seemed to many as additional confirmation of the truth of this evaluation.

In particular, neo-orthodox or Barthian theology over the past nearly two generations has taken a strong stand on this issue with the radical, almost ultimate distinction which it generally affirmed between the Hebraic and the Hellenistic world views. In this context of understanding it concentrated its fulminations in a special way against the movement it called Gnosticism, which it saw as emerging solely out of Hellenism (with possible earlier sources in Iranian religious thought) as a kind of *bête noire* to distort and sully the purity of Hebraic faith and its world view. As a result of the widespread influence of this school of thought, it appears that most Christian theologians and ministers still have a decidedly negative view of the terms Gnostic and Gnosticism and the concepts and activities which they connote. I believe that such is the case even though a consensus of specialists in Gnostic studies has recently emerged which sheds quite new light on the problem. This is the discovery that Palestinian Judaism, particularly in its sectarian or heterodox forms, was the source, or at least the main channel, through which the larger activity centered around the term *gnōsis* entered the Greco-Roman world.[7]

Let us at this point, however, endeavor to clarify both definitions and issues; by so doing we may hope that some order will be brought into this most complex area of studies. Part of the

---

6. Adolf von Harnack, *Lehrbuch der Dogmengeschichte*, 4th ed. (Tübingen, 1915), p. 250. Quoted in Robert Haardt, *Gnosis* (Leiden: E.J. Brill, 1971), p. 11.
7. Menahem Mansoor, "The Nature of Gnosticism in Qumran," in *Le Origini dello Gnosticismo* (Leiden: E.J. Brill, 1967), p. 390. Cf. Haardt, *op. cit.*, p. 16.

difficulty in twentieth-century treatments lies in a restricted, pejorative use of the very terms Gnosis and Gnostic (*gnōstikos*) which would have been surprising to almost all Christians of the apostolic or later generations of the early church.

The basic term is the Greek word *gnōsis*, which is regularly (and properly) translated into English as "knowledge." The use of the term, or of its English derivatives Gnostic and Gnosticism, to designate heretical forms of Christianity is a development with only limited backing in the first centuries of the church. Irenaeus of Lyons, in writing around A.D. 180 against certain Christian groups of whose teachings and practices he disapproved, and which he did not always fully understand or fairly report, entitled his chief work of this genre "The Refutation and Overthrow of Knowledge (*gnōsis*) Falsely So Called." This language, of course, implies that there is a knowledge rightly named, and such was the almost universal understanding of the church in the first three centuries of our era.[8]

In the ancient world the word *gnōsis* generally had a wider meaning than our modern Western post-Enlightenment tendency usually grants to the term "knowledge." That is, in place of our common restriction of the sense to cognitive knowledge of empirical data or "facts" apprehended through sensory perception, the meaning of *gnōsis* in the early centuries of our era was extended to include the dimension of spiritual insight or perception at a higher level of consciousness. In the New Testament knowledge is an attribute of both God (Romans 3:11) and man (I Cor. 8:1, 7, 11). It means specifically Christian knowledge, that is, not only knowledge of the historical events of the Gospel story, but, even more, existential experience of God through the risen, living Christ, an awareness that is an ongoing reality and a developing possession (II Cor. 10:5; Luke 1:77). Paul in particular gives the term *gnōsis* the meaning of knowledge of supersensible realities, awareness of dimensions of the unseen realms, a significance which the word commonly carried in both Christianity and the pagan mystery cults of the time. In I Cor. 13:2 he places it after "prophecy" and "mysteries" as being an element of the "riches" of the Gospel.

Paul regularly employs the word *gnōsis* as a characteristic of

8. Cf. R.M. Wilson, *Gnosis and the New Testament* (Philadelphia: Fortress Press, 1968), pp. 6-12.

9. Romans 15:14; I Cor. 1-5; 8:1; 12:8 (cf. 13:8-13); 14:6; II Cor. 6:6; 8:7; 11:6; Phil. 3:8; I Peter 3:7 (in the Greek); II Peter 1:5-6. For ΕΠΙΓΥΝΩΣΙΣ see Romans 10:2; Phil. 1:9; Col. 1:9-10.

the mature Christian, a vital element of the growth or development process of the life of faith.[9] He regards *gnōsis* as a gift of God and a privilege, although it carries with it the danger of spiritual pride (cf. I Cor. 8:1). To the Roman Christians he writes warmly that he is satisfied that they are "filled with all knowledge." (Romans 15:14)

In the first-century Christian work the *Didache* (10:2) there is a prayer form which uses *gnōsis* in the sense of the message of the Gospel. In the second century, Clement of Alexandria, also in the mainstream of the church's tradition, uses the adjective *gnōstikos* (Gnostic) as a term specifically designative of the enlightened, mature Christian.[10] Indeed, in this passage Clement speaks of Christian love as properly "knowledgeable" (*gnōstikē*). Clement, in writing critically of a certain Prodicus and his adherents, who apparently held a rigid view of divine predestination, insists that they falsely call themselves Gnostics. He is concerned to retain the word in its older sense of knowledgeable or mature Christians.[11] Neither does Origen, Clement's great successor in the Alexandrian theological tradition, denote as Gnostics those against whom he writes critically; he calls them heretical, which at that period in the history of the church approximately meant "sectarian."[12]

Thus we must distinguish, as a narrower group, those persons and writers who were critically opposed by Irenaeus and his Roman contemporary Hippolytus and, from a somewhat different perspective, by Clement and Origen. Probably we must continue to denote them as Gnostics because of long historical usage. But it is vital for our understanding of the issues of the time, and, indeed, for our comprehension of the nature of the Christian faith itself, that we do not assign pejorative meaning to the words *gnōsis* or *gnōstikos* themselves.

Who, then, were the Christian leaders and groups whom later tradition has designated as Gnostics? The term actually was used as a means of self-designation by only a very small number of persons, and the whole discussion was carried on in a context wherein distinction between the words "orthodox" and "heretical" did not have the implication of repudiation that later centuries were to give them.[13] Indeed, from the standpoint of the

---

10. Clement, *Stromateis* IV, 2; J.P. Migne, *Patrologia Graeca* VIII, cols. 1340-1341.
11. Clement, *Stromateis* III, 30. Cf. John E.L. Oulton and Henry Chadwick, eds., *Alexandrian Christianity* (Philadelphia: Westminster Press, 1954), p. 54.
12. Jean Daniélou in his otherwise perceptive and balanced account of Origen regularly denotes Origen's "eternal enemies" as Gnostics. *Origéne* (Paris: La Table Ronde, 1948), pp. 23-24, 203-204, 273.

pagan world, Gnosticism of every stripe was included within the larger spectrum of Christianity.[14] This is to say that the problem was and is a familial one, an issue within the family of Christian faith. In this context of understanding, then, we may cite Basilides, Valentinus, Ptolemy, Heracleon, Marcus, and Theodotus both as Gnostics and also as among the most spiritually perceptive and intellectually capable Christians of the second century. Comparably able were men like Cerinthus, Marcion, and Epiphanes. Indeed, it has been said that the Gnostic movement originated "as the reaction of an educated minority to the emerging phenomenon of 'popular Christianity.'"[15] My preference, however, as I shall endeavor to justify below, is to stress at least the intent of these Christians to give priority to spiritual perception rather than to mere intellectual power or skill in our modern sense of the word. We shall see that probably most adherents of the movement called Gnosticism emerged as spiritual critics of what they saw as not so much a popularization as a vulgarization of Christianity.

The problem of understanding is further complicated by the fact that a wide variety of views and practices came to be included within the category of Gnosticism, to the extent of making it impossible for a discriminating thinker to use the term casually. On the one hand, we find extreme ascetics like Marcion of Pontus and Rome or Tatian of Syria, who both came to reject the concept of the physical world as being the creation of the God and Father of Jesus Christ (i.e., the high and good God) and, as one consequence of this understanding, forbade sexual relationships in any context. Tatian considered marriage as fornication. On the other hand, we find extremists who were accused by their contemporaries of being morally licentious, as, for example, the Carpocratians.[16]

There were, however, other personages and groups called Gnostic who clearly belonged to neither of these extremes. Two noted Christian Gnostics of this category were Basilides, who taught at Alexandria *ca.* 120-140, and Valentinus, a native of Alexandria and perhaps the ablest of all Christian Gnostics, who taught in Rome *ca.* 140-160. Basilides and his son Isidore did not consider marriage a sin, although they taught, like Paul (I Cor.

13. Cf. Elaine H. Pagels, *The Johannine Gospel in Gnostic Exegesis* (Nashville: Abingdon Press, 1973), p. 58.
14. Arthur Darby Nock, "Gnosticism," *Harvard Theological Review*, LVII, October, 1964, p. 261.
15. By Samuel Laeuchli, as reported in Pagels, *op. cit.*, p. 11.
16. Oulton and Chadwick, *op. cit.*, pp. 22-30.

7:8-9), that celibacy was the more perfect way. Their followers, however, are reported to have fallen into licentious ways after Basilides' death.

The Valentinians warmly approved of monogamous marriage, believing marriage on earth to be a means of honoring celestial unions. According to Tertullian, they held a man to be inhuman and false to the truth if in this world he did not faithfully love a woman and join himself to her.[17] Clement of Alexandria, we may note, was in considerable sympathy with the teaching of Basilides and more particularly with that of Valentinus.

2

With Valentinus we are now able to move into a different mode or level of analysis. Prior to the Second World War our knowledge of Christian Gnostic thought and practices was largely limited to quotations and analyses of these activities by their theological opponents. We have reason to believe, as in the case of Irenaeus and Hippolytus, that the "heresiologists" of the church did not always understand their Gnostic Christian opponents correctly nor even agree as to the content of their teaching. But a new situation has emerged as a result of the discovery in 1945/46 near the village of Nag Hammadi in Upper Egypt of thirteen papyrus codices writen in Coptic and consisting of at least fifty-one separate treatises in complete or near complete form. One of the most important of these is the remarkable meditation on the Christian Gospel called the Gospel of Truth. Here we are no longer dealing with fragments quoted by opponents but with a treatise in full. In this work, which may have been written by Valentinus himself, instead of the Godhead being pictured as a thirtyfold complex of Aeons (Grades of Divine Emanation distinguishable in the spiritual realm), as the Valentinians were alleged by Irenaeus to have believed, we find a description of God as Father, Son, and Holy Spirit.[18] We shall consider this work more in detail after a preliminary summary of the criticisms made against Christian Gnostics by their opponents.

The chief contentions against Christian Gnostics of critics like Irenaeus, Hippolytus, and even Clement of Alexandria and

---

17. Tertullian, *Adversus Valentinianos* XXX, 3; Irenaeus, *Adversus Haereses* I, 6, 4.
18. Cf. Kendrick Grobel, *The Gospel of Truth* (Nashville: Abingdon Press, 1960), pp. 21-22. Tertullian states that the concept of Aeons was used by Valentinus to denote "movements" of awareness and feeling within the Godhead (substantias...quas Valentinus in ipsa summa divinitatis ut sensus et affectus [et] motus incluserat). *Adversus Valentinianos* IV, 2.

Origen are essentially similar. One of these is that the Gnostics do not give sufficient weight of religious meaning to historical events recorded in the written Gospels and otherwise communicated in the traditions of the church. As a basis for this charge the contention is that the Gnostics are actually hostile to the whole realm of materiality and claim that the physical world is not the creation of the good or high God, the Father of Jesus Christ, but that matter is in itself evil. Hence the opposite although theologically related extremities of consequence in moral license and ascetic self-denial. Hence also the charge of Docetism, viz., that the Gnostics teach that the Christ did not really come in the flesh but only "seemed" to do so. A further contention is that the Gnostics teach a doctrine of absolute determinism, that men are predestined by their "natures" to eternal salvation or destruction. Objection is also made that the Gnostics are overly preoccupied with identifying and defining, by means of mythopoetic terminology, the nature not only of the Godhead but of the entire unseen realm.

Whether there is any degree of truth to these contentions can only be determined, of course, by an examination of the Christian Gnostic materials themselves, to the extent that these are available. But it is vital to clarify as best we can what seems to have been the intent of Gnostic Christian leaders and writers, indeed of all theologically sophisticated Christians of the second and third centuries. We may for this purpose concentrate upon Alexandria, which was a center of the best Christian thought of the time. The intent of the Gnostics was evidently to urge all Christians who were open to seek a higher level of understanding or perception (*gnōsis*) than that accepted by "many" as sufficient. Put in another way, this is a view of the Christian life, and in particular of salvation through the Gospel, as involving more than a passive hearing and believing of the events of salvation history as though they were realities external to the present self; this view denies that, apart from certain quasi-legalistic responses in rite and morals, salvation through Christ is to be personally realized only in an eschatological future. To the contrary, Gnostic Christians contended that, while the historical reality of the Christ event was not to be gainsaid, the primary issue for the present was the appropriation and application of the cosmic significance and effects of the event to and within the lives of believers. Of even greater significance was relationship with the central actor of the event, the risen Christ perceived as the Eternal Contemporary, unto the transformation of the human self, of human consciousness, of human character. This transformation was further seen as an ascending process of growth, wherein the "now" of the time of salvation becomes daily repeatable, both in this world and in other dimensions beyond.[19]

Another important concern of many Gnostic Christians was hermeneutical, the proper interpretation especially of the Old Testament Scriptures. In one sense this concern was rooted in the desire to move from what was felt to be Jewish racial, national, and cultural particularism to authentic Christian universalism. Perhaps the most significant element, however, in this concern was moral and spiritual, the wish to distinguish from Christian faith what were regarded as theologically and morally unworthy concepts of God revealed in certain of the more anthropomorphic depictions of Yahweh in the Old Testament. This approach was one example of the larger Gnostic Christian sensitivity to the fact of evil in the world and the apparent contradictions which this fact poses to belief in a God congruent with the person of Jesus the Christ. Jesus Himself had clearly employed a selectively critical approach to the Hebrew Scriptures,[20] and the bulk of early Christian theological and exegetical writers had come to use variations of Philo's (*ca.* 20 B.C.-A.D. 42) allegorical method of interpretation in order to make the Old Testament contemporarily acceptable and useful to the Christian church. One of the most sophisticated examples of early Biblical hermeneutics, however, is that found in the Gnostic Christian Ptolemaeus' Letter to Flora. Ptolemaeus' discriminating interpretation of the Pentateuch and other parts of the Old Testament may be the first example in the history of the Christian church of the conscious use of a form of the historical-critical hermeneutical method.[21]

Let us then briefly consider in the light of the criticisms offered, as well as of the apparent intent of the Gnostic Christians themselves, those writings which we now have in largely complete form. The work referred to above, the Gospel of Truth (*Evangelium Veritatis*), is evidently a meditation, dating from perhaps the middle of the second century, on the deeper meaning of the Christian Gospel which presupposes and in no way intends to displace the four Gospels of the church's tradition. To repeat, one of the charges made was that the Valentinians taught a

---

19. Cf. Pagels, *op. cit.*, pp. 13-15, 52-57; Henry Chadwick, *Early Christian Thought and the Classical Tradition* (London: Oxford University Press, 1966), pp. 53-54, 75-76.
20. Matthew 5:21-48; Mark 10:2-9; 12:28-34.
21. Haardt, *op. cit.*, pp. 144-150.

Docetic form of Christianity, viz., that the Christ did not really manifest in the flesh but only "appeared" as such, and that while He entered the man Jesus at His baptism by John at the river Jordan, He withdrew from Jesus at the time of the latter's crucifixion so as not to participate in His suffering.

Actually we find in this work a veritable *theologia crucis*. Jesus is the Christ, "He was nailed to a tree" and thereby "became a fruit of the Father's knowledge." (18:16, 25-27) He was killed, and His "death would be life for many." "Jesus, the merciful and the true, had mercy, assumed in patience the sufferings." "Jesus appeared... and was nailed to wood, He nailed the deed of disposal of the Father to the cross." "He humbled Himself to death and was clad in eternal life." (20:7-29) The Word (Logos) "had taken body." (26:8) We find language reminiscent of the first Epistle of John (I John 1:1) in the statement that the Father "allowed them to taste, feel and touch the beloved Son." (30:21-23)

This Valentinian work affirms that the Gospel is joy and hope (16:31; 17:3). As Cullen Story has put it, its movement is "always forward and upward."[22] There is a recurring emphasis in the Gospel of Truth that Jesus the Christ brings men back to the Father (24:6-7).[23] Those who respond to Jesus' call by turning again to the Father not only receive divine instruction, but receive themselves from the Father (21:7-8). *Gnōsis* clearly meant to acquire knowledge both of God and of one's true self.[24]

In the Gospel of Truth we note that Jesus the Son and Word has overcome the enemy Error and become a way for the straying, *gnōsis* for those who lack knowledge, strength for the weak and purity for the defiled. Jesus is the good shepherd who sought the one sheep that was lost, who worked even on the sabbath to lift out the sheep fallen into the well. He continues to bring salvation to men even as He did when He was on earth, for "the work of salvation must never stop." (31:28-32:25)

The warmth of the Father's love is intended not only to demolish the wall separating Him from His world, but to warm

---

22. Cullen I.K. Story, *The Nature of Truth in "The Gospel of Truth" and in the Writings of Justin Martyr* (Leiden: E.J. Brill, 1970), p. 1. This book is probably the most thorough study of the *Gospel of Truth* which has yet appeared.

23. In 24:7 we note the phrase "to the Father and the Mother."

24. In the Gospel of Thomas, also included in the materials discovered near Nag Hammadi, we find repeated references to the fact that self-discovery and self-knowledge become a means and indeed another dimension of knowing God (80:26; 93:18-20, 30; 99:8-10). A. Guillaumont *et al.*, trans., *The Gospel According to Thomas* (New York: Harper & Brothers, 1959), pp. 3, 39, 41, 55.

up that which is cold (34:26-34). Immortality was given breath (in Jesus) to follow the sinner, with intent not to punish, but to give him peace. As a doctor hurries to the place where a sick man lies, God, through His Word, "is at work with the light of His forgiveness in the very place of lack or need, i.e., in the material world." (35:15-31)[25]

The Father is loving and good, and therefore those who accept the divine call have the responsibility to witness by word and life. Above all, not what men do but what they are bears witness to the Father. Those who are united to Him are urged to support those who stumble, reach out their hands to the sick, feed the hungry, help the suffering, aid those trying to stand, and awaken those who are spiritually asleep (33:1-8). For "strength grows in action." This practical approach is coupled with the teaching that such witness is particularly made possible by the practice of meditation. Each person finds himself through the divine Unity, is integrated from the confusion of multiplicity and moves toward the goal of union with the divine Oneness. To this end, "we then above all take care to see that the house (of the self) may be holy and silent for Unity." (25:1-21)

3

I have quoted rather extensively from this work in order to make it clear that, according to my view, the author is properly to be included within the larger spectrum of Christian faith. Basic to his faith-understanding is recognition of the incarnation of the Son of God, the Word, in Jesus the Christ, and affirmation of Jesus' historical life and teaching, of His death, resurrection, and ascension.[26]

With regard to the issue of determinism or free will, we may say that there are passages in the Gospel of Truth which seem to point in both directions. The charge of determinism or rigid divine predestination, however, is one which, I would suggest, should be made only with the greatest caution. We need to remember that Augustine, Luther, and Calvin either denied the freedom of the human will or at least disallowed its role in any way in the salvation of human beings, and we usually do not call them Gnostics.[27]

---

25. Story, *op. cit.*, p. 29.
26. *Ibid.*, p. 50.
27. Augustine taught that God predestines whom He will, "to punishment and to salvation," with the number of each class already fixed (*Enchiridion* 107). In his

I say caution is needed because historically not a few interpreters have taken Paul's language in Romans 9:14-33 as part of a basis for a rigid doctrine of "eternal election, by which God has predestined some to salvation, others to destruction."[28] But Paul only asks questions (9:21-24) in order to affirm the sovereign right of God to will as He would. Paul does not actually say that God prejudges the eternal destiny of men arbitrarily. To the contrary, the culmination of his argument is his hope, which he calls a mystery, that all Israel will be saved, indeed that God may have mercy upon all men (Romans 11:25-32). This example suggests the need for comparable scrutiny of like passages in the Old Testament as well as in the New. Isaiah 45:9-13 at first sight might seem to affirm a rigid divine determinism, but the larger context of both the author and the tradition clearly does not support such an interpretation.[29]

Valentinian Gnosticism is generally recognized as teaching a tripartite anthropology, a division of mankind into "hylics" (material-level persons), "psychics" (mental-level Christians) and "pneumatics" (spiritual-level Christians). Actually these distinctions may primarily represent present levels of human consciousness and not necessarily unchangeable products of divine predestination.[30] In fact, there are a number of passages in the Gospel of Truth which suggest not only that "psychics" may ascend to the level of "pneumatics," but that the Father has acted to grant grace to and satisfy "whoever is in need." (36:1-3)[31] Indeed, there are also verses which clearly imply the possibility of falling away or returning to what had been once rejected (33:7-15).

The whole problem of alleged determinism in Christian Gnosticism, however, is given a different coloring by reason of the fact that many writers within this category taught the pre-existence of souls or, more specifically, metempsychosis or the

controversy with Erasmus, Luther insisted that man is like a donkey ridden now by God and now by the Devil—although he generally did not preach as if he believed this, nor did Calvin. Cf. Roland H. Bainton, *Here I Stand* (New York: New American Library, 1955), pp. 196-197.

28. Most notably John Calvin, *Institutes of the Christian Religion*, III, pp. 21-24.
29. We may note that Gospel of Truth 37:19-38:6 constitutes a strong affirmation of divine sovereignty which is in fact no different from Irenaeus' own position. Irenaeus' view is given in the Latin as follows: "Homo etenim a se non videt Deum. Ille autem volens videtur ab hominibus, a quibus vult, et quando vult, et quem admodum vult." *Adversus Haeresus* IV, 20, 5; II, 2, 1-6.
30. Pagels, *op. cit.*, pp. 13-15, 52-57. Cf. the review of Professor Pagels's book by William R. Schoedel in *Journal of Biblical Literature*, XCIII, June, 1974, pp. 315-316; Haardt, *op. cit.*, p. 8.
31. Cf. *Gospel of Truth*, 26:30; 27:22-28:3; 31:16-32:27; 35:19-36:23.

reincarnation of souls. By affirming the possibility of a succession of human lives upon earth, this doctrine, in addition to teaching the ancient, spiritual origin of the soul, clearly widens the possibilities of final salvation.[32] It may be surprising to modern Christians to learn that this doctrine, in one form or another, was widely held in the early church, even, indeed, by Christians who could not be classed as Gnostic in the narrower sense of the word.[33]

The author of the Gospel of Truth, like almost all Christians of the first three centuries, taught a strong doctrine of divine providence. This is that nothing ever happens without Him (the Father), nor does anything happen outside His will (37:19-21). The Father has appointed the destinies of all who have their roots in Him. But this understanding seems to be in the context of allowing each believer to grow within the divinely given framework of limitations, "so that by their thought they might be perfected." Their destiny is the country where they have their root, "which lifts them upwards through all heights to the Father." (41:15-24) The manner of aspiration is to strive for the one who is unique, striving that is effortless in Him "who is rest without straining." (42:9-22)

We may perhaps legitimately criticize some of the Christian Gnostics for a generally negative view of the world of matter. The author of the Gospel of Truth refers to the flesh which Jesus put off through His resurrection as "rags and tatters." (20:36) He seems to assert the creation of the material world by "the forces of confusion." (17:13-16) Other Christian Gnostics, like Menander, Saturninus, and Basilides, are said to have taught the creation of the material world through mediation, as of angels or emanations from the high God.[34] We recall, of course, that the New Testament with its teaching of the creation of the world by the mediation of the divine Logos, in the context of a certain subordinationism of the Logos and the Spirit, represents a position not really alien to this latter one.[35] There appears to have been a significant distinction between those Christian Gnostics,

---

32. Cf. *Gospel of Truth*, 22:14; 36:35-38; 41:4-7. Among the references in Haardt, *op. cit.*, we may cite pp. 33, 53, 58-59, 70, 84-85, 194, 202, 216, 232, 237, 251, 253, 257, 262. In *The Epistle to Rheginos* (Malcolm L. Peel [Philadelphia: Westminster Press, 1969], pp. 29-36) we find similar intimations: 46:12-13; 47:5-8; 49:35.
33. Jerome (*ca.* 340-420) writes in one of his letters (CXXX, *Epistula ad Demetriadem* 16) that the concept of reincarnation was widely held, especially in the churches of the Greek-speaking East.
34. Haardt, *op. cit.*, pp. 33, 39, 40, 41-42, 57.
35. Cf. John 1:1; Col. 1:16; Eph. 2:10; Heb. 1:2.

like Cerinthus, the Barbelo Gnostics, and the Sethian Ophites, who taught the creation of the material world by supernal beings opposed in will to the most high God, and the larger number, who averred the material creation through mediation but believed the mediators to have acted in accord with the will of the Highest. In this latter category we may include Simon Magus, Menander, Saturninus, Basilides, Carpocrates, the Naassene Gnostics, the Peratae, Ptolemaeus, and the author of the Apocryphon of John.[36] We at times find strong language, as in the Gospel According to Thomas, urging disciples to be wary of "the world"; but, just as in the New Testament, the distinction is primarily moral and spiritual, between differing qualities of mind and spirit, rather than an ontologically and fixedly dualistic distinction between matter and spirit.[37]

4

We do not have space to pursue this subject in more detail. Suffice it to say that the problems are many and complex and require further study and discussion. My primary intent in this paper is to clarify the issues, above all to identify what I see as the practical religious concerns of the Christian personages called Gnostics. One of the basic issues is, of course, that of the nature of salvation as understood in the New Testament and the early church. My contention is that there seems to have been a specific understanding of the nature of salvation held by almost all those Christians, who comprise not a few varieties, for whom the terms *gnōsis* and *gnōstikos* held positive meanings. This is the understanding of salvation as focusing not primarily upon a single unrepeatable event, but upon a succession of events in the lives of believers. This is not to say that Gnostic Christians held either what is popularly called the linear view of time or the early Greek concept of eternal recurrence.[38] But they were evidently concerned to affirm salvation as a repeatable "now," as a

---

36. Haardt, *op. cit.*, pp. 33, 39, 40-42, 57, 93, 97, 102, 150, 194. Cf. The Hypostasis of the Archons, 3.b.30, Bentley Layton, "The Hypostasis of the Archons, or the Reality of the Rulers," *Harvard Theological Review*, LXVII, 1974, pp. 396, 400, 420.

37. *The Gospel According to Thomas*, pp. 21, 22, 27, 42, 56, 80, 110. It is in order to recall that relatively negative views of the physical world are found in a number of places in the New Testament, e.g., Romans 7:24; 8:22; James 4:14; I Peter 1:24.

38. Cf. Henri-Charles Puech, "Gnosis and Time," in *Man and Time,* Bollingen Series XXX, vol. 3 (New York: Pantheon Books, 1957), pp. 38-84; Malcolm L. Peel, "Gnostic Eschatology and the New Testament," in *Novum Testamentum* (Leiden: E.J. Brill, 1970), vol XII, fasc. 2, pp. 141-165.

meaningful process of spiritual and moral growth both on earth and in the unseen realms beyond. This process was envisaged as possibly extending through a number of lives on earth and ultimately through the heavenly spheres.

The time has surely come, therefore, to correct the older, facile dismissal of Christian Gnostic mythopoetic depiction of the heavenly spheres as "fantastic speculation" and recognize it for what it is. It represents, first, a concern which was in fact faithful to the ancient Hebraic affirmation of Yahweh as Lord of the heavenly hosts—realities to be not denied but "known"—and, second, imagery symbolic of the moral and spiritual growth of the soul in this and other dimensions of life.[39] This growth process, we may add, was seen by most Christian Gnostics not as some kind of titanic effort to penetrate by man's own power the unseen realms, but as a journey homeward made possible by grace from on high, most specifically by the cosmic significance and power of the Christ event.

I would affirm that this faith-understanding is similar to the main thrust of the New Testament witness. This is to perceive not only the Christian life but the concept of salvation itself, however sudden or dramatic a single conversion experience may be, as properly a long-range growth process in faith-understanding and in moral quality of life.[40] This view, I believe, is the proper interpretation to be derived from Jesus' parables of the kingdom of God as growth.[41] Paul's rephrasing of Jesus' teaching on the losing and finding of the self led him to employ the imagery of crucifixion and resurrection and then write, "I die every day."[42] Paul's initial conversion to Christian faith on the road to Damascus was dramatic, indeed traumatic. But in one of his last letters, that written to the church in Philippi, he has revealed his mature understanding of the nature of salvation as comprising both initial divine acceptance and subsequent human

39. Haardt, *op. cit.*, pp. 47, 52-54, 59, 87, 93, 96, 98, 103, 135, 141, 174-175, 196, 200-201, 227, 237-239, 265, 268, 275-276. We may also properly recall that in the Greek text of Matthew, "the kingdom of Heaven" more commonly has the pluralized form, "Heavens." Matthew 4:17; 5:3, 10, 12, 16, 19, 20, 45, etc. Cf. II Cor. 12:2.
40. New Testament usage of the words for "save" and "salvation" in a theological sense shows a frequent alternation between the present and future tenses. Salvation is to be fully realized in the future but clearly has present dimensions. The rather frequent use of the present tense of the verb in a continuative sense is particularly instructive. Cf. Gerhard Friedrich, ed., *Theological Dictionary of the New Testament* (Grand Rapids, Michigan: Eerdmans, 1971), vol. VII, pp. 989-999.
41. Mark 4:26-29, 30-32; Matthew 13:18-23, 24-30, 33.
42. Matthew 10:39; 16:25; John 12:24-26; I Cor. 15:31 (cf. II Cor. 4:16); II Cor. 6:9; Gal. 2:20.

appropriation-in-process ("in Christ" and through the Holy Spirit). Here, at the end of his life and in prison, we find him writing: "Not that I have already obtained this [the eschatological goal of resurrection from the dead] or am already perfect; but I press on to make it my own, because Christ Jesus has made me His own. Brethren, I do not consider that I have made it my own; but one thing I do, forgetting what lies behind and straining forward to what lies ahead, I press on toward the goal for the prize of the upward call of God in Christ Jesus. Let those of us who are mature be thus minded."[43] We may add that also for the author of the Johannine literature truth is both an unveiled reality and a process. The promise of the Spirit of truth is as one who will guide—presumably step by step—into all the truth.[44]

This understanding of Christian faith and life can be found, although with many variations, in the most representative Christian writers of the first three centuries of the life of the church. I should like to conclude this article with brief accounts of the relevant views of the two great Alexandrian theologians, Clement and Origen, who, although they wrote critically of some of the Christians called Gnostics, themselves gave positive interpretaions to the terms gnōsis and gnōstikos.

Clement depicted the Christian life with the imagery of a ladder of ascent. The soul progresses from faith, as one step on the way, to knowledge (gnōsis), as another. By control of the passions and by positive attitudes and deeds of love, the soul ascends, step by step, to the beatific vision and union with God. This is a moral as well as a spiritual progress. Clement put as strong an emphasis upon sanctification as did the early Protestant evangelicalism. Like other Christians of his time, he saw this process as also involving heavenly dimensions (we may recall Paul's reference to "the third heaven" in II Cor. 12:2). Clement wrote: "Leaving behind all hindrances and scorning all the distractions of matter, he [the Gnostic, or mature Christian] cleaves the heavens by his wisdom, and having passed through the spiritual entities and every rule and authority, he lays hold of the throne on high, speeding to that alone, which alone he knows."[45]

---

43. Phil. 3:12-15. Paul's admonition in the same letter (2:12-13) to "work out your own salvation with fear and trembling; for God is at work in you" is clearly to be understood in the same context of thought. Cf. I Cor. 2:6-3:2.
44. John 16:13. Cf. Story, op. cit., pp. 195-197. We note that the Greek of Gal. 2:14 may mean "to progress toward the truth of the gospel." In Gal. 5:7 the present tense of the verb implies obedience as an ongoing process.
45. Clement, Stromateis VII, 82. The translation is quoted from Oulton and Chadwick, op. cit., pp. 38-39.

Origen (*ca.* A.D. 182-251) was certainly the greatest scholar and perhaps the most influential theologian in the Greek-speaking church within the first six centuries of our era. Like Clement, his predecessor in the tradition of theological teaching in Alexandria, he employed the term Gnostic positively as denotative of a mature, knowledgeable Christian.[46] Origen, like Clement, was a churchman in fact and intent all his life; he believed this material world to be beautiful and good, the creation of a beneficent God.[47] "But it is not comfortable and is not intended to be." Man is placed here under divine providence for ultimately spiritual and moral purposes; that is, he is given "educational" opportunities that he may return to perfect fellowship with his Maker. Jean Daniélou has called Origen's doctrine of *Pronoia* and *Paideusis* ("la Providence éducatrice") the central theme of his theological system. This involves perception of two presuppositions of Origen's thought, a gracious and beneficent divine providence and free creatures, free to choose either evil or good. The saving plan of God, in which Jesus the Christ, the Logos of God, is the central instrumental element, works unto the progressive restoration of all beings.[48]

To return, then, to our point of departure, I believe that we are now in a position to understand, it is to be hoped with a measure of appreciation, the favorable posture toward Christian Gnostics in their wider range taken by Edgar Cayce, Carl Jung, and Rudolf Steiner. Christian Gnostics, as we have seen, by no means present a uniform front of doctrine or practice. From our present point of view, certain of their opinions and practices require appreciable correction, if not rejection. Yet in terms of intent and often of teaching, an impressive and in many ways "true" understanding of the nature of Christian faith and life emerges, one which certainly suggests Christianity without shortcuts or notions of "cheap grace." This is to see, on the one hand, the Christian Gospel as declarative of God's total openness to humankind, and the Christ event as God's utterly gracious work of redemption— liberation quite beyond the merits or deserts of any person. It is also to see, on the other hand, the proper response of man as involving not one but many conversions or commitments of faith

---

46. The view long current in the Middle Ages that Origen was condemned by the Sixth Ecumenical Council in 553 has been shown to be erroneous. See F. Prat, "Origen and Origenism," in *The Catholic Encyclopedia* (New York: The Gilmary Society, 1939), vol. XI, 306-312.
47. Cf. Daniélou, *op.cit.*, p. 208.
48. *Ibid.*, pp. 203-205.

and obedience. This means a daily death and new birth of the self. It means that each day constitutes the ever new "now" of salvation, not as an eternal recurrence, but as an ascending path. Each day has its mercies and its renewals, its opportunities to grow in the service of God and humanity—all in the context of the grandly cosmic plan of God, the God who in Christ has made possible our daily appropriation and application of these opportunities. This is to believe in an open-hearted God and an open-ended universe.

PART II

I
Jesus the Christ

In the context of this, the most important subject given to human beings to consider, it is appropriate to reflect once more upon the methodology basic to the discourse. We are to consider here aspects of both the historical life and the theological meaning of Jesus the Christ as they appear in the readings of Edgar Cayce. We need to remind ourselves again that the readings of Edgar Cayce are the results of his clairvoyant activity; they consist of his responses to questions asked and suggestions made after he had put himself into a trance.

This means that the data on the life and theological significance of Jesus the Christ which will be presented here have their origin in clairvoyant perception and not in the more common materials of historical and theological research. This is to say that neither historical documents, nor archaeological investigation, nor theological reflection based on either the Judeo-Christian Scriptures or historical materials are themselves the source or sources of the data to be presented. As has been discussed elsewhere in this collection of essays, the sources are referred to in the readings themselves as "universal." The authenticity of these sources, however—or, more particularly, the truth of the content of the materials allegedly given by these sources—needs to be tested, I believe, in the same way that other statements of fact or larger truth are tested. That is, the materials must be tested in terms of both their inner coherence and consistency, and their conformity to facts and truth already known and tested by the same means.

By this method of reciprocal comparison and testing, not only scientific and historical truth, but also truth in the realm of religion and philosophy, is normally sought. "Thus you will know them by their fruits." (Matt. 7:20) It is necessary, however, to recognize that for most people the quest for historical facts or theological truth through clairvoyant perception is a new way of investigating either history 'or theology.[1] And as the Japanese sociologist of religion Minoru Kasai has put it, a new epistemology is needed for this—as for most—new methodology I personally would contend that a study of the nature and grounds of the knowledge gained in this way is very much worth the attempt, and that the validity of such knowledge can be reliably ascertained by the very tests which are applied to data of comparable content but obtained by other means. In this essay I shall attempt to suggest some points of comparison with related data known through more common procedures of investigation as a first step in what will no doubt prove to be a long and arduous task of testing and verification.

A further point of methodological clarification needs to be made. The limits of space do not allow even an attempt to set forth the totality of the material on the life and meaning of Jesus the Christ as given in the Cayce readings. My task here will be to give the main lines and structures of the whole, with particular focus on the quality or "spirit" of understanding that emerges, I believe, with remarkable consistency throughout.

1. Cf. Trevor Ravenscroft, *The Spear of Destiny* (New York: G.P. Putnam's Sons, 1973), pp. 203, 272-289.

II
The Preparation

As described in the Edgar Cayce readings, the Christ event occurs in the context of a panorama of divine purpose and activity vast in range but unified in nature. In the beginning God "moved,"[2] God who from the beginning could be called multiple, for "in the beginning was the Word, the Word was God, the Word was with God." As God moved, "souls—portions of Himself—came into being." (263-13; cf. John 1:1) This concept, which is given in many readings with somewhat varying expressions but identical meaning, constitutes a subtle variation of the usual doctrine of creation. Creation is forthrightly affirmed, and, in a sense, there was a "point" or "time" when souls, as separate foci of consciousness or awareness, were not. But as in the primary element of their nature they participate in consciousness, they are of the same nature as God, although derivatively so. The phrase "portions of Himself" or "portions of God" occurs frequently in the readings, and there is no essential variation in this perception.[3] Also, all individual entities or souls now in existence, a phrase intended to include all human beings both living and "dead" (those in realms beyond the earthly), were created "in the

---

2. God is described in the Cayce readings with rich profusion of predicates or epithets, of which typical examples are: "...God, the Father, the Universal Influence, the Creative Energy, the I AM THAT I AM..." (262-87); "Life is an essence of the Father" (5749-4); and "God is love; hence occupies a space, place, condition, and *is* the Force that permeates all activity." (5749-4) With reference to the phrase "God moved," it may be of interest to compare *Rig-veda* 10:129; *Chāndogya Upanishad* 6:2, 1-2; 3:19, 1; with Gen. 1:1-2.
3. "...ye are part and parcel of a Universal Consciousness or God—and thus [of] all that is within the Universal Consciousness, or the Universal Awareness..." (2794-3) In the Cayce readings, however, this perception by no means belongs to the category of what is called "pantheism" or philosophical monism in the strict sense of the term. The distinctive relationship of the soul, as a part, to God, as the Whole, is clearly revealed in the following words, which were given in answer to the question of what the purpose of an entity's existence is: "That it, the entity, may *know* itself to *be* itself and part of the Whole; not the

beginning." (5749-14) We have the further statement that "man was created a little bit higher than all the rest of the whole universe, and is capable of harnessing, directing, enforcing, the laws of the universe." (5-2; cf. Heb. 2:6-8; Ps. 8:4-6)

Cayce thus shares with the great Alexandrian theologian Origen the conviction that all souls preexisted; that is, they all had their origin in God the Father but existed in a spiritual realm prior to their appearance in this world, when all were "in the spiritual force. . ." (2497-1) rather than constituting later individual and temporally separate creations. He also shares with Origen a strong emphasis upon free will as a gift given by God to souls in the beginning and never taken from them.[4] The origins of sin, according to the Cayce readings, lay in souls "seeking expression of themselves outside of the plan or the way in which God had expressed same." (5749-14) Elsewhere (5749-3) Cayce refers to sin as error, which brought the consequence of death (which he also frequently spoke of as only a transition, as "God's other door"). More commonly, however, sin is described in practical terms as selfishness (254-87). In this earth "Man alone is given the birthright of free will. He alone may defy his God!" (5757-1) Evil is thus also designated as rebellion, in the context of personal relations between God and His creation, first in the realm of celestial beings and then in that of human beings. "As there is, then, a personal savior, there is the personal devil." (262-52)

The purpose of creation lay in "God's desire for companionship and expression" (5749-14) and was for souls to be "companions with the Father-God" (1567-2), "a co-creator with Him. . ." (2794-3). "The universe He called into being for purposes that the individual soul, that might be one with Him, would have. . .those influences for bringing this to pass or to be in the experience of every soul. For hath it not been given that the Lord thy God hath not willed that any soul should perish? but He hath prepared with every temptation a means, a way of escape." (1347-1; cf. II Pet. 3:9; I Cor. 10-13) "Giving of will to His creation, man, that man might be one with Him. . ." (900-20)

Jesus the Christ, according to the Cayce readings, is the central instrument of God to make it possible for all souls—specifically those who have sinned or erred from the will and plan of the Father—to fulfill the original purpose of their creation. Jesus the

Whole but one *with* the Whole; and thus retaining its individuality, knowing itself to be itself yet one with the purposes of the First Cause that called it, the entity, into *being*, into the awareness, into the consciousness of itself. That is the purpose, that is the cause of *being*." (826-11)

4. Origen, *Contra Celsum* VII, 50; *De Principiis* I, 7, 4; I, 8, 1; I, 8, 4; III, 3, 5; III, 5, 5.

Christ, however, is both God and man in a sense subtly different from the Athanasian formula. Cayce affirms the Godhead to be three-dimensional, as Father, Son and Holy Spirit (5749-3), when viewed from the level of earth consciousness, which itself is a "three-dimensional plane in one." (4035-1)[5] The Godhead in Its multiplicity or richness of content may conceivably, when viewed from the perspective of higher levels of consciousness, be perceived as more complex than three-dimensional. Nevertheless, the Christ, whether one speaks of the Godhead as three-dimensional or multidimensional, is seen as an essential, an integral part of the Godhead.

Jesus, who became the Christ,[6] is also man—specifically, a soul created with other souls in the beginning and, like them, a part of Universal Consciousness. "This man, as man, makes [his] will the will of the Father, then becoming one with the Father and the model for man." (900-10) This understanding, we should note, is not to be confused with the position of Arius in the early church, who taught that the Christ, or second Person of the Trinity, is ultimately a created being, in distinction from the uncreated Father. In the Cayce readings the Christ is integrally one with the Father. Jesus as the first man "was created—brought into being from all that there was in the earth. . ." but this form of creation was in fact "an encasement for the soul of an entity. . ." who was in turn "a part of the Creator. . ." although derivatively so (2072-4). The union of the Christ and the man Jesus constituted, according to the readings, a unique divine-human unity, although this relationship is properly the ultimate goal of all entities and one, therefore, that is ontologically as well as spiritually possible for all. In the Cayce readings the elevated view of man, as a soul or entity created in the beginning as a part of divine consciousness, gives a dimension of ontological "appropriateness" or "fitness" to the divine-human union in Jesus the Christ, differentiating it from the stark, paradoxical "union of opposites" posited in the traditional theologies (cf. John 10:34-35).

The precise nature of the initial form of the union of Jesus with the Christ is not discussed in the Cayce readings in terms beyond

5. Cayce relates the three-dimensional mode of consciousness of human beings on earth to the three concepts of "time, space and patience." (4035-1) He adds, however, that none of these "exists in fact, except in the concept of the individual as [he] may apply [self] to time or space or patience." The addition of "patience" to the duality of time and space is a very interesting phenomenon. Both time and space are held to be human concepts or modes of organizing perception, but their role is seen as properly fulfilled only when the mental attitude of patience is added.

6. We shall consider the significance of this term in more detail later.

that of union of will. But, as we shall see later, the union, once effected, became a permanent cosmic reality of universal scope and consequence. Theologically, then, Cayce's position would seem at this point to be similar to that of the Sixth General or Ecumenical Council, held in Constantinople in 680 and 681, where, in contradistinction to the so-called Monothelite heresy, there were affirmed to be two wills—divine and human—in Jesus the Christ.[7] Yet Cayce attributes a richer background and meaning to the human will and individuality of Jesus than the Council would perhaps have allowed. The fact is that Jesus is flatly stated to have been also the first Adam.

It is well known that the apostle Paul wrote of Adam as "a type of the one who was to come" (Rom. 5:14) and drew between Adam and the Christ a parallel that was also a contrast: "The first man Adam became a living being; the last Adam became a life-giving spirit." (I Cor. 15:45; cf. 15:22) The Christ is thus seen as the last Adam, who was typologically prefigured in the first, the "one man" who by his obedience undoes, with a far greater richness of good effects, the results of the disobedience of the first (Rom. 5:12-21). This theme is also developed in the "recapitulation" theology of Irenaeus (active in the latter half of the second century A.D.), who describes Jesus the Christ as "recapitulating" the stages of Adam's fall, but in reverse order and quality.

The language of Paul is almost invariably understood by modern interpreters of the Bible as no more than figurative, a rhetorical device useful for highlighting the superlative nature of the person and work of the Christ. It is therefore astonishing to most contemporary Christians when they read that according to the Cayce readings Jesus was indeed the same entity who as Adam "fell in Eden."[8] (2067-7) Most shocking, perhaps, to orthodox Christians is the implication, indeed the clear statement, that the Jesus whom they have always believed to be sinless had been not only guilty of sin, but the very person who has been traditionally regarded as the author of sin on the human level.

But once again the remarkable subtlety of the Cayce perceptions takes away much, if not all, of the initial shock, if the reader is willing to read on. To my knowledge, nowhere in the Cayce readings is it stated that Jesus as the Christ was guilty of sin

---

7. Cf. Williston Walker, *A History of the Christian Church,* rev. ed. (New York: Charles Scribner's Sons, 1959), pp. 146-147.

8. *Q-19. When did the knowledge come to Jesus that He was to be the Savior of the world?* A-19. When He fell in Eden. 2067-7

of any kind. At that stage of His personal and cosmic development His obedience was flawless, His relationship with the Father perfect. Thus we read of "the perfect relationship to the Creative Forces or God, the Father—which the man Jesus attained when He gave of Himself to the world, that through Him, by and in Him, each entity might come to know the true relationship with the Father." (3357-2) Therefore His coming as Jesus of Nazareth is to be contrasted in its quality of perfect fulfillment with His coming "on other occasions [when He] failed to keep the whole law." (2072-8)

The Cayce readings, however, go on to speak of the singular appropriateness of Adam finally emerging as Jesus to become the Savior of the world. That is, in conformity with the commission given him in the first chapter of Genesis (1:28), Adam "must become the savior *of* the world, as it was committed to his care. 'Be thou fruitful, multiply, and *subdue* the earth!'...the first Adam, the last Adam, becomes—then—that that is *given* the *power over* the earth..." (364-7) The basic principle involved is one which in a certain sense is applicable to all human beings: "...as in each soul the first to be conquered is self—then *all things,* conditions and elements, are subject unto that self! That is a universal law..." (364-7) Only Jesus, the second Adam, however, has as yet perfectly fulfilled this condition, and only He was fit to become the Savior of the world: "...self, death, hell and the grave even, become subservient unto Him *through* the conquering of self in that made flesh..." (364-7) It should be added, however, that the readings affirm a certain saving dimension also in all the previous incarnations of Him who was born last as Jesus of Nazareth (288-29). Indeed, since in the readings sin is asserted to have its origin in spiritual realms before even the creation of the earth, we appropriately find intimations that there was redemptive intent also in His coming to earth as Adam (262-115; 262-57).

Clearly we are dealing here with a world view which includes reincarnation as an integral element of its understanding of God's ways with man and the world. Since this element of the Cayce readings has been treated with relative fullness in previous chapters of this book, I shall not discuss it in detail here. It will suffice, I believe, to refer only to those aspects of the concept of repeated human lives on earth which particularly relate to Jesus who became the Christ.

It should be stated at the outset, however, that the perception of Jesus the Christ as having had previous human incarnations on earth did not originate in the Cayce material. For example, the early Jewish Christian group known as the Ebionites, possibly direct descendants of the pre-Christian Essenes, taught that the Spirit, whom they considered superior to the angels and yet able to descend to the earth as He willed, had come as Adam and later reincarnated as Jesus.[9] The influence of the Essene Ebionites reached beyond the Transjordan area and extended over a large part of southwestern Asia well into the fourth century. According to the church father Hippolytus of Rome (170?-235), another Jewish Christian group, known as the Elkasaites, taught that when the Christ was born of a virgin He was not making His first appearance on earth; He had been incarnated previously and frequently, the same soul being born in different bodies.[10] The same view was held by the early Jewish Christian Nasoreans, or Nazarites.

A documentary source of major extent and importance for early Jewish Christianity is that known as the Clementine Homilies. Here we find expressed in the most unequivocal language the contention that the Christ as "the True Messenger" or "the Only Prophet" had from the beginning of the world incarnated again and again, "changing His forms and names," appearing as different historical personages at various times.[11] According to the Clementine Homilies, the Christ had been incarnate in Adam, Enoch, Noah, Abraham, Isaac, Jacob, Moses and, lastly, Jesus. Moses is at times eliminated from this list, making Jesus the seventh in the series.[12] The list given in the Cayce readings, though at points similar, is notably different: Adam, Enoch, Melchizedek, Joseph, Joshua, Jeshua (the scribe chiefly responsible, according to Cayce, for the work of collation leading to the later form of the Hebrew Bible) and Jesus (5749-14); this list is also made up of seven names, the sacred number.[13]

A further point of great significance is made by the Cayce readings regarding the wider work and influence of Jesus: "...the

---

9. Epiphanius, *Adversus Haereses*, lib. 1, vol. II, 30, 18. J.P. Migne, *Patrologia Graeca* XLI, col. 455. Cf. Thomas O'Shaughnessy, S.J., "The Development of the Meaning of Spirit in the Koran," *Orientalia Christiana Analecta*, no. 139, p. 19.
10. Hippolytus, *Ante-Nicene Fathers*, vol. V, p. 132.
11. *Clementine Homilies* III, 20. This concept plays an important role in Manichaean and Mandaean teaching and, later, in Islam. Cf. C.H. Dodd, *Interpretation of the Fourth Gospel* (Cambridge: Cambridge University Press, 1955), pp. 122, 239.
12. Cf. F.L. Cross, *The Early Christian Fathers* (London: Gerald Duckworth & Co., 1960), pp. 98-99; W.D. Davies, *Paul and Rabbinic Judaism* (London: S.P.C.K., 1955), pp. 50-51.
13. The Cayce readings indicate that the soul who incarnated as Adam and last as Jesus also had incarnations outside the direct line recorded in the Hebrew Scriptures. Not all of

entity—as an entity—influenced either directly or indirectly all those forms of philosophy or religious thought that taught God was One." (364-9; cf. "In all those periods that the basic principle was the Oneness of the Father, He has walked with men" [364-8], that is, in union with the Spirit of the Christ He walked with men [364-9]) This statement was made in answer to a question regarding the wider role of Jesus in His previous incarnations. It refers, of course, to direct and indirect influence on the historical plane. The answer in its larger compass, however, makes clear that the work and influence of the entity who became Jesus of Nazareth functioned also from spiritual realms between incarnations and was felt with special effect after the Christ event, by which He had become one with the Christ. The methodology of direct spiritual influence was by association "with—in the meditation or spirit of—that one guiding. . ." (364-9) or leading the historical activity or movement. The readings assert that this combination of influence on the historical plane and spiritual association from a higher dimension has not been limited to the Judeo-Christian context; in the same way that many things have been added to the original expressions of Judaism, much has been added to Confucianism, Buddhism, Platonism and Islam "from that as was given by Jesus in His walk in Galilee and Judea. In all of these, then, there is that same impelling spirit." (364-9)[14]

---

these incarnations are named, but a significant one was as Zend, the father of the Persian prophet Zoroaster (364-7). Also, the soul who became Jesus apparently incarnated first as one Amilius in the Atlantean period, which, according to the readings, preceded the coming of Adam. Adam, however, was the first man of flesh and soul in the present sense of the word. In one reading it is stated that in all Jesus had thirty lives on earth. The book of Job, incidentally, is said to have been written by Jesus in a previous incarnation, as Melchizedek (262-55).

14. The possibility of influences of this kind is, of course, not merely a fanciful thought. As careful a scholar as Edward Conze argues that for a proper understanding of the development of *Mahāyāna Buddhism,* parallels between historical events in the eastern Mediterranean area and India should not be ignored. Specifically, Mahayana literature appears first about the time of the Christian era, and Conze calls it an unresolved historical problem that Buddhism "just at the time when Christianity itself arose, underwent a radical reform of its basic tenets which made it much more similar to Christianity than it had been before." Edward Conze, *The Concise Encyclopedia of Living Faiths,* ed. R.C. Zaehner (New York: Hawthorne Books, 1959), p. 296.

Rudolf Steiner, in speaking of the wider influence of the Christ as operative from higher realms, writes that "the Christ is interwoven with the evolution not only of humanity but of the whole world." He sees "the Christ Event as the single point on which the scales of world-evolution hinge and . . . there can be no repetition of it." This larger activity has so functioned that "in hidden worlds the union has meanwhile taken place between Buddhism and Christianity." This result is also at least in part the consequence of the activity of "the Buddha, who has moved onwards and from spiritual realms exercises an enduring influence upon human culture." Rudolf Steiner, *Background to the Gospel of St. Mark* (London: Rudolf Steiner Press, 1968), pp. 155, 164, 158, 156.

III
Preparations for the Birth

At this point it would be well to leave further theological discussion until later and focus on the data in the Cayce readings concerning the birth of the Christ Child and certain elements of the preparation and environment that help to give understanding of the larger significance of the event. It should be said at the outset that the Cayce readings repeatedly affirm that "*He* came, the Master, in flesh and blood..." (1152-1) There is no trace in the readings of what has been called Docetism, or the doctrine that the Christ only "appeared" to be in the flesh, that incarnation in the flesh was not real. To the contrary, the strongest language is used to assert Jesus' manifestation in flesh and blood and the reality of His physical and mental suffering on the cross, a point which we shall consider in greater detail later. The life of the "man called Jesus" was a real human life: "This man [Jesus], as man, makes the will the will of the Father, then becoming one with the Father and the model for man." (900-10) But Jesus, as man, is also described, in conformity with what we have already noted, as being "of His [God's] own being made crucified even in the flesh." (5749-14)

The birth of the man Jesus is seen in the Cayce readings as the final state of the earthly development of this central instrument of the Father's work for the salvation of mankind. This process of personal development, however, is one in which all human beings must also participate—through realms both earthly and trans-earthly, although an earthly incarnation is required as a part of each particular stage of development. Thus we read: "For, without passing through each and every stage of development, there is not the correct vibration to become one with the Creator... Then, in the many stages of development, throughout the universal, or in the great system of the Universal Forces... each stage of development is made manifest through flesh, which is the testing portion of the Universal Vibration." (900-16) Jesus, however, is described as "the soul who first went through the cycle of earthly lives to attain perfection, including perfection in the planetary lives also." (5749-14) And His work as Jesus the Christ is described as "a voluntary mission [on the part of] One who was already perfected and returned to God, having accomplished His Oneness in other planes and systems." (5749-14)

The concept, then, is that of One who, according to the purposes of God, passed through all the needed "periods of preparation in the flesh. . ." (5749-6) and "completed the cycle for the necessary manifestation in the earth of the holy influence necessary for the sustaining of a backsliding world. . ." (5749-3) And He came—through His own choice (5749-7). The preparation was also being made on the historical plane in a specific way to receive the Holy One properly. According to the Cayce readings, the primary focus of this latter preparation was the religious sect or order of the Jews called the Essenes, which, like other religious groups within Israel, had its "adherents and near adherents. . ." (1602-4) This sect has become the object of special public and academic interest since the discovery of the first Qumran (or Dead Sea) Scrolls in 1947, for the scrolls are generally held to be the product of the Essene community. The Cayce readings, incidentally, revealed first in 1936 the existence as well as the location of the Qumran community.

The readings specifically take issue with the oft held notion that nothing of spiritual significance had occurred in Israel in the four hundred years between the last Biblical Hebrew prophets and the birth of Christ. They contend that such would imply that no historical preparation was necessary to make "the setting for the place and for the entering in of that consciousness into the earth that *ye* know as the Son of man, the Jesus of Nazareth, the Christ on the cross. . ." (262-61) To the contrary, there was a specific group, the Essenes, who "dedicated their lives, their minds, their bodies, to a purpose, to a *seeking* for that which had been to them a promise of old. . ." (262-61) Their purpose was to raise up people who would be fit channels for the birth of the Messiah. They were, according to the Cayce readings, in the direct line of spiritual descent from the school of prophets established by Elijah, though in a sense begun by Samuel, who in turn drew upon the teachings of Melchizedek. And surprisingly, the contention is that the

Essenes, at least in the period just prior to the birth of Jesus, "took Jews and Gentiles alike as members..."(254-109) As we shall see, the Essenes are said to have had notable international associations and were regarded as not orthodox by the rabbis of this later period (2067-11); the Essene meetings were all secret, according to the Cayce readings (2067-11). We find also the statement that the Essenes were seen by "many of the peoples, especially of the Pharisee group..." as rebels and radicals (1815-1).

The sect of the Essenes is also said to have had a special connection with Mount Carmel from the time of Elijah. It is not without significance that the present Carmelite Order of the Roman Catholic Church has preserved a tradition of the Eastern Orthodox monastics who had long lived on Mount Carmel and who welcomed as brothers the monks who came from the West with the Crusaders. The tradition asserts that their order had in fact been founded by Elijah and that with the name of the Sons of the Prophets they had prepared on Mount Carmel for the birth of the Messiah. When the Messiah came, they accepted Him as such and continued to live on Mount Carmel, becoming in time a recognized order in the Eastern Orthodox Church. From the union of this ancient lineage with the monks from the West there developed, the tradition claims, the present Carmelite Order.[15]

The Cayce readings state that Mary and Joseph and Mary's cousin Elizabeth were Essenes and raised their children accordingly.[16] The readings, particularly the 5749 series, are rich

15. Cf. Robert A. Adriance, "The Journey," in *Journey to Mount Carmel*, ed. Violet M. Shelley (Virginia Beach: A.R.E. Press, 1972), p. 7. In the context of the Cayce affirmation in 1936 of the existence of the Essene Community in the area where the Qumran Scrolls were later discovered, another significant perception of the readings may be noted. In a reading dated May 6, 1939 reference is made to one of the so-called holy women who ministered to Jesus and His disciples. Her name is given as Salome, and she is said to have been associated with the event of Jesus' raising Lazarus from the dead. (1874-1) In 1958 the American scholar Morton Smith discovered in the Monastery of Mar Saba in the Judean desert a letter which he and the larger academic community in general have come to acknowledge as a genuine letter of Clement of Alexandria (A.D. ca. 150-215). In this letter a quotation from a Secret Gospel of Mark, a main item of reference in the content of the letter, identifies Salome as present with the family of Lazarus shortly after the miraculous event. There is no reference to Salome in the Biblical account (John 11:1-57). Cf. Morton Smith, *The Secret Gospel*, New York: Harper & Row, 1973, pp. 1-17; *Clement of Alexandria and A Secret Gospel of Mark*, Cambridge, Mass.: Howard University Press, 1973, pp. 452-453.

16. The readings state that Zechariah, as a member of the orthodox priesthood—i.e., a priest of the temple in Jerusalem according to the orthodox or Aaronic tradition—was not at first an Essene but became at least a sympathizer toward the end of his life, as the result of his visions in the temple. The readings also identify Zechariah, the father of John the Baptist, with the Zechariah who was murdered "between the sanctuary and the altar" (Matthew 23:35; Luke 11:51); and they state that the murder occurred precisely because of

in their depiction of the process of preparation for the birth of the Christ Child. They culminate in a description of the selection and training of Mary and, of course, in the birth itself. We find that the readings not only affirm the virgin birth of Jesus but also insist, going even beyond ancient Eastern tradition,[17] that Mary herself was born of a virgin, that her mother Anne bore her without a human father (5749-7; 5749-8). The readings have a consistently high view of Mary; they not only state that she was immaculately conceived but include the mysterious expression that "so far as the earth is concerned ... " Mary was "the twin-soul of the Master in the entrance into the earth!" (5749-8)[18]

It appears that as part of the continued preparation and dedication of potential channels through which the Christ might enter materiality, "in Carmel—where there were the priests of this faith—there were the maidens chosen that were dedicated to this purpose, this office, this service." (5749-7) Twelve young girls were originally selected as candidates for this training. At that time Mary was only four years old. She was "between twelve and thirteen" (5749-8) when she was designated as the one of the twelve who was to be the specific channel for the Master's coming. The readings describe in a singularly beautiful way the mode by which it was revealed that she was the chosen one.

The training of the twelve maidens comprised physical, mental and spiritual dimensions, including "chastity, purity, love, patience, endurance" (5749-8), as well as proper diet; it was a discipline that could be called severe for the sake of physical and mental strength. The focus of this training was the temple of the Essenes on Mount Carmel, and the revelation of the chosen channel occurred one morning as the maidens were going to the altar for prayer and the burning of incense:

On this day, as they mounted the steps all were bathed in the morning sun; which not only made a beautiful picture but clothed all as in purple and gold.

Zechariah's open proclamation of the content of his visions and, presumably, because such proclamation signified a commitment to the Essene position (5749-8). The content was evidently a prophecy of the coming Messianic events largely according to the Essenes' expectations (2167-1).

17. Cf. *The Protoevangelium of James* (2nd century) 1-5; *The Gospel of the Nativity of Mary* 1-5. The dogma of the Immaculate Conception of Mary as defined by Pope Pius IX on December 8, 1854, refers not to birth from a virgin but to freedom from original sin from the very moment of conception. See also footnote 19.

18. Protestants may be taken aback by this fact, but the Cayce readings affirm that Mary, like Jesus, was "without original sin from the moment of her conception in the womb..." (5749-8) This is in effect to confirm the correctness of the Roman Catholic dogma of the Immaculate Conception of Mary.

As Mary reached the top step, then, there were the thunder and lightning, and the angel led the way, taking the child by the hand before the altar. This was the manner of choice, this was the showing of the way; for she led the others on *this* particular day.   5749-8

As a result of this event, Mary was "separated and kept in the closer associations. . ." (5749-7) with the teachers or mentors who were responsible for the preparation. The Cayce readings affirm that this event or series of events constitutes the beginning or foundation of the Christian Church (5749-7).

"Then, when the days were fulfilled that the prophecy might come that had been given by Isaiah, Malachi, Joel and those of old, she—Mary, espoused to Joseph. . .became with child." (5749-7) Mary was "between sixteen and seventeen [when] she was found with child" (5749-8), and thus there had been a further period of training "of some three to four years. . ." from the time of her final designation until the conception (5749-8). Joseph is said to have been thirty-six at the time of their marriage, performed in the Essene temple at Carmel, himself a "chosen vessel" for this role, selected from among the priests of the Essene faith (5749-7).[19]

The nature of the previous relationship of Mary and Joseph was such that the marriage could properly be called an arranged marriage in traditional Middle Eastern or Oriental fashion. According to the Cayce readings, however—contrary to the custom of most Jewish families of the time, whereby "the arrangements were made by the parents of the contracting parties. . ." (5749-8)—this relationship was arranged to a

19. It should be stated that the Cayce readings, while unequivocally affirming the virgin birth of both Jesus and Mary, do not support the doctrine of the "eternal virginity" of Mary, a concept which even Martin Luther apparently favored. The readings assert that for approximately ten years after the birth of Jesus—while He was still under their roof and in their direct care—Mary and Joseph did not have conjugal relations. But after Jesus' departure for further training by the Essenes and later, as we shall see, abroad, they took up the normal life of a married couple (5749-8, A-12, 15).

In the course of time, in conformity with the affirmations of the New Testament (Mark 6:3; cf. Gal. 1:19; Acts 12:17), Mary gave birth, by the paternity of Joseph, to other children. The readings, however, limit their number to three: James, Jude and one daughter, Ruth (5749-7; 1158-2, 4, 5, 9, 10; 137-4, 64). The readings also contend that the bearing of these three other children by normal means was in order to fulfill her physical karma, and that in bringing perfection by balancing the spiritual, mental and physical, she made it possible for all women to have that opportunity. The chains of transgression slipped from all womankind, and from that day forward they have been a guiding influence in the civilizations of the world. We shall consider later the significance of the contributions of the work of Jesus to the emancipation of women and the enhancement of their role, but it is clear that the readings assign a certain redemptive significance, even if secondary to that of Jesus the Christ, to the work of Mary. A similar concept of the redemptive role of Mary appears in Irenaeus, who sees Mary as "recapitulating" the acts of Eve in reverse order and quality to become a "cause" of human salvation (et sibi et universo generi humano causa facta est salutis). Irenaeus, *Adversus Haereses,* III, 22, 4.

substantial extent by leaders of the Essene religious community, although not without the consent of both parties. Mary and Joseph had previously known each other to the extent normal for fellow members of the same religious community (5749-9). The readings state, however, that Joseph at first demurred at the suggestion of the Essene leaders that he become the husband of Mary. This demurral was of course in the context of Essene expectations of Mary's becoming the mother of the Messiah, but at least part of Joseph's concern was over public opinion about the disparity of their ages.[20] He agreed, the readings say, only after he himself had had confirmation through his own personal religious experience—first in a dream and then by a "direct voice" experience—that the arrangement was indeed according to the divine will (5749-8). The readings also indicate that Joseph not only had initial hesitancy about the proposed plan but later felt consternation when Mary was found to be with child while yet a virgin. Thus he followed through with the Essene program at both points only after his own religious experience gave him the needed confirmation (cf. Matt. 1:18-25). The Cayce readings, we should note, forthrightly state in a number of instances that the birth of Jesus was "a conception through the Holy Spirit" (1158-5); it was an "immaculate conception." (5749-7)

A bit more needs to be said about these activities "that brought the Prince of Peace, the Christ, Jesus, into the earth." (1222-1) It appears from the Cayce readings that the Essenes were conscious of being preparers for "the new race" to be inaugurated by the Messiah. This elusive term is not explained, but it appears more than once. It seems to have had physical—although not primarily ethnic—as well as mental and spiritual dimensions. Not only Mary but all of the twelve maidens were dedicated as "channels for the new race" (254-109), and the regimen of training, which included physical and mental "cleansings" was to ensure that "bodies [plural!] were to become channels for the new race, or the new preparation [preparation for the New?]. . ." (254-109) Incidentally, the readings state that the true meaning of the term "Essene" was "Expectancy" (254-109) and the word "Israel" also had a greater meaning, namely, "those called of God for a service before the fellow man." (587-6)

The Essenes clearly had, according to the readings, a higher concept of the position and role of women than was common among the Jews of the time. About the place of women in the Essene order, the readings state:

---

20. To my knowledge, the readings nowhere state that the Essenes expected the birth of the Messiah to be virginal. To the contrary, we read that it was not generally believed in the Essene community that Mary's birth from Anne had been virginal (5749-8, A-2). Therefore, it came as a particular surprise to Joseph, as well as to the others, that Mary became pregnant before the marriage had been consummated (5749-8, A-9).

This was the beginning of the period where women were considered as equals with the men in their activities, in their abilities to formulate, to live, to be, channels [of the Divine].

They joined [the order] by dedication—usually by their parents.

[But] It was a free will thing all the way through... they were restricted only in the matter of certain foods and certain associations in various periods—which referred to the sex, as well as to the food or drink.

254-109

The readings also tell us that it was John the Baptist who first taught the larger public that "women who *chose* might dedicate their lives to a specific [religious] service." (540-4) It may be that women ministered in the temple services of the Essenes on Mount Carmel (1391-1). The Essenes, according to the readings, clearly had prophetesses as well as prophets. The Essene outlook thus constitutes the particular background for the fuller development seen in "the teachings of Jesus, that released woman from that bondage to which she had been held since the ideas of man conceived from the fall of Eve or of her first acceptance of the opinions..." (2067-11) In this connection it also may be properly noted that, according to the readings, the totality that was Jesus Christ is not to be seen as merely a projection of His Essene background. In comparison with His cousin, John the Baptist, it is specifically said that "John was more the Essene than Jesus. For Jesus held rather to the spirit of the law, and John to the letter of same." (2067-11)

The Cayce readings also affirm that the Essenes were in effect a kind of international brotherhood, although the base and focus were in Israel. The nature of the ties did not preclude those of different backgrounds from following their own religious rituals, as the Jews did theirs. "Those of the other groups, as the Egyptians or the Parthians, were not refrained from following the customs to which they had been trained..." (254-109)[21] In the case of the Essene leader Judy, who became the teacher of Jesus as a youth and whom we shall consider in more detail later, we note that in her work of developing records she drew upon the traditions of Egypt, Persia and India, as well as those of Israel (1472-3).

---

21. There is a statement in this passage which seems to suggest that these practices of non-Jewish origin were conducted not in the Essene temple at Mount Carmel but at another place, "the general meeting place of the Essenes as a body-organization." (254-109) One wonders, of course, whether this is a reference to the location at Qumran. Incidentally, the readings indicate that there were differences or divisions of thought among the Essenes as to whether God's providence allowed human freedom within divine order or precluded it. "One held to—that it can happen—the other that God makes it happen." (2072-15)

94

This then was the background, in its main lines, of the birth of Him whom the Cayce readings call "the Savior, the Messiah, the Prince of Peace, the Way, the Truth, the Light. . ." (1010-17); "that beloved Son, who would make the paths straight, who would bring then *man out* of darkness into light. . .that shepherd [who] must lead forth His flock, His brethren again into the light of the countenance of an all-merciful Father." (587-6) ". . .the purpose of the entrance of the Son *into* the earth [was] that man might have the closer walk with, yea the open door to, the very heart of the living God!" (1472-3)—that all may know that "the Lord thy God is One!" (587-6; cf. Mark 12:29; Deut. 6:4)

IV
The Birth

The two main dates given in the Cayce readings for the birth of the Christ Child are the twenty-fourth, twenty-fifth of December (5749-8) (the birth occurred "Just as the midnight hour came. . ." [5749-15]) and the sixth of January (5749-15). These two dates are, respectively, the dates held and celebrated by the two great branches of the Christian faith, the Western (including both the Roman Catholic and Protestant Churches) and the Eastern (Orthodox). The readings state that each date has a legitimate basis, depending upon the calendar used or the period in which evaluation is made.[22]

The arrival of Mary and Joseph was in the evening, the weather cool. There were crowds of people on the way, many from the hills of Judea and others from the north. Varied also were their occupations: shepherds, husbandmen of flocks, farmers and different kinds of craftsmen. Some in the group from Nazareth were "helpers to Joseph—carpenters' helpers. . ." (5749-15) A number of the readings state that Joseph was a carpenter-builder of some means and substance. The purpose of the trip, according to the account in Luke (2:1-5), was that each Jew had to return to his ancestral birthplace in order to be registered for the Roman tax. According to the readings both Joseph and Mary, as members of the sect of the Essenes, were questioned, apparently on this occasion as on others, by those in religious authority in the land as well as by the Romans (5749-15).

The Cayce readings indicate that the journey of the Holy Family to Bethlehem at the time of the impending birth of the

22. Another reading affirms that the date of Jesus' birth was March 19th and the year 4, based on the Julian calendar, or the year 1899, based on the Mosaic calendar (587-6).

child was by no means undertaken without the concern and care of the larger group of Essenes. Upon their arrival at the inn the couple found there a number of these people. Therefore "there was consternation outside, among those who had heard that Joseph and Mary had arrived and were not given a room." (5749-15)

[They had been told] "No room in the inn"...
...They began to seek some place, some shelter...
Thus many joined in the search for some place. Necessity demanded that some place be sought—quickly. Then it was found, under the hill, in the stable—above which the shepherds were gathering their flocks into the fold.   5749-15

...in the evening—just before the sun in all its glory of the Palestine hills gave forth almost into the voice of nature, proclaiming the heralding of a new hope, a new birth to the earth, and the glorifying of man's hope in God—the spectre of His star in the evening sky brought awe and wonder to all that beheld.   1152-3

There the Savior, the Child was born; who, through the will and the life manifested, became the Savior of the world—that channel through which those of old had been told that the promise would be fulfilled that was made to *Eve;* the arising again of another like unto Moses; and as given to David, the promise was not to depart from that channel. But lower and lower man's concept of needs had fallen.
Then—when hope seemed gone—the herald angels sang. The star appeared, that made the wonderment to the shepherds, that caused the awe and consternation to all of those about the inn...   5749-15

Laughter and jeers followed [upon the negative answer of the innkeeper], at the sight of the elderly man with the beautiful girl, his wife, heavy with child...
...some making fun, some smitten with conviction that those unkind things said must needs be readjusted in their relationships to things coming to pass.
All were in awe as the brightness of His star appeared and shone, as the music of the spheres brought that joyful choir, *"Peace on earth! Good will to men of good faith."*
All felt the vibrations and saw a great light—not only the shepherds above the stable but those in the inn as well.
To be sure, those conditions were later to be dispelled by the doubters, who told the people that they had been overcome with wine or whatnot.
Just as the midnight hour came, there was the birth of the Master.
                                                                                                    5749-15

According to the Cayce readings this was a real, physical birth: "He came, the Master, in flesh and blood, even as thou didst come in flesh and blood." (1152-1)[23] A special dimension of this phenomenon affirmed by the readings is that "the Prince of Peace came into the earth. . ." not only to become the Savior of all mankind—although this first aspect constituted the ultimate purpose—but also "for the completing of His *own* development in the earth. . ." For this latter purpose also "*He* overcame the flesh *and* temptation." (1152-1)

Like the account in the Gospel of Luke (2:8-20), the readings affirm the historical reality of the story of the shepherds in the fields at the time of the birth of the Christ Child. They speak of "those shepherds who had *experienced* that cry of the heavenly hosts, 'Behold a son is given and his name is wonderful, counselor!'" (587-6) The same reading also states that the experience of the shepherds was a reflection of the fact that not only all the heavenly hosts but also "all nature. . .proclaimed that glorious period for man." (587-6; cf. Is. 9:6)[24] The shepherds are variously described as those "who heard the cry of 'Glory to God in the Highest—Peace on earth and good will to men'" (1815-1; cf. Luke 2:14) and as those "who heard the voice, who saw the light, and who experienced the choir of the angelic hosts that pronounced His advent." (2562-1) A man, aged thirty-nine, was told by Edgar Cayce in a reading given in 1934 that in a former lifetime he had been "among the shepherds that were in the hill country, and among those that heard the song of the angels, 'Peace on earth, good will to men.'" Later in that same lifetime this entity was said to have come "very close in touch with the activity of the Nazarene, the Prince of Peace, the Savior of men, as He walked in the earth. . ." (519-1)

The Cayce readings give surprisingly full accounts of the Wise Men who appear briefly but significantly in the Gospel according to Matthew (2:1-23). The fullness of these accounts is due to several reasons. One is that, according to the readings, the Wise Men are concrete representatives of the international contacts of the Essenes and symbols of the wider meaning of the birth of the

23. The view of the Cayce readings with reference to the proper relationship between flesh and spirit, particularly in the case of Jesus Himself and His message of God's will for human beings regarding this relationship, is given in the sentence which immediately follows the one quoted above: "Yet as He then proclaimed to thee, there is a cleansing of the body, of the flesh, of the blood, in such measures that it may become illumined with power from on high..." (1152-1)

24. This same reading also states "how all nature—the face in the water, the dew upon the grass, the tint and the beauty of the rose, the song of the stars, the mourn of the wind, all proclaim—*now*—the mighty words of a merciful, a loving God." (587-6)

Christ Child. This was not merely a local or ethnically restricted occurrence, but an event international, historical and, indeed, cosmic in its full significance.

The Wise Men came "to do honor, to give of their substance. . ." (587-6) and to give "blessings. . .upon the infant in the manger" (5749-2); but their coming was representative of more than their personal perceptions and inclinations. Incidentally, we are told that they came to Bethlehem during the days of purification—the twenty-nine days during which the Holy Family remained in Bethlehem—but were presented to the mother only after she was purified according to the laws of the Jews (5749-7). The purification ceremony, the consecration of the child, the blessings, and the circumcision, according to the readings, evidently took place in the temple in Jerusalem and not in the Essene temple on Mount Carmel (2166-1; 5749-15). And it was here in the temple, then, that both mother and child were presented to "the magi, to Anna and to Simeon." (5749-15) The Wise Men, who came "with their ladened beasts or camels. . ." (1152-3) were three in number, coming from Persia, India and Egypt. But the readings insist that there was later a fourth and a fifth Wise Man and then a second group, among whom there were those who came from Chaldea, the Gobi (desert) area and what is now Indochina or Southeast Asia (2067-7; 587-6). These men were among the sages, or wise and holy ones, in their own lands. They were seekers for the truth, in particular for "this happening" (5749-7), for "the day, the hour when that *great purpose*, that event, was to be in the earth a literal experience." (1908-1) They came "to the place 'where the child was'" (5749-7) in and through the application of those forces which today would be termed psychic. The readings specify that the tradition of the sages from which the Persian Wise Men came included the study of mathematics as well as astronomy and astrology and the other laws of nature (5749-7, 1908-1). In Persia "the studies were of the influence of stellar space or the sojourns of souls in the environs about the earth that made—and make—for the mental urges in the souls of men." (256-5)[25] Moreover, the readings state that "those indications" of the birth of the Christ Child had been proclaimed in Persia not only by the seers of old but also "by the

---

25. This sentence also contains a frequently affirmed insight of the readings into the nature of man, namely that the "mental urges" which characterize the experience of every human being are not the result of heredity and environment alone, nor of arbitrary divine creation, not merely of on-the-spot upsurges of feeling, otherwise uncaused, but are to a substantial extent the result of each entity's own choices and activities in both earthly and other realms preceding the present.

new visions." (1293-1) This is to say that we have to do here with a long tradition of learning that was specifically religious as well as "scientific."

The Wise Men came, then, with relatively clear perceptions of the significance of the birth of the Christ Child. They had been among those who had participated in "the seekings for an understanding and a comprehension of what was to take place in the experience of the *world* by the entrance of an unusual, unheard of as it were. . .influence from another source upon human experience, human relationships, human activities. . ." (1297-1) Furthermore, the Cayce readings make it clear that the Wise Men came not without previous contacts with the Jews, in particular with the Essenes. And we learn that the Essenes had specifically been drawing upon the spiritual tradition of Persia "as handed down by the old Persian teacher, Zoroaster." (1297-1) Also of interest is the assertion of the readings that it was the Romans who gave the order for the Wise Men to be conducted to the place which they sought, and that the Romans later attempted to stay the killing of the babes commanded by the edict of Herod (1220-1).

V
The Flight to Egypt

The Cayce readings state that the flight of the Holy Family to Egypt was in fulfillment of Old Testament prophecy (5749-16; 1010-12). At the same time they give considerable detail with regard to the human activities and circumstances surrounding the event. It should be noted in this context that the readings were always given in response to requests made by persons living during the lifetime of Edgar Cayce; and as a part of the information given, especially in the case of the so-called life readings, references were frequently made to the particular entity's previous incarnations or lifetimes on earth. This term *entity* was consistently used by the Cayce readings to denote the essential asexuality, or perhaps presexuality, of the individual soul and to allow for the fact that souls often were of one sex in a particular lifetime and of the other in a subsequent lifetime—a change generally made, according to the readings, in conformity with the larger educative plan of divine providence, for the sake of developing the particular virtues or aspects of character that are more commonly associated with one sex or the other.

Thus there are several persons who are stated to have been in or related to the court of Herod the Great at the time of the massacre of the male children. It is significant that the readings are at times critical, although always constructively so, of the past life or lives of the individual for whom the reading was given. For example, it is said of a man who was forty-five years of age in 1928 that he had been among the higher officials in Herod's court and, in accordance with Herod's decree, had participated directly in the search for male children. "The entity lost and gained and lost [i.e., in terms of soul or character development] through this experience, for in the service as rendered gain came. In the exercising of personal gain, through the oppressions brought, the entity lost. Through the ability to have presented that which was truth, and rejecting same for those of power, the entity lost." (1629-1) Incidentally, the readings state that only children of the household of David in Judah were killed, by being beheaded (but cf. 1602-4). The search was for children of the "age from six months to two years. . ." (1010-1) "of that line from which there would be the calling of the ruler." (775-1) Accordingly, families of the territory under Herod's jurisdiction, "especially in that region from Bethany to Nazareth" (1010-17), were questioned as to which household they belonged, Ephraim or Judah, Benjamin or Issachar. . ." (775-1)

Of particular interest is the series of readings given from 1939 to 1941 for a woman who was said to have been Herod Antipas's third wife "in the land of the Master of masters' sojourn in the earth." (2067-1) Her mother was Jewish, her father a Roman soldier, and her life extended from 28 B.C. to 6 A.D. (2067-2). In answer to a specific question, she was described as being "five feet six inches in height, *black* of hair, and almost blue of eyes; prominent cheeks but a great deal of color in the general or whole figure and makeup; in weight, a hundred and twenty-nine pounds." (2067-2) She married Herod when she was only fourteen years old (2067-2), as a consequence of political relationships between her family and those in power in the court.

The readings state that this wife of Herod, Thesea by name, came to have knowledge of and contacts with the Essene movement through "one of those in the household [of Herod] who had been so set aside for active service. Through the manner and conduct of life of that individual, and the associations and activities, the entity gained knowledge of that group's [i.e., the Essenes'] activities." (254-109) This information certainly suggests that the placing of trusted members of the Essene community in strategic positions in the larger Jewish society was part of the plan of operation of the Essenes. As a result of this relationship, the readings relate, this wife of Herod became "well acquainted with many of that group of the Essenes during that time. . ." (2067-2)[26] In this context Thesea not only "reasoned with

26. Some insight into the nature of the activities of the Essenes is given by the statement that Thesea was "a seeker . . . for the mystical powers proclaimed by many of that group through those periods of activity." (2067-2) At this point no further explanation is given of the meaning of the phrase "mystical powers," but, as we have already noted, they apparently included a wide range of religious activities and experiences, including prayer and meditation, the cultivation as well as the study of prophecy, the analysis of dreams,

the Essenes [but also] conversed with the Wise Men who came with the new messages to the world. . ." and "sought a closer comprehending of the Wise Men." Incidentally, it is stated in another reading that the Wise Men came not only with material gifts but also with spiritual teachings (1581-1), which were evidently largely in harmony with the views of the Essenes.

The personal relationship of Thesea to her husband Herod, whom the readings describe as "this debased ruler—that only sought for the aggrandizement of self. . ." (1472-3) naturally became strained, even though "these were never very close. . ." (2067-2) "He was cruel. . .because of the *non*-activity or non-conformity to any general rule. . . "(2067-2); we would say that he was unprincipled. And when Herod gave orders for the killing of the infants, "these brought abhorrence, and the turning away from the close associations with the activities of the companion [Herod] at the period." (2067-2) This deterioration of the personal relationship, plus the fact that Thesea was able to save a number of children by having them taken out of the area secretly, led to her death, in compliance with Herod's order, "by exposure and starvation." (2067-6; see also 2067-2)[27]

According to the Cayce readings, the decision of the Holy Family to flee to Egypt was made in consultation with leaders of the Essene brotherhood. As a consequence, the event occurred in the context of specific plans and preparations for the sake of the needed physical protection of the family, especially of the mother and child. Both Mary and Jesus were under the care of an Essene woman named Josie, to whom the brotherhood had assigned the special task of "care and attention to the child and the mother. . ."; she became "the handmaid or companion of Mary, Jesus and Joseph [i.e., she was both nurse and governess], in their flight into

---

visions, and voices, physical and mental healing, dietary training and what is now called astrology. Apparently the Essenes themselves were divided, like others among the Jews, as to whether determinism (by divine predestination) or limited freedom characterizes the human historical experience (1472-3; 2072-15). The world view of the Cayce readings themselves, however, is consistently that of seeing human beings as possessing freedom of the will to make real choices (3976-29; 262-86, A-1; 5749-14, A-10). The divine intent, however, with regard to human freedom is "that each man will live for his fellow man!" (3976-29) The other aspect of this divine purpose is that each person will be "one who uses that [his or her own] living soul as a companion with God. That's God's purpose. That should be man's purpose." (3976-29)

27. The readings state that Herod died "of sarcoma" (2067-2), that is, a malignant or cancerous growth of tissue of mesodermal origin. A further point of interest is that when the sleeping Cayce was specifically asked why "historians like Josephus ignore the massacre of the infants, and the history of Christ, when they record minute details of all other historical events. . ." the answer given was simply: "What was the purpose of Josephus' writing? For the Jews or for the Christians? This answers itself!" (2067-7)

Egypt." (1010-17) But for the larger physical protection needed "there were other groups [of Essenes] that preceded and followed..." the Holy Family itself. The flight "began on an evening, and the journey—through portions of Palestine, from Nazareth to the borders of Egypt—was made only during the night...The period of sojourn in Egypt was in and about, or close to, what was then Alexandria," the duration "a period of some four years—four years, six months, three days." (1010-17)

The readings state that "Josie and Mary were not idle during that period of sojourn..." in Egypt, but that in addition to care of the child Jesus, Josie, as well as the parents, gave some time to study of records "preserved in portions of the libraries..." (1010-17) in Alexandria.[28] These records, according to the readings, included what we would today call astrological forecasts and gave important details regarding the expected Messiah, even to "the nature of work of the parents...their places of sojourn, and the very characteristics that would indicate these individuals..." The readings affirm that the child "was in every manner a normal, developed body, ready for those activities of children of that particular period." At the same time, they state that "the garments worn by the child would heal children." This statement of course brings to mind the accounts given of miracles wrought by Jesus as a child recorded in the so-called apocryphal gospels, although the Cayce readings contain none of the bizarre elements which are found in some of these gospels.[29] The readings explain the phenomenon by stating simply that "the body being perfect radiated that which was health, life itself" and go on to say that even today "individuals may radiate, by their spiritual selves, health, life, that vibration which is destruction to dis-ease in any form in bodies." (1010-17; see also 2067-7)

The return to Palestine, according to the readings, was to Capernaum, not to Nazareth, one of the very few instances in

28. The libraries of Alexandria were the result of a process initiated in the beginning of the third century B.C. by Ptolemy I. They were largely destroyed in the third and fourth centuries A.D. by both accident and design. Perhaps a half million or more volumes were included in the libraries, mostly in Greek but possibly including books in other languages. The original ideal was to create an international library which included translations into Greek from the other languages of the Mediterranean coastlands, the Middle East and even India.

29. Cf. M.R. James, *The Apocryphal New Testament* (Oxford: The Clarendon Press, 1924), especially "The Arabic Gospel of the Infancy of the Savior," 36; 47.

It is interesting to note that in the early seventh century A.D. the great Arab prophet Muhammad took seriously the apocryphal account of Jesus as a child molding from clay the figure of a bird and then causing it to fly away *(Qur'ān 5:110; 3:49)*. This kind of miracle, however, is not reported in the Cayce readings.

which the Cayce readings venture to correct a statement of fact given in the Bible (cf. Matt. 2:23; Mark 1:9; Luke 2:51; but cf. Mark 2:1).[30] The reasons given for going to Capernaum were partly political, a result of the division of the administrative area after the death of Herod; but, perhaps more importantly, Capernaum was evidently the proper place for the early instruction of Jesus under the auspices of the Essene brotherhood, instruction which was to be supervised by a woman named Judy. It is also stated that Capernaum was the place "where dwelt many of those who were later the closer companions of the Master." (5749-7) The woman Judy appears with considerable prominence in the Cayce readings as the highly respected leader of one group of the Essenes, those at Mount Carmel. Josie, however, who had gone with the Holy Family to Egypt, continued, under the supervision of Judy, to be "active in all the educational activities as well as in the care of the body and the attending to those things pertaining to the household duties with every developing child. And Josie was among those who went with Mary and Joseph when they went to the city, or to Jerusalem, at the time of the age of twelve. It was thought by Joseph and Mary that it was in the care of Josie that He had stayed, when He was missed, in those periods when there was the returning to find Him in the temple." (1010-17; cf. Luke 2:41-51)

It is also stated that Josie was the one who brought the spices and ointments in preparation for the burial of the body of Jesus. She never married and was known as one of the holy women among the disciples of Jesus (cf. Luke 23:55-56). She was also the one, by reason of her long intimacy, who had gone to Galilee to persuade the mother, Mary, to come to Jerusalem after the arrest of her Son. She died, apparently without suffering violence herself, during "those periods of riots following the beheading of James, the brother of John." (1010-17; cf. Acts 12:1-2)

---

30. A brief reference in one of the readings suggests that a miracle of multiplication of food occurred when an unexpected delay developed en route as the Holy Family was returning to Palestine from Egypt (5749-15).

VI
The Years of Further Education and Preparation

The Cayce readings do not deny a close relationship between the Holy Family and Nazareth, and they not infrequently refer to Jesus as the Nazarene. After the birth in Bethlehem and the purification and dedication in the temple in Jerusalem, the Holy Family are said to have returned to Nazareth, and from there, as a result of Herod's edict, they fled to Egypt (5749-7). Jesus is stated to have lived with His parents until He was twelve and even after, but for all or at least most of the period after the return from Egypt the place of residence, according to the readings, was apparently Capernaum. From the age of twelve, however, evidently after the experience of "disputing or conversing" (2067-7) with rabbis or teachers in the temple in Jerusalem, He is said to have studied in the home of Judy, who lived with her husband and mother in Carmel (2067-11). These studies apparently were pursued from time to time from "His twelfth to His fifteenth-sixteenth year. . ." (2067-11)

The Cayce readings contain a considerable amount of information about Judy, who was clearly a remarkable woman, to say the least. Her position as a leader of one group of the Essenes testifies to the role of women in that tradition. The readings state not only that both Jews and Gentiles alike were taken in as members, but also that "This was the beginning of the period where women were considered as equals with the men in their activities, in their abilities to formulate, to live, to be, channels." (254-109)[31] Judy is said to have been "the first of

---

31. We read of Judy "in those periods soon after the crucifixion not only giving comfort but a better interpretation to the twelve, to the holy women; and understanding as to how woman was redeemed from a place of obscurity to her place in the activities of the affairs of the race, of the world, of the empire—yea, of the home itself." (1472-3) This is a most significant passage, affirming that Judy, as a woman, not only instructed the twelve apostles themselves—who, the passage suggests, needed such instruction—but was the

women appointed as the head of the Essene group. . ." (3175-3); this particular group was, evidently, in some contradiction with other Essenes, in that it was more given to the honoring of religious experiences such as communications "in voices, in dreams, in signs and symbols. . ." (3175-3) Judy is referred to as a teacher, healer and prophetess. Her own training by "The Holy Spirit, and . . ." (2067-11) her parents, who were themselves Essenes, was not only that "of rote and writ" but also, in keeping with primary concerns of the Essene tradition, "the study of those things that had been handed down as a part of the *experiences* of those who had received visitations from the unseen, the unknown—or that worshiped as the Divine Spirit moving into the activities of man." (1472-3) Here we are clearly dealing with a stream of profound spirituality within Judaism, one in which the practicing members not only revered and studied the words of the prophets, lawmakers and psalmists, but also emulated the human experiences of the Divine that lay behind them. We read that the Essenes "had cherished not merely the conditions that had come as word of mouth but had kept the records of the periods when individuals had been visited with the supernatural or out of the ordinary experiences; whether in dreams, visions, voices, or whatnot. . ." (1472-3)

Also in keeping with the practice of the Essenes, Judy's own education included studies of "the traditions of Egypt, the traditions from India, the conditions and traditions from many of the Persian lands and from many of the borders about same. . ." (1472-3) As an adult she continued this activity, since an important element of her service to the Essene community lay in the making and keeping of records for the community. In the course of this work she "came in contact with the Medes, the Persians, the Indian influence of authority. . ." and it was in consequence of the weighing of the traditions of these lands with her own that she came to "that new understanding." (1472-3)[32]

person who took the already high position of women in the Essene tradition and gave it a new theological undergirding and extension as a result of the cosmically significant events of the crucifixion and the resurrection of Jesus the Christ. This development was, of course, also in accordance with the teaching and practice of Jesus during His public ministry.

32. The limited number of extant historical documents from this period makes it impossible to give specific confirmation of this kind of cross-cultural communication in the case of a person like Judy; but the tradition of Greek travelers abroad—from Pythagoras and Solon to Herodotus and Strabo—as well as recent archaeological finds of large quantities of Roman coins of the early empire in South India, make it clear that such communications were a real possibility. Strabo, the Greek historian and geographer who claimed to have traveled widely throughout the Mediterranean and Middle East, died about a dozen years before the crucifixion of Jesus.

This was the person, then, who is stated by the Cayce readings to have had formative influence upon Jesus from His twelfth to sixteenth years. The primary content of her teaching was the whole range of prophecies as contained both in the Hebrew Scriptures and in the Essene tradition, with special focus upon the prophecies of the life of the Messiah (2067-11). And it was Judy who, according to the readings, was primarily responsible for sending Jesus abroad for the completing of His studies and training. It should be emphasized that these studies were not merely academic in the modern sense of the word, but included spiritual training of the most direct and personal kind. Judy herself is stated to have had many experiences and visitations of angels, and yet it is also affirmed with equal emphasis that her daily life concerned itself in entirely normal fashion with material needs and realities, including "the faculties and desires for material associations—as indicated in the lack of celibacy." (2067-11)

Thus we learn—quite contrary to the romantic, long-held notion that Jesus, as the son of a poor and presumably not well-educated carpenter, had few opportunities for formal education—that Jesus studied abroad "in first India, then Persia, then Egypt. . ." (5749-2) from His thirteenth to sixteenth years.[33] One reading states specifically that "it is not as so oft considered, that the family of the Master lacked material opportunities. For, from many sources there had come the opportunities for those in the household of the Master to have the greater training." (1179-7) It is said of Jesus' sister Ruth that she "was educated not only in the best of the land but in other lands. . ." (1179-7) The total duration of Jesus' travel to and stay in Persia is said to have been a year; the period of stay in India was three years. The content of the teachings which Jesus received in India was evidently in keeping with the religious traditions of other peoples as had been collected and combined by the Essene schools—as, for example, by Judy herself—but the teachings themselves were not "the true Essene doctrine as practiced by the Jewish and semi-Jewish associations in Carmel." (2067-7) The content more particularly had to do with "Those cleansings of the body as related to preparation for strength in the physical, as well as in the mental man." (5749-2) We learn that a major concern of Judy was that

33. There is a slight discrepancy in the different Cayce accounts of the order in which Jesus visited these countries. In one case it is said that Jesus visited "in first India" (5749-2), and in another that " . . . He went to Persia and then to India." (2067-11) In either case, Jesus is stated to have returned to His parents' home before going to Egypt.

Jesus in His studies abroad should particularly study "What you would today call astrology." (2067-11) The intent was also "that there might be completed the more perfect knowledge of the material ways in the activities of Him that became the Way, the Truth!" (1472-3)[34] Incidentally, Jesus is said always to have registered under the name Jeshua in His educational travels abroad (2067-7).

In Persia Jesus' studies and practice are said to have focused on the "unison of forces" (5749-2), physical, mental and spiritual, according to the traditional teachings in the land. Once again, it must be emphasized that these studies were not merely academic in the modern sense of the word. For example, in one passage in a reading which gave answers to questions regarding Jesus' educational experience in Persia, it was stressed that in Jesus' case, rather than learning from these teachers, He was "*examined* by these; passing the tests there. These, as they have been since their establishing, were tests through which one attained to that place of being accepted or rejected by the influences of the mystics as well as of the various groups or schools in other lands." (2067-7) This seems to suggest that Jesus' educational experiences, "the travels of the Master during the periods of preparation" (5749-7), were certainly broad rather than narrow. Clearly these experiences involved an educational process of the profoundest kind, one that culminated in the event or process of personal transformation called initiation. This term is in fact the one used by the Cayce readings with regard to the culmination of Jesus' educational experience, and we shall dwell briefly upon the meaning and reality of the word, particularly as it relates to the period in Egypt, where this culmination was achieved.

First, however, it must be stated that Jesus, according to the readings, returned to Palestine before going to Egypt. The primary reason was the death of Joseph, at which event Josie was present, and she "closed the eyes and laid him to rest." (1010-12) The readings state that Jesus was specifically called back home from Persia at the death of Joseph "and then into Egypt for the

34. We shall return to this point later, but let it be noted once again that, according to the Cayce readings, while Jesus *became* the Christ in conformity with the plan of God, this was the result also of a long process of moral and spiritual training, discipline and service. This preparation included many previous lives on earth, as well as experiences in other realms, before the culmination of the whole in Palestine in the first century of the present era. It is in the context of this understanding that we are asked to view the earlier education of "...Jesus who became the Christ...[and] gave Himself a ransom for *thee* and thy friends; for thy world in which ye labor!" (1010-12) "Through that ability to make Himself one with the Father, He has gained that right, that honor to declare Himself unto as many as will harken." (5749-13)

completion of the preparation as a teacher." (5749-7) It was at this point that Jesus' educational experiences converged in a special way with those of his cousin John, who became the Baptizer: "He was with John, the messenger, during the portion of the training there in Egypt." (5749-7) It is said that "...John first went to Egypt—where Jesus joined him and both became the initiates in the pyramid or temple there." (2067-11) The readings state, incidentally, that an Essene woman named Sofa, who was also one of the "holy women"[35] and became the nurse and instructor of John, "during a year...gave most of the time to indicating to the child Jesus the life, the preparation, and the character of John." (2175-6) This statement would suggest that John was also regarded by the Essene community as having, according to prophecy, a specifically predesigned role in the messianic activities and that Jesus was instructed as to this fact at an early age.

The Cayce readings state that "as indicated oft through this channel, the unifying of the teachings of many lands was brought together in Egypt; for that was the center from which there was to be the radial activity of influence in the earth. . ." (2067-7)[36] It is particularly interesting to note that the Cayce readings, upon specific questioning, deny that Jesus had ever studied under Greek philosophers in Greece, or that, as some have believed, Greeks later came to Him to beg Him to come to their country when the Jews cast Him out (2067-7).[37]

The readings affirm that the initiation of Jesus in Egypt involved a literal passage through the tomb or chamber in the pyramid, symbolic of the tomb of the soul, which in turn was indicative of "the crucifying of self in relationships to ideals that made for the abilities of carrying on that called to be done." (5749-

---

35. These "holy women" are stated, among other things, to have "acted in the capacity of the mourners at the various functions of the order, as would be called, of the Essenes." (2175-6) Although one or more of these women did not marry (2173-1), the readings emphatically state that "They didn't take the vows of celibacy! Not to have children during those periods was considered to be ones not thought of by God!" (2175-6) This sentiment, of course, is in accord with the Biblical witness (cf. Luke 1:25, 58) and suggests that the celibacy of both Jesus and John was primarily functional, i.e., a life commitment made in keeping with the needs of their particular callings, and not in itself representative of a higher spiritual state.

36. Probably not enough attention has been paid heretofore to the larger cultural significance of Egyptian influence upon the formation of Greek civilization of the classical period. The travels to Egypt of the Greek statesman and lawmaker Solon in the early sixth century and of the philosopher Plato at the beginning of the fourth are surely indicative of extensive contact.

37. This reading further comments, in effect, that such an appeal would have been very unlikely, for "Jesus, as Jesus, never appealed to the worldly-wise." (2067-7)

2; cf. Matt. 10:39; 16:25-26) That is, the emptying of self, the complete and utter dedication of self to the Father and His will—which according to the Cayce readings was at once the essence of Jesus' relationship to the Father and the basis of His entire life and ministry—was in a deep sense both formalized and realized in this initiation experience. This event, however, was not an isolated one, divorced either from Jesus' previous training, of which it was the culmination or from His subsequent discipline and service. The readings indicate that Jesus' baptism in the Jordan by John was a kind of fulfillment of His "passing through the initiation. . ." (2067-7) This all is to say that, according to the Cayce readings, the whole process of Jesus' educational training and spiritual discipline was necessary not only for the perfecting of Himself to serve the Father's purposes in behalf of others, but also for the fulfillment of His own personal needs; it was, in a word, the final recapitulation in reverse (upwards rather than downwards) of His experience as Adam (2067-7).

There is, it would seem, a deep-rooted distaste for the term "initiation" among many, both clergy and laity, in the Christian churches of the present day. The origins of this distaste appear to lie in clerical disapproval of and rivalry with various non-ecclesiastical religious orders, such as the Masonic and the Rosicrucian, which have traditionally made significant use of the term "initiation" and developed extensive practices in the context thereof. One objection, especially among certain Protestants, is theological, being the disapproval of language that might suggest "synergism," or human cooperation in the divine work of salvation. More generally, however, and also more recently, objections have been made to secularizing trends in some of these non-ecclesiastical orders, and perhaps there is some justification for criticism as a consequence of the superficiality of understanding or dubiety of intent with which the rite of initiation may sometimes be participated in. In all honesty, however, one would have to say the same with regard to not a few instances of participation in the ecclesiastical rites of confirmation or adult baptism. In any case, the Cayce readings affirm the central significance of the event of initiation in the life and work of Jesus the Christ. His age at the time was evidently sixteen.

Indeed, the readings assert that this kind of initiation is "a part of the passage through that to which each soul is to attain in its development. . .each entity, each soul, as an initiate. . ."(2067-7) must pass through the same kind of tomb or pyramid in order to obtain its release and fulfillment of its goal of being a companion

111

with the Father. This teaching is of course in accord with the Biblical accounts of Jesus' statements regarding the need for every disciple to take up his cross and follow the Master, to lose his life in order to find it (Matt. 10:38-39; 16:24-26). The Cayce readings, however, emphasize that there was a unique redemptive dimension to Jesus' experience of initiation. That is, His initiation was also a kind of prefiguration of His later three days and nights in the tomb (Matt. 15:46, etc.), and in relation to this initiation it is stated that only Jesus was able to break the power of the tomb, or death. The empty tomb "has *never* been filled. . ." (2067-7) since then.

A number of readings refer to Jesus as the Great Initiate, who took "those last of the Brotherhood degrees with John, the forerunner of Him, at that place" (5748-5), that is, in the pyramid now called Gizeh (5748-5; see also 5749-2). He was "the Great Initiate, the Holy One, the Son of man, the Accepted One of the Father." (5749-2) The readings in effect acknowledge a certain continuity between the so-called Mystery Religions of pre-Christian antiquity at their best and the life experience of Jesus the Christ, in that He participated personally in the traditional rites and at the same time fulfilled them so that they henceforth could bear a deeper significance and have more powerful effects—and not just for the few, but for all mankind.[38]

As indicated above, the Cayce readings affirm that Mary and Joseph did not enter into conjugal relations until after Jesus left their household to begin His educational experiences under the guidance and protection of others. This period evidently lasted until ten years after the return from the flight to Egypt. This restraint, the readings state in answer to a specific question, was not from some external requirement; "it was a choice of them both because of their *own* feelings." (5749-8) But then they began normal or natural associations, and the children "came in succession; James, the daughter [Ruth], Jude." (5749-8) The readings go on to describe some of the feelings of the children, especially of the daughter, Ruth, who was born in Capernaum

38. Knowledgeable readers may be aware that this understanding is essentially similar to that of the Austrian philosopher, educator and clairvoyant mystic, Rudolf Steiner. See his *Background to the Gospel of St. Mark, The Gospel of St. Luke* and *Christianity as Mystical Fact.* Thus Steiner writes: "In Jesus of Nazareth, in whom the Christ was present, something happened which had been witnessed again and again in the Mysteries, but never as an historic event, concentrated into a few years. It was now an historic reality, yet it was a repetition of the temple-rituals. The life of Jesus could therefore have been described by specifying the states passed through in other circumstances during the process of Initiation." *Background to the Gospel of St. Mark* (London: Rudolf Steiner Press, 1968), p. 62.

(and evidently raised there; see 1179-7), as to what it meant to be born and raised in such a family. The circumstances surrounding Jesus' birth were evidently fairly well known, at least among those of Essene affiliation, as indicated in this excerpt:

> There was awe in the minds of the peoples as to what had taken place at the birth of the mother's, or Mary's, first son.
> Hence the entity, Ruth, was rather in awe of the suggestions, the intimations that surrounded that experience; and questioned the mother concerning same.
> As the entity grew into maidenhood, and after the birth of Jude, then the death of Joseph brought that brother—Jesus—home! and there were those activities that surrounded the entity concerning that unknown, that strange kinsman; that kinsman whom the peoples held in awe, yet said many unkind things about. .   1158-4

The readings also record some of the doubts and questionings of Ruth concerning her brother Jesus; we are told that she often asked Mary, "How *can* such things be? How *can* He without father come into the world?" (1158-9) At the time of the death of the father, Joseph, when in fact Jesus returned to see her for the first time "as a stranger. . ." Ruth asked, this time more within herself, "If He healed, why did He let Father die? If He is such as so many proclaim, *why* hath He been so long away? *Why* does He continue to go here, there? Why do those that are in authority appear against Him?" (1158-9)

The readings also state or suggest that the cost of the education of Jesus outside the home both in Palestine and abroad, combined with the death of Joseph, brought about a certain adverse "change in the material or financial status of the family. . ." (1158-4) This situation apparently became somewhat more pronounced during the latter teen years of Ruth—and therefore the late twenties of Jesus—with the result that she, and presumably all the brothers, expended "self's efforts mentally, materially. . ." (1158-4) for the aid necessary for the family as a whole. Ruth is said later to have married a Roman supervisor of tax collecting in Palestine and to have been present at both the crucifixion and resurrection of Jesus; we are also told that she was a source of appreciable aid of various kinds to the young churches in Rome and Athens, where she later resided with her husband and family (1158-4; 1158-5).

References in the Cayce readings to James, the young brother of Jesus and older brother of Ruth, are relatively sparse in content. One interesting passage, however, speaks of him as Ruth's elder brother who "became as the head of what is termed the church; not as that *ye* understand in thy present surroundings as an elder, a teacher, a minister. For how has it just been given? He, thy brother James, was exalted to the position of the leader because the *honor* was to Jesus, the Christ, to Him to whom all honor and all glory are due; to whom all patience, all suffering, all humbleness became so much a portion of His demonstration in life..." (1158-5) This passage suggests rather strongly that the late Pope John XXIII's understanding of his own role as *servus servorum Dei* was truer to the early church's understanding of the proper nature of ecclesiastical leadership than was the princely image held during some of the intervening periods.

A few references are also made to Jude, the youngest brother in the family. The Cayce readings state, however, that Jude came to have faith in "the Master as the Master of the entity..." (137-64) for the first time about a year and a half after the death of Jesus. He was then only nineteen years old. The statement is also made that Jude particularly leaned upon the disciple John at the time of his own experience of being in "chains and bonds..." He was later "Freed ... and then sent into the wilderness for thy tenderness." (137-125) The latter point probably refers to some kind of regimen of spiritual discipline. The readings also state in effect that the book in the New Testament attributed to Jude was in fact composed by him, evidently when he was in confinement in Achaia, for he "wrote much in the confinement at that place now called Achaia..." (137-121)

VII
The Public Ministry

1

In one sense the public ministry of Jesus can be said to have begun with the events immediately preceding it, namely, His baptism in the river Jordan at the hands of His cousin John, and His subsequent temptation. The Cayce readings have much to say about John, as the "kinsman who had been spoken of and held in awe, his mother having been a chosen vessel by the priests of the Essenes, and he, John, being the lineal descendant of the high priests of the Jews..." (1158-4) He is further described as "one that had renounced his position as a priest that might serve in the temple, to become an outcast and a teacher in the wilderness..." (1158-4) The readings identify John's father Zechariah with the Zechariah "murdered between the sanctuary and the altar," (Matt. 23:35) and they also affirm that the cause of his death was his public proclamation of his religious experience and committal to the Essene cause; thus it appears only natural that John would renounce the priestly role when his own father, who was of course a priest of "the division of Abijah" and therefore of the Aaronic line, had been so ruthlessly treated by the religious establishment. For Jesus to inaugurate His public ministry by baptism at the hands of this John is particularly significant as a symbolic indication of the direction of His primary loyalties and aspirations. Viewed in the context of the time and place, this action could hardly be interpreted as meaning anything other than that the main direction of this ministry would be, from the standpoint of the religious establishment, sectarian or even heterodox. This is not to say, however, that the Cayce readings affirm either the teachings or the life style of Jesus to be completely in conformity with that of John the Baptist. In

115

contrast to the extreme degree of physical abstinence for the sake of purification of the body that John taught and practiced, Jesus allowed indulgence "in those things that to some became questioned..." yet in such a way as to keep "the body for those purposes alone whereunto He had called same to be beautiful in its relationships..." (609-1) We read also that "John was more the Essene than Jesus. For Jesus held rather to the spirit of the law, and John to the letter of same." (2067-11)

The baptism in the river Jordan as described in the readings was evidently by immersion, for Jesus' bodily position is said to have been "not standing in it and being poured or sprinkled either!" (2067-7) This point is communicated simply as interesting information, without any doctrinal or ecclesiological conclusions being drawn. Rather than the form, however, emphasis is placed on the meaning of the event. The readings state that the baptism was for the fulfillment of Jesus' initiation (2067-7). And from there He went out into the wilderness to pass through what are called "the tests in the wilderness..." (1158-4) But the purpose of this latter activity is also described as having been "to meet that which had been His undoing in the beginning." (2067-7) This is, we may note again, reference to the need to recapitulate, this time as the second Adam and with full victory, the earlier experience of temptation as the first Adam.

The readings then speak of the return of Jesus, "after those periods of the tests in the wilderness, after His meeting with John..." (1158-4) The place of return, however, is cited as Capernaum.[39] Jesus' first preaching in the synagogue is described as being "as to the prophecies of Isaiah, Jeremiah, and the teachings of the lesser prophets, and as to how they applied in the experiences of that day." (1158-4) As we shall see in more detail later, this statement is fully in accord with the Cayce readings' consistent emphasis upon the application of truth to life as being a central aspect of Jesus' teaching and practice.[40] The result of this

---

39. The fourth chapter of Luke states that the return of Jesus from the experience of temptation was to Galilee, where He taught "in their synagogues." Following this, He is described as going to Nazareth, and the content of His sermon is given in some fullness, together with the angry response of many of the hearers. Luke then writes of Jesus' going to Capernaum, where He preached and healed on the sabbath and where He healed Peter's mother-in-law in Peter's house. It is significant, we may note, that Peter's home is said to be in Capernaum. Incidentally, a reading states that "...Andrew had told Peter of the happenings at the Jordan..." (5749-15; cf. John 1:40-42) In Mark 1:21 the first instance cited of Jesus' preaching in a synagogue is in Capernaum.

40. A representative statement is that "unless one makes the application...healing of the physical without change in the mental and spiritual aspects brings little real help to the individuals in the end." (4016-1)

first preaching after the return from the wilderness was that "a tumult was raised owing to the utterances of that new teacher..." (1158-4)

Perhaps it would be well at this point to observe that the Cayce readings at no time attempt to give a full and ordered report of the life of Jesus the Christ. The readings were given in response to requests of specific people, then living on the earth, and in most cases the data on the life of Jesus emerge in the context of information given a person who in a former incarnation had been somehow associated with Jesus and His contemporaries. These people did not always play a heroic role, nor did they by any means perform only deeds worthy of approbation. For instance, one person, a man who was forty years old at the time of his reading in 1940, is stated to have been one of the ten lepers who met Jesus on the way to Jerusalem and were healed (Luke 17:11-19). This entity, however, "was one who was healed; but did not return to give thanks..." (2181-1) Often the statement was made that in a given life experience an entity had "lost and gained," had "gained, lost, gained," or even had lost more than gained, although we read also in other cases that "the entity gained throughout." One instance is given of an entity who "blew hot and cold through the periods of development." (3360-1) But with reference to the events and experiences of these persons living at the time and in the place of the Christ event, only that information was given which was considered to be of present practical help to the individual concerned. For example, the statement is made "Much might be given as to the activities and associations of the entity during that sojourn..." (1188-2); and in another case, in which information regarding the life of Jesus was specifically requested, it was forthrightly stated that "A great deal... is being skipped over." (5749-15) Hence we must clearly understand that we are dealing with materials that in their original form constitute purposely selected and therefore limited data.

2

The Cayce readings state that while "the first of the outward miracles of healing..." (3175-1) was the healing of Peter's mother-in-law, the first recorded miracle was that of turning water into wine in Cana of Galilee, which is said to be "nigh unto Capernaum." (5749-16) This is one of a number of instances where the Cayce materials prefer the order of events as given in the Gospel of John. The miracle at Cana (the readings do not hesitate to denote either this event or the physical healings with the word "miracles") is said to have occurred "soon after the return of the Master from the Jordan, and His dwelling by the sea, His conversation with Peter—after Andrew had told Peter of the happenings at the Jordan; and there was the wedding in Cana of Galilee." (5749-15)

The readings very suggestively put this event in the context of various questionings by Jesus' mother, "with her son returning as a man starting upon His mission." (5749-15) She had continued to reflect upon the events surrounding Jesus' birth, the pronouncement of the angel Gabriel, the strange experiences incident to her visit with Elizabeth, and the later unusual events in Egypt and on the return to Palestine. "This might be called a first period of test. For, had He not just ten days ago sent Satan away, and received ministry from the angels?" (5749-15) Evidently Mary had already heard of these matters through others, and her first meeting with her son after the temptation experience was on this day of the wedding feast. Jesus' primary purpose in coming to Cana was to speak with His mother, who had this "natural questioning of the mother-love for the purposes; this son— strange in many ways—had chosen, by dwelling in the wilderness for the forty days, and then [by] the returning to the lowly peoples, the fishermen," (5749-15) to fulfill His calling in ways that were still puzzling to her.

The bride at this wedding feast is said by the readings to have been a daughter of a younger sister of Elizabeth, therefore a daughter of a cousin of Mary. Her name was also Mary, and she later came to be spoken of as "the other Mary." She is said to have been one of those who gave of their material means and service that the teaching activity of Jesus and His disciples might be carried on (609-1). We find numerous references elsewhere to "the holy women who followed Jesus from place to place when there were those periods of His Palestine ministry," (3175-3; cf. Luke 8:1-3; 23:49; 55-56; 24:10) Mary the mother of Jesus was in a primary way responsible for the preparation of the wedding feast, and when Jesus came with His followers—apparently a few such had already emerged—He and His disciples were invited to remain at the feast.

The groom is said to have been one of the sons of Zebedee, an older brother of the "James and John who later became the close friends and the closer followers of Jesus."[41] (5749-15) The Cayce

---

41. The Cayce readings consistently affirm the identity of John the "one beloved of the Master..." (2946-3) with John the son of Zebedee and brother of James. He is also stated to be the author of the Gospel as well as the Epistles of John.

readings insist that "the sons of Zebedee were among those of the upper class, as would be termed [today]; not the poorer ones." (5749-15) As another reading points out in reference to their later participation in Jesus' ministry, "the sons of Zebedee were among those sufficiently able financially, as would be termed in the present, to leave their work, their home [as were] all of the apostles, save Matthew; for these, the sons of Zebedee, were in favor with those in political authority." (2946-3) This was "the household that entertained the Master oft..." (2946-2) and, according to the Cayce readings, Zebedee's son John was the person to whose care the mother of Jesus was entrusted after the crucifixion.

The readings describe the context in which the wine ran low and Jesus turned water into wine:

The customs required that there be a feast, which was composed of the roasted lamb with the herbs, the breads that had been prepared in the special ways as were the custom and tradition of those who followed close to the faith in Moses' law, Moses' custom, Moses' ordinances...

Much wine was also part of the custom. The day was what ye would call June third. There were plenty of flowers and things of the field...

The day had been fine; the evening was fair; the moon was full. This then brought the activities with the imbibing more and more of wine, more hilarity, and the dance—which was in the form of the circles that were a part of the customs...[42]   **5749-15**

Another reading speaks of the event as "when water saw its Master, blushed and became wine even by activity! Remember, only as it was poured out would it become wine. Had it remained still, no wine could have filled those conditions where embarrassment was being brought even to the friend of the entity in that experience." (3361-1) The entity referred to here is said to have been a sister of James and John and acquainted with the bride.

The larger meaning of the event at Cana, however, is indicated by the statement in another reading referring to "the blessings of having the Master present at the wedding." (2946-3) This reading goes on to discuss the divine significance of human marriage, which is affirmed as involving "the unions of hearts and minds

---

42. Some readers may reflect at this point that the description sounds like the work of an imaginative historical novelist. Indeed it does, but it is also true that the description, even as literature, is in keeping with known historical data. It is appropriate, however, to observe that Edgar Cayce in his ordinary waking consciousness was not given to flights of rhetoric such as this.

and bodies..." The reading concludes by saying, in a direct address to the person for whom it was given, "Know, in thine heart of hearts, as bodies and minds are drawn together, these are not purposeless but purposeful; that the glory of God may be made manifest."

3

The next event in the public ministry of Jesus given some prominence in the Cayce readings is His healing the fever of the mother of Simon Peter's wife (Mark 1:29-31). The healing is noteworthy not only as the first of the miracles of this kind recorded as performed by Jesus, but also as "one of the few instances where healings were performed among His own people, among His own kindred." (5749-16) To my knowledge, however, the readings do not indicate in what way either Peter's family or his wife's were among Jesus' larger circle of "kindred." More, on the other hand, is said of Martha, the much younger sister of the mother of Peter's wife. This Martha, who is to be differentiated from Martha the sister of Mary and Lazarus, became, according to the readings, the wife of Nicodemus.

...and then when the message was given out that Martha's older sister had been healed from a terrible fever by this man, Jesus, this brought about great changes in Nicodemus and Martha, as they had to do with the temple and the service of the high priest. Martha began the weaving of the robe that became as a part of the equipment the Master had. Thus the robe was made especially for the Master. In color it was not as the robe of the priest, but woven in the one piece with the hole in the top through which the head was to be placed, and then over the body, so that with the cords it was bound about the waist.

This robe Nicodemus presented then to the Master, Jesus, after the healing of the widow of Nain's son, who was a relative of Nicodemus.

3175-3[43]

It is said that "Though Martha was an Essene, Nicodemus never accepted completely the tenets or the teachings of the Essenes group. [But] These were a part of the principles and applications of Martha." (3175-3) This, then, was the context of

---

43. We read further, "The color of the robe was pearl-gray, as would be called now, with selvage woven around the neck, as well as that upon the edge, as over the shoulder and to the bottom portion of same; no belts [probably "bells"; cf. Ex. 28:34], no pomegranates, but those which are woven in such a manner that into the selvage portion of the bottom was woven the Thummin and Urim. These were as the balance in which judgments were passed by the priest. But these were woven, not placed upon the top of same. Neither were there jewels set in same." (3175-3)

events and developments within which "...Nicodemus went to the Master by night [John 3:1-21] and there became those discussions in the home; for Nicodemus and Martha there began the communion as man and wife rather than man and his chattel or his servant. They were more on a basis of equality..." Here, once again, we come upon information indicative of Jesus' directing influence in the elevation of the status of women and in the purification and ennoblement of family relationships.

This Martha is said to have been "one particularly honored even by the Master." (3175-3) She came to be considered one of the leaders among the early disciples, and at the time of the crucifixion she was "one of those upon the right hand of Mary, the mother of Jesus..." She was "gathered with those in the upper room looking for the promise of the coming of the outpouring of the Holy Spirit." She was present at the day of Pentecost "Among those who heard all of the various places announce their hearing Peter in their own tongue."[44] Martha "later was among those who aided Stephen and Philip, as well as others of the various lands." She became an advisor and teacher as well as helper, especially to the younger ministers and workers in the early church. Her "home became more and more a place of refuge and help for all of the young of the church" and apparently her two sons and one daughter became ministers in the church in Antioch. This daughter later was wed to Silas, one of the missionary companions of Paul. Martha herself "lived to be an elderly person, something like seventy-nine years of age in the experience, and was not among those ever beaten or placed in jail..." (3175-3) although she knew persecution in other forms.

We find several references in the Cayce readings to the meeting of Jesus with the Samaritan woman by the well of Sychar (cf. John 4:1-42). Incidentally, we learn from a reading that there were also Samaritans who were "from the land of the Galileans..." (5328-1); that is, as might be expected, those of the Samaritan faith were not confined to the geographical limits of Samaria proper. The readings stress particularly the individual and larger consequences of this meeting by contrasting the quality of the Samaritan woman's life before and after her encounter with the Master:

...for as the entity had wielded its influence for that which brought those of distorted emotions and ideas in the minds of individuals during

44. The careful reader will note that this sentence adds a slightly different detail to the event on the day of Pentecost (cf. Acts 2:1-13).

that period, so with the awakening of the water of life springing anew in the hearts and souls of those that made Him as the ideal, did the entity bring into the minds, hearts and souls of those first of its own household, then of the multitudes, then of the greater masses, that of the *beauty* of *life* in Him, of the glories of the Father in Him, as may be manifested in the lives of individuals who have Him as their ideals, whether pertaining to the secular things of life or otherwise—for the crust of bread glorified by Him feeds in the physical body those things that bring glories in the hearts and minds of individuals, where the sumptuous board of those that wander far away must bring dimness of eye, solemness of feeling, want and desire in the hearts of those that follow such...   451-2

It may be properly noted at this point that, with reference to the old controversy over the interpretation of the meaning of the life and person of Jesus the Christ as either example and ideal or savior and redeemer, the Cayce readings consistently maintain a "both and" stance. That is, Jesus is understood as both ideal and redeemer.

We read also that members of the immediate family of this Samaritan woman later "became messengers and understanders of that being taught." (451-2) Of her sister it is stated that reflection—coupled "with the faith that was implanted by this meeting—brought peace, joy, understanding, and the ability to suffer, even in silence, whether in physical, in mental, or the material things of life..." (428-4) This sister is said to have given much to others in that period, "bringing peace to her own household, quietude to those disturbed in body and mind..." (428-2)

We read of another person who "came in close contact with the Master when the Master spoke to the woman at the well and many of those in the city who came out to see Him." (1552-1) This person, "Though then young in years...was impressed...by the gentleness and kindness of the disciples, especially the Master..." (1552-1) We learn in the same context that "as His teachings had advanced..." (1552-1) the Samaritans came to participate more and more in the great festivals in Jerusalem, evidently the result of a significant degree of reconciliation effected between Jew and Samaritan. An even stronger statement of the immediate effect of Jesus' meeting the Samaritan woman is given in another reading, where reference is made to "that city which later turned a great deal of its activity because of the visit of the Master to the woman at the well." (1592-1) This was the visit "of the man of Galilee, the man who walked among His fellow man that others might be shown the way for the more perfect understanding" (379-3), the one who also "came as the lamb to the world." (933-1) This is He who also said, "...'Not of myself'...'but [from] the Father that worketh in and through me do I bring thee health, do I bring thee hope, do I bring thee the living waters.'" (1152-4; cf. John 4:10, 13; 5:19)

Among the reports of events in the early public ministry are various references, mostly fragmentary, to the first disciples. Sometimes we have telling vignettes of the Master's followers, as when "the staid Andrew" is contrasted with "the boisterous Peter." (4016-1) A member of the seventy found that "he argued with Peter and reasoned with Andrew." (4016-1) The physical appearance of Jesus Himself is briefly described in at least two passages in the readings. One speaks of His profile as being neither distinctively Jewish nor Aryan. His appearance was "clear, clean, ruddy, hair almost like that of David, golden brown, yellow-red, but blue eyes [described in reading 5749-1 as being "blue or steel-gray"] which were piercing; and the beard, not cut, but kept in the proportion at the contour of the face, and the head was almost perfect." (5354-1)[45] This was apparently the way He appeared to "those throngs that gathered at times for the interpreting of the new teachings, and the watching of their application in the experience of Him—who gave such hope to the world." (3360-1)

This point of application, as has been noted, is a fundamental element of the Cayce readings' perception of Jesus' own activity and of the content of His teachings. One brief summation of the meaning of Jesus the Christ is "that in Him is the life and the light, and that His whole command is *sincerity* and love." (2015-3) His teaching is said to have dealt primarily with principles rather than individual problem cases, but when a person asked the sleeping Cayce, "How may I be most useful to Jesus Christ?" the answer came: "In applying principles...in thy daily life, in dealing with thy fellow men." (1646-2) The leper who was one of those healed but did not return to give thanks is said to have "gained and lost through that experience..." gained through the entity's awareness but "lost in not making a practical application of same in its experience among its fellow men, not bearing witness to those assurances, those experiences, in its activity." (2181-1)

---

45. We find in a reading given with regard to the Lord's Supper, which we shall consider in more detail later, the following description of Jesus: "The Master's hair is 'most red, inclined to be curly in portions, yet not feminine or weak—*strong*, with heavy piercing eyes that are blue or steel-gray. His weight would be at least a hundred and seventy pounds. Long tapering fingers, nails well kept. Long nail, though, on the left little finger." (5749-1)

The Cayce readings make several references to Jesus' traveling in His early public ministry, not only in the northern sections of Jewish Palestine but also for "the edifying of the peoples in the outer areas of Palestine." (3640-1) There were those in these areas who experienced and "ever gave thanks for the manner in which the Master indicated His interest in others, their sorrows, their joys, their uprisings, their littleness and their abilities to appreciate." (3640-1) In this spirit and manner the "Prince of Peace entered into [the country of the Gadarenes]..." (2481-1) and journeyed into the territories of Tyre and Sidon, "the upmost coast of the land." (513-1) References are made also to people who came from long distances, that is, from outside Jewish Palestine, "hearing of the healings and of the Master's activities through portions of the land." (3640-1) There were those who "brought their loved ones to the Master for healing" and found that "... He supplied that as would bring happiness and joy; not gratification but contentment and peace to the hearts and souls of those that sought to know His biddings." (3216-1) We note that Jesus, "the Teacher of teachers, the Lord of lords, the Brother of man" (2035-1), He who "was...is, the life, the light in this material world..." also sojourned in what the readings call "the land of the Saracens..." (2661-1) This term, although not much used in contemporary English, is derived from a late Greek word which came to designate Arabs in general and finally all Muslim subjects of the caliphate. More narrowly, however, the term Saracen appears to have been used for a nomadic people of Semitic stock and language living in the deserts between Syria and Arabia proper. The terminology of the readings seems to be in accord with this narrower usage and points to a specific area outside Jewish Palestine where Jesus taught and healed.

With regard to the power and effect of these teachings, a reading given in 1939 to a woman fifty-eight years old offered the following advice: "Practice in thy daily life in the present, and in the telling of them ye will not only find Him alive in thine own heart and consciousness, but that His words become *living* water, quenching the thirst of those who are disturbed or troubled as to the meanings of His parables, His lessons that He taught." (2035-1) "For He has promised to come to thee, to all who seek, who live, who act in such a manner that His presence is *acceptable* to those who seek." (478-4)[46]

---

46. We note in this final quotation another example of the discriminating subtlety of the

6

There are several references in the Cayce readings to the mission of the seventy who were sent out in the early public ministry. We read how "the Master blessed the seventy that were to go abroad and teach and minister to others and preach repentance, that the day of the Lord was at hand." (1529-1) Another reading states that members of the seventy were "able, by the blessing of the Master, to heal physically and mentally..." (5328-1) We read also of "each individual being commissioned by the Master, Jesus Himself..." (3395-3) Elsewhere we are told that "those that had become the leaders and the teachers...were tested, trained, taught by Him..." (857-1) One sentence describes their being "sent as emissaries through the land to proclaim periods in which there would be activity of the Master as combined with the teachings and ministerings of many of the apostles." (2285-1) Incidentally, we learn elsewhere that the "apostles" were at first called only "disciples," the term "apostles" evidently being given later as some of the "disciples" came to be assigned specificially missionary tasks (2459-1). In any case, the mission of the seventy seems to have included the specific function of preparing a place or area for the later arrival of Jesus and His co-workers. We read also that they were sent out on at least two different occasions, "during the Galilean as well as the Judean ministry." (622-4; see also 3347-1) The readings suggest that the mission of the seventy—one to be repeated again and again in the present day—could be described as follows:

...to bring into the hearts of men again and again *hope*, encouragement; and to *sow* again and again the seed that bear the fruits of the Spirit—patience, gentleness, kindness, brotherly love, long-suffering! For against such there is no law.

For it is the law that as ye sow, so shall ye reap.[47] And ye are the sower; but leave what may be the results to thy Father!

For He alone may increase. For unless the souls be quickened by the precept and example, and the Father calleth, how can they know Him?
1529-1

Cayce readings with regard to the divine-human relationship. Here the presence of the Lord is stated to be conditioned not by any limitation of will or power on the divine side, but by the nature or quality of the human quest and response, whereby the presence of the Lord can be "accepted" or not.

47. We shall later consider in more detail how the Cayce readings perceive Jesus' understanding and practice of the Law, in the sense of the Law of God as believed and practiced in the Jewish tradition. Let it be said here, however, that Jesus is described as

This is obviously missionary advice superbly appropriate to any time or place. The missioner is both to teach and to give example, in the context of the Father's own work. The readings emphasize that Jesus Himself both taught and exemplified, telling us of "that truth which He so thoroughly exemplified in the experiences of man; namely, to love the Lord thy God with all thy heart, thy mind, thy body, and thy neighbor as thyself—which is the whole law." (2031-1; cf. Mark 12:28-31)[48]

The Cayce readings state that it was after the return of the seventy to Jesus that He taught that people "must eat of the body and drink of the blood if they are to know the Lord." (cf. John 6:48-71) And the person to whom this reading was given was told that he had been present at that time and place and "like many others the entity went away, but kept in touch with the activities; and with the day of Pentecost, when many were turned, the entity again became one of those associated with organized work. For then the entity understood, when there had been explained how on the night He was betrayed He took bread and broke it saying, 'This is my body,' and with the cup, 'This is my blood.'" (5328-1) Another person was also said to have been "among those who could not interpret upon the return. 'Except ye eat of my body, ye have no part in me.'" (4016-1) The explanation was then given: "Literal, it becomes disturbing. Mentally and in a spiritual sense, it may be interpreted."

The nature of what in fact is involved in the Lord's Supper as an ongoing reality of spiritual communion is further explained as in a sense including both physical and spiritual dimensions. "For the Christ, as manifested in Jesus, was the first, is the foremost, is the

focusing on the essence of the Law; He does not abolish it. The Cayce readings frequently use the word "law" to denote the complete integrity and essential regularity of God's ways in the universe, as of the processes of nature under His ultimate control. With reference to the much debated question of divine judgment, we find that "He [Jesus] condemned not ..." but at the same time He is said to have stated more that once that "Indeed offenses must come, but woe unto them by whom they come." (2031-1; cf. Matthew 18:7, etc.) The Cayce readings here as elsewhere insist that Jesus never condemned anyone in the sense of closing off his future, but yet He made clear the operation of the law of cause and effect, or sowing and reaping, in the moral and spiritual as well as physical realms. At the same time, He also pointed to the open door and the transcendent power of God's mercy, which in an ultimate sense takes precedence over all other laws and functions. See the Gospel of Matthew, chapter seven, which in a graphic way reflects the various facets of this reality of the dual working of "the kindness and the severity of God." (cf. Rom. 11:22)

48. This same reading states that an appropriate contemporary reenactment of the activity of the seventy would be to "keep this experience [as one of the seventy] in such manners that, day by day—not so much by proclamation of thyself, but by thy gentleness, by thy kindness, by thy tenderness of words, of hope, of cheer, of that ever giving of creative forces in their experiences—others may be led to know that ye walk and talk with Him!" (2031-1)

essence of both bread and of wine. For that element which is life-giving physically of bread, or that giveth strength to wine, is the source of life itself. Thus in partaking, one does literally partake of the body and of the blood in that communion." (5328-1) This statement or explanation is an extremely subtle one. On the one hand, it is not "pantheistic," for neither here nor elsewhere in the Cayce readings is it claimed that all is God without distinction of priority or differentiation of quality. The fact, in particular, of individual consciousness and freedom of will in human beings is consistently maintained.[49]

According to this quotation (5328-1), the "life-giving" element in bread or wine—presumably any kind of bread or wine—is the "source of life itself" and is to be identified with the Universal Christ Spirit, who was manifested in Jesus of Nazareth. This evidently means that the Godhead, as Life, is present and constitutes the essential element in *all* "life-giving" realities or things, and yet is not to be totally identified with them.

On the other hand, however, it would be a mistake to interpret this quotation as indicating that partaking of the elements of the Lord's Supper has some magical efficacy apart from the mental attitude or fundamental intent of the participant. This would be another form of *ex opere operato* religion—to use the medieval Latin phrase—which implies automatic spiritual, even salvific, effects regardless of the quality of faith or sincerity of intent of the worshiper. To my knowledge, nowhere in the entire corpus of Cayce materials is an affirmation of this kind made. According to the readings, God always respects the integrity of the human consciousness and will and never forces Himself upon that consciousness apart from human consent and willing openness. As stated in a reading given at the request of those present at the Tenth Annual Congress of the Association for Research and Enlightenment, in 1941:

> ...we are joint heirs with that Universal Force we call God—if we seek to do His biddings. If our purposes are not in keeping with that Creative Force, or God, then we may be a hindrance. And, as it has been

---

49. "It should be understood that Life is One, that each soul, each entity is a part of the Whole, able, and capable of being one with the Source, or the Universal Power, God, yet capable of being individual, independent entities in their own selves. As He has given, to those whom He calls does He give the power to become the Sons of God." (294-155) This is to say that in the mystery of the relationship of human beings to God, the Author, the Creator, of all life, there is both dependence and freedom, but for that relationship to reach its proper form or destiny the dialogic reciprocity of divine call and human response, of particular appeal and willing cooperation, is necessary. "*Open* then thy heart, thy consciousness, for He would tarry with thee!" (5755-1)

indicated of old, it has not appeared nor even entered into the heart of man to know the glories the Father has prepared for those that love Him. Neither may man conceive of destruction, even though he is in the earth a three-dimensional awareness. Neither may he conceive of horror, nor of suffering, nor even of what it means to be in outer darkness where the worm dieth not.   5755-2

In this way both the fact—and the possible variations of consequence of the fact—of human freedom are graphically affirmed.[50] "Only they that seek shall find!" (5755-1) Another reading puts it thus: "He comes not unbidden, but as ye seek ye find; as ye knock it is opened. As ye live the life is the awareness of His closeness, of His presence, thine." (5749-10; cf. Matt. 7:7-8)

Thus the literal partaking of the body and blood in the communion of the Lord's Supper is a participation—through the physical eating—in the Source of life itself, in the Christ of the Godhead. But for this participation to have spiritual and moral significance—ethically transforming or saving power—questing, requesting human aspiration for the Godhead (one aspect of this aspiration may of course properly be called faith) is necessary. "He that would know his own way, his own relationships to Creative Forces or God, may seek through the promises in Him; as set in Jesus of Nazareth—He passeth by! Will ye have Him enter and sup with thee?" (5755-1; cf. Rev. 3:20)[51]

7

To return, then, to events in the public ministry of Jesus, we note that in the case of Jesus' healings of the sick and infirm, a distinction is made in the readings between the physical and the moral-spiritual dimensions involved in healing. Thus in the case of the "leper at the gate" (cf. Matt. 8:1-4) who was healed by Jesus, the statement is made that "the entity was *healed* (physical), made clean (moral)... [that he might] gain the better understanding of self, through those lessons taught by that Teacher..." (2482-1)

In the 5749 series of readings we note the following statement:

---

50. In at least two readings an extra-canonical saying of Jesus to this effect is quoted: "As the tree falls, so does it lie." (5755-1; 5755-2) This phrase would seem to communicate the same truth as Paul's "whatsoever a man sows, that he will also reap," (Gal. 6:7) a phrase which the Cayce readings repeat, with slight variations of language, many, many times.
51. Another reading that stresses the same point makes use of the famous scriptural passage, Rev. 3:20: "...know that He stands at the door of thy heart and thy mind and knocks, and would enter and sup with thee! if ye will but invite Him! Not by might, not by power, 'but by my word' saith the Lord of hosts!" (1641-1; cf. Zechariah 4:6)

Respecting the miracles of healing, there were many instances where individual healings were of the nature as to be instantaneous—as that when He said to him sick of the palsy, "Son, thy sins be forgiven thee." [cf. Matt. 9:1-8] When the questionings came (as He knew they would), He answered "Which is it easier to say, Thy sins be forgiven thee, or Arise, take up thy bed and go into thine house?" *Immediately* the man arose, took up his bed and *went* unto his house! Here we find that it was not by the command, but by His own personage. For, the question was not as to whether He healed but as to whether He had the power to forgive sin! The recognition was that sin had caused the physical disturbance.   5749-16

One implication of the interpretation given within this passage seems to be that while the healing was instantaneous and indeed "miraculous," the entire event was not effected by mere *fiat*; rather, it involved particularly the power and quality of the influence of Jesus' person, to the end that the individual being healed cooperated fully in the process with both faith and obedience. As another reading puts it, "He that is called to service must indeed obey." (294-155) A second point made in this passage is the flat statement that in this particular case "sin had caused the physical disturbance." This statement is in accord with other affirmations in the readings that moral wrong or sin may be the cause of physical illness.[52]

Several references are made in the readings to the restoration to life of the widow's son at Nain (cf. Luke 7:11-17), "when the widow of Nain was stopped by the Master..." (5248-1) We read that "the entity received back alive the son—as they walked from Nain at those periods of His ministry there" (601-2), and "the son was delivered again to the mother." (2454-3)

A reference is also made to a person who was "among those groups chosen as companions upon many of the missions which the Master took." (5276-1) This person was present at the time of Jesus' stilling of the storm, for "The entity saw that experience of the wind, of the storm, the elements, the thunder, the lightning obey the voice of the Master..." In this context we find Jesus spoken of in the most exalted terms as "... Him, who is the God

---

52. A significant discussion of the relationship between miraculous healing and the forgiveness of sins in the ministry of Jesus is given by the German Biblical scholar Otto Betz in *What Do We Know About Jesus?* (London: S.C.M. Press, 1968), p. 62. Another reading gives further suggestive material in this context. Cayce was asked to "explain why the Master in many cases forgave sins in healing individuals." The answer was, "Sins are of commission and omission. Sins of commission were forgiven, while sins of omission were called to mind—even by the Master." (281-2)

of the storm, God of peace, God of the wind, God of the rain, yea, the Lord of the earth of whom the disciples said, 'What manner of man is this, that even the wind and the rain, the sea and the elements obey His voice?'" (5276-1; cf. Mark 4:41, etc.)

Brief references are made in the readings to the casting out of demons from the two men of the country of the Gadarenes (cf. Matthew 8:28-34). The incident is cited as another instance when Jesus came to those "in the outer coasts of the land." (1934-1) One reading describes the event as that "when the influences were driven from the man in the Gadarene land."[53] (1616-1) The event also, according to this reading, became the occasion for Jesus to teach with moving emphasis the fact that God is to be known and addressed as "Father, God!" Another reading indicates that the event had profound effects upon others than those healed, as in the case of one who "learned gentleness, kindness, patience—as was shown in the gentle manner in which *all* were answered who raised their voice in criticism of the activities of that particular experience." (1934-1)

A considerable number of references are made in the readings to the healing or calling back from the dead of the daughter of Jairus, one of the rulers of the synagogue (cf. Mark 5:22-43, etc.). In one reading the event is spoken of as that which happened to the "one whom the Master called again from the deep sleep—Jairus' daughter." (559-7) In another it is said that the parents "had their loved one given again to them as a *living* example of His indeed being the resurrection." (1968-4) In yet another the mother herself is addressed and told how she was able to see "in body the love in the flesh presented to thy arms, by the love of the Son of the Father, God!" (1968-1) In this same reading, while reference is also made to "the patience of the man of Galilee," we are told "how stern He might be when He put the entity out of the room, as well as those of the household, because of doubt..." The lesson to be gained from that experience was and is to put "the whole trust in the faith of Him that *is* the way and light and truth and understanding!" And again, with reference to the nature of Jesus' mode of healing, this reading states that "... His presence [was] to heal body, mind and soul..." Here we are also told of Jesus' "love for man, of His filling the whole life purpose of man." (1968-1)

Another reading dealing with the healing of Jairus' daughter

---

53. The readings seem to suggest that while there were two afflicted men who were from the tombs, only one of the two could be described as having been "possessed." (1934-1; 1616-1)

refers to "the blessings to be had materially and mentally from the embracing of those principles and tenets of the teacher..." (1968-4); this is a further instance of the understanding widely found in the readings that Jesus had concern for every dimension of human life and taught, as well as acted, accordingly. This same reading cites as a fact that Jairus had been previously influenced by the teachings of both John the Baptist and Jesus Himself, with the result that he was commended by the Master because of his showing an "unusual interest of man for his mate, and for the offspring, for the period or time." This attitude and practice of Jairus also brought "wonderment from his associates or companions in his office." (1968-4) It should be added that the call of Jairus' daughter back to life was a call "back to service in that experience..." (421-5) She was addressed: "Awake, my daughter, to the abilities of thyself through the might of the God-Force within thee." (1246-2) Thus "the man of might and power through Galilee" said to her, "Arise, and minister." (1246-2) She, like others, became "a changed person in those days because of the happenings there..." (3307-1)

The healing of the woman who had had a flow of blood for twelve years appears in the scriptural accounts in connection with the raising of Jairus' daughter (Mark 5:24-34, etc.). A Cayce reading describes the woman as "a very thin or pale individual, with very dark eyes and hair—and a robe of gray and purple, or the bands about same purple while the robe would be in a lighter gray." She is seen as "kneeling upon one knee and reaching for the hem of the Master's robes—and He turned as to the left to encounter the figure kneeling, see?" (585-10) This same reading also adds further descriptive data with regard to Jesus Himself, for He is pictured as "the Master with the gray robe, the beard scant, the hair—not red nor yet golden, but as of reddish golden—blessing or healing the woman with the issue."

8

The miracle of Jesus' feeding the five thousand (Mark 6:30-44, etc.) is referred to a number of times in the Cayce readings, often in connection with the blessing of children.[54] The event is singled out as an occasion when the Master blessed many, particularly the young. One reading, addressed to a woman who is said to have

---

54. A Cayce reading makes mention of the second feeding of a multitude, said in Matthew 15:38 to number four thousand and described in the reading as numbering the same (3183-1).

been among the children blessed on "that day when the five thousand were fed" (1614-2), states how as a result of that experience "the whole reliance upon the faith in those promises made manifest in Him held the entity to an experience of helpfulness to others." Then the reading tells this person, "He blessed thee in the flesh. He will bless thee again, if thou holdest to that purpose; putting away strife, jealousy, malice, condemnation. Condemn not, if ye would not be condemned." (cf. Matthew 7:1-2)

With regard to the event itself, which the readings consistently affirm as historical and physical fact, a number of significant insights are given and lessons drawn. For instance, one reading states that the entity learned patience from participation in that and related events. "For He did not lose patience with His disciples when they said, 'Should we go away to buy bread to feed this mob?' " (5089-2) Giving concrete expression to a theme often emphasized in the Cayce material—the necessity of starting where one is and with what one has in hand—the reading quotes Jesus Himself as saying to the disciples " 'What have we here?' 'What have you here?' " The account then goes on:

Did you ever hear this used to individuals? Try it! It is one of the most disturbing, yet one of the most quieting words which may be used, even to a mob. "What have we here?" And only a few loaves, a few fishes, yet in the hands of those who could realize as ye may, "Of myself, I can do nothing, but through His power," it may be multiplied into blessings. And remember, it can be multiplied in curses, also, if ye use not thy abilities aright.   5089-2

The readings therefore see the event as one that can be applied to a significant degree in the experience of all persons, but at the same time they affirm its uniqueness. Thus mention is made of the fact that "the thousands were fed as only the Master might feed, from the few loaves and fishes." (5002-1) Another reading states that participation in the experience "brought the awareness of the unusualness and the divinity of the Master..." In this latter case another factor contributing to the entity's awareness was "wonderments at His joining His disciples without means of transportation in the ship..." (2845-2; cf. Mark 6:45-52, etc.) This event is referred to in yet another reading as "...His walking on water and...His bidding Peter to come to Him." (2829-1)

The Cayce readings interpret the feeding of the five thousand in language which is common in the Metaphysical or New Thought tradition in American life, viz., that of divine supply and increase. The readings, however, consistently affirm the reality of matter in a positive way, even though it is seen as derivative of spirit and therefore in a sense subordinate or secondary.[55] "...even as the Spirit moved, matter came into being." (1770-2) The Cayce readings also affirm the principle and fact of what may be called secondary creation, for not all things in the material world are seen as the result of the primary or original creation on the part of God Himself. Some things, such as "those things that corrupt good ground, those that corrupt the elements..."—"elementals, and pests..." for example—are in fact perceived to be "the compounds" or consequential offspring of the beings or souls created in the primary creation (364-7).

This principle of secondary creation can of course be given the very widest interpretation and application. It means that human beings, who as souls are products of the primary creation, are seen as capable of truly creative activity, which has its origin in the spiritual dimension, its direction in the mental and its manifestation in the material or physical. Thus, in a reading which refers directly to Jesus' feeding the five thousand, the statement is made, "But know, that which is material must have first had its inception in the spiritual—and has grown according to *mental* application..." (1743-1) In this same context the proper religious application of this cosmic principle is given: "...as the purpose of each soul is to be a channel through which that as held as its ideal is to be made manifest, and that the glory of God be kept first and foremost—then so live, so act as to be consistent in thy thoughts, thy acts, thy expressions. Not only in word but in deed. For being true to self will not make thee false to any." In all this, one is not to forget the Source of "*all* power as may be manifested in the earth." (1743-1)

This, then, is the context within which the affirmation of divine supply of human needs is made. He in whom we live and move and have our being "is the supply—whether it be material, the mental, the spiritual." (1770-2) Without question, at one level the feeding of the five thousand was for "the supplying of physical needs to the material man" (2549-1); but it was also the occasion

---

55. The high view of matter in the Cayce readings may be further perceived in the analogy which is used in a number of instances to explain the nature and inner relationships of the Divine Trinity. In this analogy of the Godhead, the Father is equated with the body; the Christ, the Son, with the mind; the Holy Spirit, "through which all approach is made" (1770-2), with the soul. "...the Mind became the Way, the Truth, the Light in materiality..." (1770-2)

on which "spiritual blessings came to many..." (2549-1) In fact, Jesus' "blessing and bringing abundance to others..." were means of expressing His love and showing forth "the light of the life of the Christ." (1770-2) This love and light is seen as a manifestation of the breadth and depth of the Father's compassion, for "why shouldn't a divine Father supply those worthy, and unworthy as well?" (5398-1)

However, in this particular application of Jesus' teaching about the Father—who "makes His sun to rise on the evil and on the good, and sends rain on the just and the unjust" (Matthew 5:45)—the readings, like the account given in Matthew, do not hesitate to warn against human presumption toward this divine compassion and generosity. For instance, the very "lad *from* whom Andrew obtained the loaves and fishes to feed the five thousand"—and this was an important contribution, because however small, it was precisely the material at hand which could be used by the Master for multiplication—had gained in his personal life from "that influence of increase, yet *not* too great a gainer in the experience from the lesson there. Easy come, easy go became too great an influence in that particular sojourn." (1821-1) This person was warned that participation in so great a blessing does not obviate the fact "that there are the needs each day for each soul to choose aright; that there is today, as every day, set before thee good and evil, life and death—Choose thou!" (cf. Joshua 24:15) Choices so weighted in the direction of the temporal "as to blind self to the mental and spiritual needs" bring their own consequences, "For unless the purpose, the ideal is founded in the spirituality, the increase and the growth—as ye experienced in seeing manifested to feed the *hordes* that day—*cannot*, will not be a part of the experience!" (1821-1) As an example of Jesus' "warning" others— He never "threatened"—we note in a reading what is stated as one of His extra-canonical sayings: "...as He gave, 'Being forewarned, be forearmed, and allow not thine house (thine self) to be broken up.'" (1602-4)

This is to say that having one's material needs supplied becomes a positive part of the total self experience only as the material obtains its proper place and proportion in the hierarchy of reality and value which constitutes both the cosmos as a whole and the human self in particular. Thus the following advice is offered: "Then as He hath given, and as ye heard so oft, 'The kingdom is within.' [cf. Luke 17:20-21] Turn ye within, for there in the temple of thine own body is the temple of the living God, where He hath promised to meet thee, to commune with thee, and to give thee the supply of *all* that may be needed within thine experience!" (1770-2)[56]

Thus the process of divine supply is not to be regarded as automatic or mechanical, for it requires proper human mental and spiritual participation if it is to continue functioning properly. For instance, we read, "he that follows in *His* footsteps [is] His, who said: 'Take my yoke upon you and learn of me.' And those that do such shall never—nor their seed—beg bread." (457-3; cf. Matthew 11:29) There are also wrong ways to try to use divine supply: "... there *is* the way that may seem right to a man, but the end thereof may be death." (1770-2) The opportunity and the invitation are laid before us, but only "if the heart is open, He will come and abide with thee." (1770-2) The proper way is seen in advice given to a person who was said to be present at the feeding of the multitude:

In the present walk ever closer with the Master. Let oft the deeds of thy hands be again multiplied by and through Him, and not of thyself. For, these are the manners in which ye may accomplish the most; letting that power—which ye *saw* so well demonstrated—flow through thee; by faith, yes; by works, yes; by the good will that is a part of thy whole being—but ever the power, the might in Him.[57]   **3183-1**

Or, as another reading expresses it, "If thy trust is put in the Lord of Lords, ye may indeed revel in that consciousness that 'The Lord will take care of many, as I do His biddings.'" (5002-1) A larger application of the meaning of the feeding of the five thousand is seen in the following quotation from a reading dealing precisely with the problem of man's role in securing divine supply:

---

56. With regard to the affirmation very often made in the Cayce readings that the kingdom is within, it is important to note the following: "It is *within* that there is the kingdom of heaven! The kingdom of *God* is without, but is manifested in how it is reacting upon *thee*—by the manner in which ye mete to thy associates day by day that concept of that light which rises within!" (877-27) Once again we note that the Cayce readings consistently affirm "both/and" with reference to issues that are commonly polarized as "either/or."
57. In this particular reading the entity addressed is said to have been among the early disciples of Jesus and to have served as a teacher and writer, with the name of Thaddeus. He is said to have made notes that became "a part of the records of Mark and Matthew; in Luke or John ..." and to have been a personal acquaintance of John (3183-1). Reference is made elsewhere to a woman named Esther, who had "aided in compiling many of the letters written by the writers of the Gospels in that particular period." (3667-2) Another reading mentions a person who was present in Bethsaida during Jesus' ministry there; this entity is said to have "aided others by the recording in its own terms, in its own language, the sayings and doings of the Master..." and to have "prompted Matthew to write his Gospel." (3395-2)

Does mankind consider he is indeed his brother's keeper? This is the manner in which man may answer the question. There will be no want in bread for mankind when mankind eventually realizes he is indeed his brother's keeper [cf. Genesis 4:9]. For the earth is the Lord's and the fullness thereof, and the bounty in one land is lent to man to give his brother. Who is his brother? 'Our Father' (we say)—then each of every land, of every color, of every creed is brother of those who seek the Father—God.   5398-1

The larger significance of this reading, given on August 24, 1944, less than six months before Edgar Cayce's death (January 3, 1945), will not be lost on perceptive readers.

One final point may be made with regard to the feeding of the multitudes. As noted above, the event occurred within the larger context of the blessing of many, especially the children and the young. A Cayce reading interprets the Biblically recorded teaching of Jesus on becoming as little children in a way that is helpful to our understanding of the whole. With reference to "the multiplying of things and experiences in the hand..." a young woman who had presumably been one of the children blessed was advised, "Do not let these become a selfish thing. Let them be rather as He gave, when He blessed you—'Except ye become as little children, ye shall in no wise enter in'; unless ye are as forgiving, unless ye are as generous, unless ye are as dependent as little children..." (1532-1; see also 3395-2; cf. Matthew 18:1-4, etc.) Another reading describes "how oft He used children, the young people, as the hope of the world, as to how each individual puts away those selfish desires which arise and becomes as little children, one may never quite understand the simplicity of Christ's faith; Christ-like faith, Christ-like simplicity, Christ-like forgiveness, Christ-like love, Christ-like helpfulness to others." (1223-9)

Still another reading gives us further dimensions of Jesus' teaching on this theme. "... He taught His followers, His beloved disciples, that humbleness of heart, singleness or centralness of purpose, with the very expression of same as the child; that hurts must be forgiven, that neglect must be overlooked, that dissension must be of short duration; that such, and of such, are those that are acceptable in His sight, and who will stand with Him and He with *them* before the throne of grace." (702-1) Elsewhere it is stated that Jesus knew just how to speak to and teach children in "those lessons given by Him as He spoke to the children in the childish *understanding* manner..." (665-1) Apparently at such times the lessons were illustrated by stories "of the lamb and... of the household pets..." (665-1) A number of references are made in the readings to the ongoing effect, reaching even into incarnations in the twentieth century, of Jesus' having blessed, as well as more generally influenced, persons in His Palestinian ministry. Thus a woman is told, "As He gathered thee into His arms, materially, so is there—as ye abide [now] in the presence of His love—that as may bring the security. For as goodness, as love lives on, so may thy body-soul realize... that blessing as ye magnify—in thy dealings with thy fellow men, 'Inasmuch as ye do it unto the least of these, my little ones, ye do it unto me.'" (1877-1; cf. Matthew 25:40, 45)

9

The Cayce readings include a considerable number of passages which may be grouped together as concerning the experiences and teachings given at Bethsaida by the Sea of Galilee. Bethsaida is said to be "among the places often visited by the Master... this place where the Master liked to rest." (1223-9) A number of references are made to people, including those in authority, who entertained Jesus or "made the home His resting place." (1223-4) A woman is described as giving of herself unstintingly to open her home "for the pleasure, the comfort, of a tired man—the Son of God." (1223-4) This same reading speaks of "... His face—worn at times..." indicating something of the toll taken by the physical strenuousness and the deep-level mental and spiritual giving-out of self in this itinerant ministry. In the very same connection, however, reference is made also to "that smile, that expression that brings the hope so necessary in the heart of the human—that there *is* the better way, there *is* safety in His presence, in the consciousness of the abiding faith in Him." (1223-4) To this woman Jesus was a friend as well as a Savior.[58] She is said to have become "so closely associated with Jesus as to call Him by His name, Jesus, not Master... [as she did] after His crucifixion." (1223-9)

The Cayce readings frequently describe with deeply compassionate understanding the existential needs and common problems met with in human life. Thus those who heard Jesus at Bethsaida are cited as persons "who looked for, who had come to

---

58. Another reading, given to another woman who was said to have been among the children whom Jesus held "materially in His arms," speaks of Jesus' smile: "Thou wert there, my child! Thou felt His hand upon thy brow; yea, ye saw the smile upon the Master's face; yea, ye felt within thine very soul that strength that so oft keeps thee—in thine trials—in this very day." (702-1)

expect that sometime, somewhere, God would hear the cry and answer those who were troubled by ills of body, turmoils of the struggles for life, for the meeting of the passions of the body of men, for the cries of the young for succor, for aid, yea.for bread." (3660-1) It was to these that "... He spoke gentle words—the sower went forth to sow. What are ye casting into the soil of life for those ye meet? Upon what character of soil seek ye to prepare, even in thine own life and heart and body?" (3660-1; cf. Mark 4:1-20, etc.)

This relatively free handling of Biblical passages, rephrasing—often in a variety of expressions—in order to give both the essence of the meaning and the mode of application, is typical of the Cayce readings. They also do not hesitate to give, as we have seen, what may be called extra-canonical sayings of Jesus; that is, direct quotations of Jesus' teachings which are not found in the Bible. It is indeed as if the "Source" of the reading were present at the scene and describing both its outer form and inner reality. The following is an example of the bringing together of separate scriptural passages: "... as He has given so oft, it is here a little, there a little, line upon line, precept upon precept; *sowing* the fruits of the Spirit, *leaving* the fruition of same to God!" (1877-2; cf. Isaiah 28:10, 13; Galatians 5:22-23) Another form of an extra-canonical saying is: "... as He gave, those being on guard do not allow their houses, their own selves or their mental abilities to be broken up." (1968-1) In other cases, to be sure, quotations from the Scriptures are given either verbatim or as close paraphrases thereof, as when we read, "as the Master gave Himself, 'Search the Scriptures, for in them ye think ye find eternal life and they are they that speak of me.'" (5373-1; cf. John 5:39) Even here, however, the description of fact as given in the Biblical account is subtly changed to a constructive admonition.

Further teachings given at Bethsaida include those "that the Master gave as to friendships, associations, forgiveness, the lack of common gossip about others... those warnings which were a part of the experience with Jesus of Nazareth..." (1223-9) He, "the lowly Nazarene" (1177-1), taught humility in a special way "to those who would become teachers and ministers in the experiences and lives of others." (1958-1) The readings are quite frank as to the limitations of Jesus' disciples of the time, as where we read how a person at first was inclined to dismiss them as of no account, "Because of the character or manner of livelihood of many of those who were proclaimed as disciples or adherents to those teachings..." (1877-2)[59]

Indeed, there were "in the material many things that brought dissensions and strife among even the very elect, for the satisfying of material desires..."[60] even among those of whom it is said, "how glorious to have been among those" "who were present when the Master of men, thy brother, thy Savior—yea, thine intercessor before the throne of grace, as man—walked in the earth." (702-1) We read also how "it became necessary [for Jesus] to rebuke the disciples for their attempting to rebuke the peoples." (5373-1)

Yet Jesus' sternness at times was not dissociated from "... His laughter, His care, His thoughtfulness of others." (3342-1) We shall note later the ability of Jesus to laugh even amidst the sufferings of the last week of His earthly life; this dimension of Jesus' personal character is a noteworthy contribution to the understanding of Jesus the Christ furnished by the Cayce readings. Furthermore, the spiritual truths which He taught, along with His person, "brought into the lives of those who followed in *His* way that of *joy*—though in service; *joy*—though in trial; *joy*—though in persecution for a cause and for a purpose." (2043-1) In another reading, where it is affirmed that "... His promises are sure, 'If ye seek me, I stand at the door and knock'"[61] (3089-1), the admonition is promptly added, "Not that this is to become long-facedness, but the happiness—as well as the sorrows..." is to have its proper place in the life of those who follow "the Way, the Truth and the Light." For "... He, in mercy, in grace, had overcome the world." (4065-1)[62]

---

59. It may be well to mention again in this context the emphasis placed by the readings on the varieties of views and positions held by the different "groups and sects among the Jewish population..." (1877-2), a point also revealed by the Qumran materials (cf. Betz, *op. cit.*, pp. 78-79). Also, the wisdom and restraint generally shown by the Roman overlords is duly noted: "...the Romans who were in partial political power, and refrained from an active influence in the religious—or certain portions of the social life of individuals through the period." (1877-2) In this same reading it is stated that among those who were in positions of power and influence in the land and yet deeply affected by the person and teachings of Jesus there were "periods of fear that there might be an uprising..."

60. The Cayce readings contain a number of references to "the elect" without specifying, to my knowledge, precisely who are denoted by this term. There is, however, no indication that the word has primary reference to eternal or ultimate salvation; it seems rather to refer to those chosen for particular roles in the service of the kingdom of God. This is to say that the context of meaning is more missiological than soteriological. We do, however, find references to those who were "the closer followers of the Master..." (3667-2; see also 1223-4)

61. Here again, in a slightly altered quotation from the Bible (Rev. 3:20), we find the typical Cayce emphasis upon the necessity of mutuality for a proper relationship between God and man.

62. This reading states that in fact this affirmation of Jesus' having overcome the world was a part of Jesus' own teaching at the time, and it is immediately followed by the

10

A passage in the New Testament that has long troubled commentators perhaps more than any other is the account of Jesus' healing the daughter of a Syrophoenician woman called a Canaanite by Matthew, in the district of Tyre and Sidon (Mark 7:24-30; Matthew 15:21-28)[63] In the Marcan version we read that in response to the mother's appeal for the healing of her possessed daughter Jesus says, "Let the children first be fed, for it is not right to take the children's bread and throw it to the dogs." In Matthew the language is even harsher: "It is not fair to take the children's bread and throw it to the dogs."

There are references to this incident in at least six different Cayce readings. In no case is the word "dogs" used by Jesus to denote the Syrophoenician woman or her compatriots. According to one reading, the question asked by Jesus was, "Must I give to those not of this household?" (585-2) The word "household" evidently refers to the household of Israel; according to the Matthean version, Jesus in the early part of His public ministry believed that His mission was to "the lost sheep of the house of Israel," even though in Matthew we also find an early reference to Jesus' healing Gadarenes outside the borders of Jewish Palestine (Matthew 8:28-34). In this Cayce reading, however, the initiative and charm lie not totally with the Syrophoenician woman, as in the Marcan and Matthean accounts, but also appear in Jesus. For it is said, "the Master put His hands upon the entity and loved the entity..." (585-2)

In the readings the word "dogs" is used only by the mother, as in one case: "Yea, Lord, but even the dogs eat of the crumbs from the master's table" (1159-1), or in another: "Doth not the servants—even the dogs—eat at the Master's table?" (2364-1) In both cases the response of Jesus was similar, "I have not found so great a faith, no, not in Israel." (1159-1) In these readings Jesus is twice referred to as "the Holy One." (2364-1; 105-2) And strong emphasis is laid upon the abiding effects of the ministry of Jesus in this place among the people who are said in a reading to be "of a mixed race..." (1159-1) Jesus is also said to have blessed the entire household of the woman, and reference is briefly made to the fact that the accounts of this event have "been diverted by

statement, "... it must indeed be that offenses come, but woe to those who would offend." (4065-1; cf. Matthew 18:7)
63. Jerome, the translator of the Bible into what became the official or Vulgate version of the Roman Catholic Church, offered his own solution to the problem: "O mira rerum conversio! Israel quondam filius, nos canes." This, of course, is no solution at all.

many of the writers of same..." (105-2) In this same reading, immediately following this observation we find a direct quotation of Jesus: "He that believeth in me, or that cometh to me, I will in no wise cast out, for even as I am in the Father and ye in me, we are then one with the Father that doeth His will." (cf. John 6:3537; 17:21) The last phrase would appear to mean, "We who do the will of the Father are one with Him." The intention of the reading is clearly to refuse to ascribe to Jesus any kind of racial, cultural or religious partiality. The readings frequently refer to the Jews as that "peculiar people," in the sense of having a distinct divine calling and mission, but never, to my knowledge, consider them the sole objects of God's love and care.

Reference has already been made to Jesus' blessing of the children and teaching, "Except ye become as little children, ye shall in no wise enter in" (cf. Mark 10:15, etc.), but it seems in order to reintroduce the incident, partly because of the numerous references to it in the readings and partly because several of the teachings which Jesus is said to have given in connection with it are particularly appropriate as introductory to the accounts of Jesus' treatment of Mary Magdalene. The quality in children of quickness to forgive and forget is particularly stressed. Thus Jesus is described as "one that drew children to Him and made of them and their lives an illustration of the manner in which people, men, women, everywhere, must accept those activities of their fellow associates. For if one would be forgiven as a child, one must forgive those that would—or do—err against self." (857-1) Elsewhere the meaning of the condition, "Unless ye become as a little child" is explained: "Unless you become as open-minded, unless you can get mad and fight and then forgive and forget. For it is the nature of man to fight, while it is the nature of God to forgive.[64] ...'As ye forgive, so are ye forgiven.' As ye treat thy fellow man ye are treating thy Maker." (3395-3; cf. Luke 6:37) In this same reading the further point is made that there is properly a "lesson of correction that is part of the desire for forgiveness." (3395-3) The point is then repeated to emphasize the fact that forgiveness, by God or by one's fellow human beings, is not to be presumed upon but is only truly appropriated when accompanied by openness to correction and change, including the willingness to forgive others.

The Cayce readings emphasize that Jesus taught not "dogmatic influences of an orthodox activity..." (1401-1) but "principles"

---

64. The readings, of course, do not mean this kind of phrase to be understood in the light sense of Heinrich Heine's "Dieu me pardonnera. C'est son métier."

that are in fact descriptive of cosmic process as well as of divine will. In this context of understanding the statement is made, "For the whole Gospel as He gave is, 'Thou shalt love the Lord, thy God, with all thy heart, thy mind, thy body; and thy neighbor as thyself.'" (1401-1; cf. Mark 12:30, 33, etc.) The readings, therefore, do not hesitate to give full weight to the so-called "hard" sayings of Jesus. For example, along with many quotations of "Whatever a man sows, that he will also reap" (cf. Galatians 6:7), there are many references to Jesus' teaching that "with what measure ye mete, it is measured to thee again. Even as He, the Master gave, 'the faults ye find in others are reflected in thine own mirror of life. And as He gave, 'Cast the beam out of thine eye that ye may see to take the mote from thy brother's eye.'" (3395-2; cf. Matthew 7:2-5, etc.) In a reading which refers to Jesus' parable of the seed sown in various conditions (cf. Mark 4:1-25), the individual addressed is squarely told that he was among those whose "ideals and purposes were choked out" (33081) as a result of persecutions and hardships suffered in regard to material things. And the admonition was then given, "less and less of self, and more and more of the spirit of truth should be in thy ministering, in thy attempting to direct others." With reference to the meaning of human suffering, the entity was instructed to remember, "Though He were the Son, yet learned He obedience through the things which He suffered." (cf. Hebrews 5:8) And then the profound point is made, "Count thyself then rather as being remembered, when ye suffer for His sake." (3308-1)[65]

11

The famous passage in John 7:53-8:11, which tells of the woman caught in the act of adultery and treated with remarkable compassion by Jesus in the face of her accusers, has long been known to involve textual difficulties. Although found in a few Old Latin texts, it does not occur in any Greek manuscript earlier than the sixth century, and its location varies, as it is sometimes placed at the end of the Gospel of John or after Luke 21:38. There is, however, a rather wide scholarly consensus that, even with

65. We find, however, that the Cayce readings insist upon the overall positive and constructive nature as well as effect of Jesus' teaching, as we read in a statement made of one "not only being thrilled by the presence but by the words of the Master as He gave what ye call the Beatitudes." (5089-2) This same person is told that the proper response to hearing those words of Jesus is "the kind word, the patient word, the pressing of the hand upon the brow of those who are with fever, yea those who are troubled in heart there may be brought comfort by the [same] words."

some variations in the text as well as in its location, we have therein an account of authentic tradition. The woman, incidentally, is not identified in the present form of the Biblical text.

The Cayce readings insist, however, that this passage is actually based on two different incidents in the ministry of Jesus and that in one case the woman involved is to be identified with Mary Magdalene, who is also said to be the Mary who was the sister of Lazarus and Martha. The other woman, according to the readings, had been primarily associated with Roman soldiers. We shall consider these incidents separately, giving, as the readings do, emphasis to the accounts which relate to Mary.

Mary is frankly said to have been a courtesan offering her services to Roman officers and civilians as well as to Jews (295-8). Another reading indicates that prostitutes of this class sometimes used their skills "for the gaining of information of various sorts or natures..." (5749-9) and since the Cayce text says specifically that such was *not* the case with the other woman caught in adultery and aided by Jesus—while it refrains from making such a statement in the case of Mary—it may be proper to infer that Mary was engaged in some kind of espionage activity as a part of her profession at that time (5749-9). In any case, it is said that because of her activities Mary was separated from her family in Bethany, and it was only after her experience with Jesus that she was reunited with them (295-8). Mary's family background was thus of considerable distinction; she, together with her brother and sister, is said to have been closely associated with the disciples, later apostles, John and James (5749-9). Incidentally, the readings state that John "was the wealthiest of the disciples of the Christ. His estate would be counted in the present [A.D. 1933], in American money, as being near to a quarter of a million dollars... he was a power" among both the Romans and the Jews (295-8).

The readings state that of the two incidents, the one involving Mary occurred in the earlier portions of Jesus' public ministry, while that which concerned the maid "taken in the act with the Roman soldiery..." occurred "*after* there had been the reuniting of Martha, Lazarus and Mary..." (5749-9) Mary is said to have been brought before the Jewish council, and "the whole council or court at the time asked that, according to the law, the woman be stoned." (295-8)[66] The location of the incident in the temple, as

---

66. According to Lev. 20:10 and Deut. 22:22, both of the guilty parties in a case of adultery

given in the Biblical account, is referred in the readings to the incident concerning the other woman (1436-2).

Mary is said to have been "twenty-three years old when the Christ cleansed her from the seven devils: avarice, hate, self-indulgence, and those of the kindred selfishnesses; hopelessness and blasphemy." (295-8) This means, of course, that the readings specifically associate this Mary with the Mary Magdalene of Luke 8:2. Mary is described as "A body five feet four inches in height, weight a hundred and twenty-one pounds—in the general. Hair almost red. The eyes were blue. The features were those impelled both from the Grecian and Jewish ancestry." (295-8) The reading at this point asserts that she has been "well drawn by da Vinci..."

The readings say that Jesus at that time wrote in the sand "That which condemned each individual, as each looked over His arm—or as He wrote." (295-8) That which He said to Mary was "Neither do I condemn thee—Neither do *I* condemn thee." This event became then for Mary a "cleansing of the body-mind..."—"an awakening..." It is also connected in the readings with the problem of self-condemnation, and for her present needs the entity who is said to have been Mary Magdalene is specifically told, "Do not condemn self!" The readings elsewhere frequently refer to self-condemnation as a mental and moral problem as serious as the condemnation of others. In this case it is said that "condemning self is condemning the abilities of the Master... the Christ, [who] manifested life in the earth..." (295-8)[67] She is told to "Blot *this* from *thine* experience, *through* Him who maketh all things possible." (295-1) In a question which the thirty-year-old American woman receiving the reading asked the sleeping Cayce in this connection, she inquired, "Did the entity repay any fraction of the debt owed the Master while He was in the Earth?" The answer came back forthrightly:

That's impossible!...

So, in any attempt to repay—there can be no repay! But when one lives the life that *manifests* the Christ life, love, joy, peace, harmony, grace, glory, the *joy* is in the life of the Master as He manifests—and manifested—life in the earth.   295-8

---

are to be put to death. It should be noted that the woman's accusers in the Biblical version do not bring the responsible man or men to account at all.

67. In this reading the mode of Jesus' manifestation of life—which is given in the context of affirmation that "...*God* is god of the *living*—NOT of the dead!...Life, then, is God"—was "through not only the material manifestations that were given in the ministry but in laying aside the life. As He gave, 'I *give* my life—I give it of myself, and I take it of myself.'" (295-8; cf. John 10:17-18)

After this experience "of the saving grace in the love of the Christ, the Savior of men" (295-8), Mary returned to her family and home in Bethany near Jerusalem, where "those two vital forces of such different natures—Mary and Martha, and Lazarus" (2787-1) made of their home "the center from which most of the activities of the disciples took place. . ." (295-8) in that area. In reference to "the cleansing power" manifested in both the raising of Lazarus, which we shall discuss later, and the restoration of Mary, we are told that "All those, then, that were cleansed by Him have been called—are called—for special missions, for activities in each experience in and among men that they. . . may demonstrate, may give, the blessings to many." (295-8)

This, then, is the Mary of whom "the Master said, 'She hath chosen the better part.'" (295-1; cf. Luke 10:42) The readings follow the tradition of the Gospel of John in identifying Mary with the woman who anointed the feet of Jesus with costly ointment (cf. John 12:1-8; Matthew 26:6-13). And with reference to Jesus' words "Wherever my Gospel is preached, her works will be spoken of" this reading comments, "What a heritage!" (295-1)

The readings state further that the home of Mary and Martha—Lazarus is said to have lived after his being raised from the dead "only until the first of the rebellions arose. . ." (295-8) perhaps a reference to the uprising led by Theudas about ten years after Jesus' crucifixion[68]—became a center of support for the activities of those disciples especially who were of Judean background, as contrasted with the Galileans. Also, after the return from Galilee following the ascension of Jesus, when Mary, the mother of Jesus, became "a dweller in the house or home of John. . ." this John, the beloved disciple, is said to have "joined with those in Bethany. . ." "Hence the associations of Mary and John became the closest after this (we are speaking of Mary, the sister of Martha)." Whether this statement means that Mary, the sister of Martha, married John is not clear, but it is at least possible, as the same reading later speaks of Mary Magdalene as being a part of John's household along with Mary, the mother of Jesus, and the sister of the mother of James and John.[69] The life of Mary, the sister of Martha, is said to have lasted "some twenty and two years. . ." after her experience of cleansing (295-8).

---

68. Cf. Josephus, *Antiquities of the Jews* XX, 5, 1; Acts 5:34-39.
69. In this context, reference is made to a journey to "what would be called their *summer home*. . ." on the shores of the lake of Gennesaret (the sea of Galilee), which also became a center of support for Christian workers who "came and went" at that period (295-8).

The other incident of this category, which occurred later in Jesus' public ministry, is that wherein the maid was "brought before the Master in the temple... condemned as one taken in adultery; and because of the judgment passed upon that entity according to the law, the peoples or the high priests or those of the Sanhedrin declared that He must make a statement."[70] (1436-2) At this point the readings say that "...He gave, 'Let him that is without sin cast the first stone.' Let him that has been guiltless make the first move for the fulfilling of the *letter* of the Law." It is, as we have seen, a common practice in the readings to quote a Biblical passage with relative exactitude (John 8:7) and immediately follow it with an interpretation profoundly perceptive as well as helpfully idiomatic. In this case, however, the mode of speech is that of traditional Hebraic parallelism, and the second sentence may conceivably be authentically from Jesus Himself.

The readings say that in both cases of women taken in adultery Jesus stooped and wrote on the ground. In this latter instance in the temple Jesus wrote words which called for "the expression of mercy and not sacrifice..." (5749-9; cf. Matthew 9:13), words which also revealed "the awakening in the heart of the entity of hope..." (1436-2) In the earlier instance "that written was that which made the accusers recognize their *own* activities." (5749-9) Here in the temple, with this awakening of hope, "as the cry came, 'Master, what sayest thou?' the answer came, 'I condemn thee not, daughter—go and sin no more.'" (1436-2; cf. John 8:11)

This reading then goes on to say, "Is it any wonder, then, that those days that followed made for a remolding of the entity? though the entity kept afar, and not until after those periods when the persecutions began did she venture to come nigh unto those that were classed or called of the household of faith." This girl apparently felt instinctively that even those of the household of faith created by Jesus Himself were not capable of taking her into their fellowship until they, too, had been brought low in the eyes of the world.[71]

The reading continues, "But to have had the words direct from

70. The dilemma thus laid upon Jesus was that one answer would leave Him open to the charge of "illegally inciting others to kill the woman, a charge that could be brought before the Roman authorities," and another could lead to His being accused of "condoning so heinous a sin according to the Jewish law," which later could serve to discredit Him in the eyes of religiously earnest Jews. Wilbert F. Howard, *The Interpreter's Bible* (New York: Abingdon-Cokesbury Press, 1952), vol. VIII, p. 593.
71. A reading referring to Mary Magdalene expresses very clearly the attitude that prevailed at first in at least some of the disciples: "...with the return of Mary after the

the Master of masters, the Teacher of teachers, 'I do not condemn thee, *'has* meant, *must* mean, in the experience of the entity, that which words cannot portray..." The only appropriate response, the reading says, is in relationship to others: through "the deeds of the body, the desire of the mind to bring hope, faith, *in* that Lord, that Master, who is able to *save* unto the utmost, and who hath given to all, 'My peace I leave *with* you, my peace I give *unto* you.'" It is also stated that after refusing to condemn the woman Jesus said to her, "... be thou merciful, even as I have shown and give thee mercy." Following this admonition there is given some advice that is as valid today as it was during the Master's time:

In the life of intolerability in the experience, cannot the entity find in the heart of self to say, even as He, 'They know not what they do'? and to give the cup of water, to give the healing in the hands, to give the cherishment to those that are sad?

To those that are joyous give them more joy in that the praise be given to Him who maketh life to all that seek to know His face. 1436-2

The reading paints the scene in the temple with its vivid contrasts, showing Jesus facing the questioning Saducees,[72] as "the experience when before those in penal law or authority, those with their pomp and glory—yet He in *all* His glory, His face shining as only from the Father-God itself!" (1436-2)[73] This was "the Holy One, who honored woman that she might, too, be equal with man in the redemption of man [generic] from the wiles of the devil, or the wiles of him who would cause man or woman to err in any manner." (5231-1)

---

conversion and the casting out of the demons—this brought even greater confusion to the entity. For, to the entity, how *could* anyone who had been *such* a person—or who had so disregarded persons except for the material gains—become an honored one among those, or in association with a household of ones such as Lazarus and Martha?" (993-5)

72. The readings state that Jesus was questioned at different times by different groups, now by the Pharisees, now by the Saducees or " by those in Roman authority." (5749-9)

73. This use of the neuter personal pronoun with reference to the Father-God should not be construed as meaning that the Cayce readings affirm God to be ultimately impersonal. As is shown elsewhere in this collection of materials, the readings teach that God is sublimely personal, that He is both self-conscious and conscious of us, and that He seeks companionship with His creation, above all with the souls that He created in the beginning (cf. 1567-2; 1458-1; 5064-1). "...He cares!" (1567-2) Actually, the male personal pronoun is used much more frequently, to my knowledge, than the neuter; but, significantly, the readings, like some Christians in the early church, also use the term "the Mother-God" as another appropriate designation for "the Father-God." (945-1) Another reading discusses the issue in the following terms: "...How personal is thy God? Just as personal as ye will let Him be! How close is the Christ as was manifested in the physical body, Jesus? Just as near, just as dear as ye will let Him be!" (1158-9)

12

There are relatively few details given in the Cayce readings regarding the experience on the mount of transfiguration. One is that "... He had withdrawn in the mount that there might be material evidence in the flesh to His faithful three." (3216-1; cf. Mark 9:2-13, etc.) It is stated that after this experience it was difficult for the disciples to understand why they themselves could not heal just as Jesus did. Another reading asks with reference to the experience on the mount, "Did Moses and Elias give strength to Him, or gain strength from Him?" (877-27) The context—which emphasizes that Jesus both taught and manifested the fact that the kingdom of God is within and "it is *not* a dependence upon the powers without!" (877-27)—makes it clear that the source of Jesus' power was the Father within and not worldly powers or supernal spirits, however worthy they may be. A point of considerable significance is that another reading rephrases Mark 9:1-2 as follows: "There be some standing here that will see me come in my glory. And He taketh with Him Peter, James and John and goeth into the mount, and *there* was transfigured before them." (478-4) Since Mark 9:1 contains the statement, "There are some standing here who will not taste death before they see the kingdom of God come with power," it may be that this Cayce reading indicates that Jesus was referring to the transfiguration experience as one example of His glorification.

This reading, 478-4, has an interesting reference to "the nine left in the valley..." at the time of the experience on the mount. The question is asked, "Were they not great preachers, great ministers? Did they not have a close contact with the very Truth and Life itself? Yet it is not that He had departed, not that He was withdrawn." We have here, of course, an affirmation of the meaning and value of the life and work of those of the twelve who were not taken along for this momentous experience. They are not to be less thought of, either personally or in terms of their effectiveness in the ministry of the Gospel, because they were not among the three. A brief reference is made to the fact that they, for the moment, did not have the effective power to heal that they had had formerly or would have later. The point, however, seems to be that Peter, James and John were taken along for "strategical" or "functional" reasons that are not to be viewed as implying their superior personal worth. The question is asked with reference to their participation in the experience, "Did it take from the activities or add to the activities of Peter, James and

John—their being in the Presence? Peter denied. John held to himself. James—by his very exertion—Herod laid his hands upon him." (478-4; cf. Acts 12:1-2) This reading tells the man of forty-five to whom it was addressed that these matters should be lessons in his own experience, that it should not disturb him whether he "may be either upon the mount in thine experience with Him, or in the valley with the nine. . . " for he was still "of Him. . . " (478-4)

Another reading, in speaking of the statement of Peter on the mount—"Let us make here a tabernacle"—goes on to ask, "What indeed is thy tabernacle? It is thy body, thy mind, thy soul! Present them, therefore, as things holy, acceptable unto Him who *is* the Giver of all good and perfect gifts!" (827-77) This in turn is in order that He "who thought it not robbery to be equal with God yet made Himself of *no* estate. . . might enter into the holy of holies with thee in thy *own* tabernacle!" (877-27; cf. I Cor. 3:16; Rom. 12:1; James 1:17; Phil. 2:6) In another reading we find a brief reference to the transfiguration experience: "What saw they? A glorified body? The glory of the body brought what? Communion of saints!" (262-87)

13

We come now to the numerous accounts or references in the readings to the raising of Lazarus (cf. John 11:1-57). Jesus' relationship to the family in Bethany was clearly special; He went there often, to "the rest place in Bethany." (966-1; see also 993-5) This special relationship is affirmed even in the context of statements revealing the universality "of that love shown in that experience to those peoples, wherever the *Master* walked." (2466-1) Lazarus was "the brother to those whom the Lord loved" (1924-1), and the readings contain several references to the fact that Jesus "wept with Mary, Martha and that household." (993-5) "He—the friend—wept with those of His friends in the face of criticism, in the company of the great and near great. . . " (993-5; see also 2787-1) The family was evidently one of considerable distinction in the society of the time, although not necessarily wealthy, as we read of "the little house in Bethany. . . " (2466-1; see also 1924-1) There is reason to believe that the mother—no reference is made in the readings, to my knowledge, to the father—had been "a close adherent of the Essene thought yet of the orthodox group. . . " (993-5) This statement would appear to mean that the mother's formal associations were with the religious establishment of the time but that her personal faith was that of the Essenes. The family had come, however, to be, as Lazarus, "the friend, the companion, of those who loved His [Jesus'] name, who loved His manner... " (1924-1) Lazarus is said to have been "ill of a fever—what today would be called the slow fever, or typhoid—and there was the eventual death." (993-5)

The readings agree with the Biblical account that Lazarus was "four days in the tomb." (3656-1; see also 5148-2; cf. John 11:17) The raising of Lazarus is described and interpreted with various phrases and statements. "To Lazarus we find He called, 'Come forth!'" (1158-14) A contemporary application is given where we read: "... He stands at the door and knocks [cf. Rev. 3:20], even as He did at the tomb as He called Lazarus to come forth. For He overcame death, hell *and* the grave by His wholly trusting in the love of the Father." (993-5) This same reading, which thus cites the spiritual methodology as well as the wider theological significance not only of the raising of Lazarus but also of Jesus' own resurrection, gives a representative statement of the Cayce readings' perception of the proper relationship among body, mind and soul, or spirit, in human life on earth: "The spirit is willing, the flesh is weak [cf. Matthew 26:41]—but hate not the flesh for its weakness; and know that in materiality they are one, that must coordinate as the body, the mind and the soul, if one would be creative in body, mind or spirit... It is only as ye apply that ye know that ye grow." (993-5)

This positive attitude of the Cayce readings towards materiality (not, to be sure, towards materialism!) is revealed in a most suggestive reading given in the year 1937. In this reading a woman of forty-seven asked the sleeping Cayce, "If I believe that God within is capable of meeting my every need, how can I justify my going to an osteopath for treatments?" The answer was:

How did Jesus, the Son, the Christ, justify Himself in telling the man that was healed from leprosy to "Go, show thyself to the priest and offer the sacrifice as commanded by Moses" [cf. Mark 1:44, etc.]?

Did the man remain healed because of the act or because God spoke and was sufficient?

Now: When Lazarus was dead, yea when Jairus' daughter lay dead, He spoke and they were aroused. Yet He took *her* by the hand and commanded that food and drink be given [cf. Mark 5:41-43, etc.].

For in the material world, material responses must apply to the material being.

To Lazarus we find He called, "Come forth!" yet he was not able to unbind himself.   1158-14

This emphasis upon the appropriateness of material means, together with utter trust in God, is seen in another reading, which also stresses the need for human cooperation, both individual and corporate, with the Divine to achieve truly effective results. This reading describes the raising of Lazarus thus:

...when He spoke, death itself gave up that it had claimed, even though the sister had warned that there had not been the embalming as had been the purposes of many. Instantly the activity brought life. For He *is* life. He *is* health, He *is* beauty, He *is*—not was, not will be, but *is*! For He having overcome death, hell and the grave, He is justified before God in giving to him who believes, who is in accord; that "If ye ask in my name, believing," doing, being that ye ask for, that shall be done unto thee [cf. John 14:13-14; 16:23-24].

Yet with the breaking of the bonds of death, the breaking of the material bonds—the binding about the head—must needs be done by others.   5749-16

The reading then goes on to advise the person addressed, "There is ever, then—in thy material associations, in thy seeking for help, love, health, understanding for thy brother—*something*, some effort on their part as well as *thine*. But 'Where two or three are gathered together in my name, there will I be in the midst of them.'" (5749-16; cf. Matthew 18:20)

Another reading contains the following passage:

...though there may be mechanical or medicinal applications for the welfare of the physical body, these are to attune the body to that consciousness which makes or brings it aware of its relationship to the spiritual or God-force. Just as the clay, the spittle upon the eyes of the blind had that effect to bring the awareness of the presence of the Creative Force or God to those granulated lids, in the experience of that individual.   2812-1 (cf. John 9:1-41)

In the set of readings which refer to Lazarus we find several observations about Judas Iscariot that reveal Jesus' posture toward the larger political and social environment of His day. We note that Judas did not stand alone, but had a number of supporters in the particular program of activity that he sought for Jesus. The reference states that "those groups about Judas sought to proclaim Jesus as the deliverer of the peoples from that bondage, that taxation [of the Romans]." (1179-7) The reading specifically speaks at this point of Jesus' "rebukings of the peoples that were especially about Judas at that time." Later the same

151

reading emphasizes with regard to "Him—who is the Way, the Truth, the Light..." that this is "the truth that maketh men free indeed, though they may be under the shadow of a service to a higher power materially." This profoundly significant affirmation of the power of the Christ Spirit to liberate—to be truly effective in the lives of human beings no matter what their political, economic or social circumstances may be, even, evidently, without structural changes in these circumstances— appears elsewhere as a statement of the primary purposes for which Jesus had entered into the world. "...the purposes for which His entrance into the world had been [were], as He gave, not for self, not for material gain, but that *all* should know the truth that would make *all* men free under *every* circumstance in a material plane." (1179-7) "...His [was the] ability to roll back death, even to defy same and to give to others a greater hope..." (2519-8)

One or two points need to be added regarding the raising of Lazarus, who, again, is said to have lived on "only until the first of the rebellions arose..." (295-8) One item is that of "the great feast...made for Lazarus and the Master with His disciples." (2791-1) "...the sisters—Martha, Mary—made preparations for the supper, after the resurrection or the bringing to life of the brother." (1179-2) Another reading speaks of "the great feast given to the friends and to Jesus and His disciples." (2787-1) Elsewhere this event is described as "the feast of thanksgiving to those peoples from Jerusalem, as well as Bethany, when the supper was given to Lazarus." (2519-8; cf. John 12:1-12) Then there are various references here as elsewhere in the readings to the custom then common in Palestine of hiring mourners for funerals. It is specifically stated that such were hired upon the death of Lazarus (2787-1; 3179-1; 5148-2). We have already seen that there were those who took notes and kept records even during the lifetime of Jesus (5148-2), but about pictorial art a reading tells a person who was among those who attempted to "make or draw upon the walls of the meeting places of some of those groups the activities of that Teacher" that "the first one drawn was the raising of Lazarus." (2398-2)

14

We find in the Cayce readings references to the rich young ruler who came to Jesus (cf. Mark 10:17-22, etc.). The young man is said to have been "a student of the law, which means a student of the unwritten as well as that interpreted from the penal, the spiritual and the marital code." (2677-1) It is interesting that this reading refers to later problems of interpretation of the Biblical account, for the young man is characterized as "that one about whom much speculation has been in the minds of many, over what is written there in the records, concerning which many a verbose orator has proclaimed much about which he knew so little." The reading goes on to describe the incident succinctly:

> ...the rich young ruler who declared, "These have I kept from my youth up. What lack I yet?" "Sell that thou hast, come and follow me." "And he went away sorrowing."
> But remember another line, "The Master loved the young man."
> He whom the Master has favored, in mind or in purpose, may count his soul indeed fortunate. Remember one of those eternal laws, "He hath not willed that any soul should perish." 2677-1 (cf. II Pet. 3:9)

This reading further states that the young man later came to follow Jesus; he was among those influential in the stimulation of Nicodemus' quest of the Lord, and he contributed to the care of Jesus' body after it was taken down from the cross. "...he came, later, and followed. Who prompted Nicodemus to seek the Lord? Who prompted those that cared for the body when it was placed in a new tomb yet unused?" (2677-1) The young man's experience with Jesus, the reading also affirms, became a source particularly of the virtue of tolerance, which "is the basis for patience, and in patience—my son—even as He gave, ye become aware of thy soul and its relationships to the purposes of infinity with the finite." The Cayce readings have much to say of the importance of patience, both as a significant element of Jesus' teaching and as an indispensable part of a wise and balanced life before God. As we have noted earlier, patience is cited, along with time and space, as one of the three integral structural elements of the cosmos experienced by human beings on the three-dimensional plane.

As another reading emphasizes, "Blessed indeed is the entity to whom or about whom it was said, 'As the Master looked on him, He loved him.'" (1416-1) This reading gives contemporary advice that may provide some insight into the meaning of the original appeal which Jesus Himself made. After urging this person to "Hold fast to that thou hast heard..." specifically affirming the rightness of following the commandments which the rich young ruler had confessed, the reading then says, "... 'Give that thou hast'—not all of thy worldly goods, but that thou hast attained, by bringing hope and help in the experiences of those who have lost their perspective, who have lost their way."[74] We should add that another reading states, "... He wept with the young man who turned away... He was sorry for the young man... the fear of lack, the fear of the lack of the medium of exchange—or of wealth—hindered." (2533-7)

A few readings make mention of the blind Bartimaeus, who was healed by Jesus at Jericho (cf. Mark 10:46-52, etc.). Two readings refer to Bartimaeus as having been a physically strong man, and his loss of sight is said to have occurred as a result of his craft, that of a metal worker (2124-3; 688-2). The readings emphasize that though the Biblical accounts give no information regarding the later activity of Bartimaeus, his services and their influences were indeed great. In particular he sought, through the name of the Christ, to "bring the awakening of the inner man, to the abilities of that contact as may be made by the calling *on* His name." (2124-3) Bartimaeus' response to his own healing was pointedly that of one "mindful that those so aided are not ... spongers upon the good graces of those that would aid ... " (2124-3; see also 5277-1)

In one of the readings related to Bartimaeus we find a brief description of the movement focusing on Jesus of Nazareth as "a cause that reached into and awakened all those promises [of God] that have been set from the beginning ... " (688-2) This is another way of stating what we have noted earlier, that in Jesus the Christ we find the recapitulation as well as the fulfillment of all that had gone before in the experience of man within the economy of God. In this same reading we find a high Christology which affirms, in the context of the Cayce readings' understanding of and emphasis upon the cosmic Christ, the wider work of God in the world, the indispensability of the role of the Christ in every authentic spiritual activity in human history.[75] Thus we read, "Only in Him

74. This pair of readings constitutes a situation of which there are very few instances elsewhere in the total corpus of Cayce readings. That is, we have two persons addressed ([2677] was a male twenty-one years old when the reading was given on January 27, 1942; [1416] was a male of thirty-four on July 27, 1937), each of whom is alleged to have been in a former lifetime the rich young ruler of the Biblical incident. On the basis of our present understanding, this fact would appear to indicate either a mistake in the readings or a contradiction for which we have no adequate explanation at present.

75. This understanding has been summed up elsewhere in this book, in the statement that "every man in every place has ongoing access to spiritual channels that may be used and blessed by the Spirit of the Christ, by the Holy Spirit, whether these channels bear the name Christian or not." In the case of this reading (688-2), this universal work is put in the context of Jesus' affirmation of His return to the Father, from which "place" of work His

may the cleansing come ... for His name is above *every* name, for through that name thou may approach the throne of grace itself ... " (688-2; cf. Phil. 2:9-10) In the same reading something of the meaning of Bartimeaus' experience of suffering is given in the statement that he learned "the ability to suffer in body that the soul might be made alive in Him." Incidentally, it should be noted that in one reading brief mention is made of the healing of the son of the Roman governor Pilate as occurring after the healing of Bartimaeus (324-5).

In the Bartimaeus readings we find further material on the teaching of Jesus with regard to the proper relation of self to God and others. Much may be done "if self is put entirely aside ... " (5277-1) In one primary sense we meet God, or the Christ, within: " ... the lesson of the Teacher, the Christ, the Master is to look within *self;* 'for of myself I can do *nothing,'* [cf. John 5:19] but it is the God that worketh within thee!" (688-4)[76] At the same time we are told, " ... 'I [the Christ] will meet thee in thine own activities toward thy fellow man.' " (688-2) The affirmation is thus that the meeting "within" entails both communion in prayer and meditation and fellowship in the midst of activities related to our fellow human beings. And one central element of these activities toward others is the way in which we judge or evaluate them; our persistent posture should be that of "not condemning any, for thine own self would condemn thee. Dost thou make for self's own aggrandizement through those relationships in this or that with thine fellow man, thou hast thine reward—and so must meet that thou sowest." (688-2) This principle of meeting again in the economy of God that which one has sown is a frequently affirmed truth in the Cayce readings, even to the extent that "Thou must meet every word thou hast uttered in thine experience." (688-2)

The teaching of humility may not be currently popular, but the Cayce readings consistently follow the New Testament pattern of including this theme as an element of great significance: " ... hold fast to that love that He gave, and ye will find peace and harmony, much strength and much power ... " (688-4) But this statement is

saving relationship may be made available to all: " ... as He has given, 'I go to prepare the place, that where I am there ye may be also.' " (cf. John 14:2-3)

76. It should be noted again in this context that there are many, many references in the Cayce readings that give singular emphasis to the fact that the kingdom of God is within (cf. Luke 17:20-21); for example, "the consciousness of His abiding presence is within, even as He gave, 'The kingdom of heaven is within thee.' " (1456-1) To my knowledge, in spite of the large number of references to this theme, it is never once rendered as "the kingdom of God is in the midst of you," the translation which is found in the text of the Revised Standard Version of the Bible (Luke 17:21), as contrasted with the Authorized, or King James, Version.

interpreted to mean that humility is needed for these results to be realized, for the "love that He gave" is manifested "only in *humbling* of self and self's own emotions, self's own self!" The woman who was the mother of Bartimaeus is told, "In the application in the present, then, mind not high things; condescend rather to things of low estate [cf. Rom 12:16]. Humble thyself as one to another, as ye did through those experiences, and so manifest in Him—how that the King even of kings suffered with those that would betray even His fellow man." (688-4) The deep-going, perhaps severe-appearing, application of this principle is "that if credit is taken here, or if it is sought that others thank thee or bless thee or praise thee for the efforts that ye put forth, then ye are seeking *self*-glory; the ego of self is seeking expression!" (688-4) Another reading discusses the theme of humility in the context of Jesus' teaching: "... 'He that is greatest among you will be the servant of all.' [cf. Mark 10:43, etc.] Learn then *humbleness* and *believe* ..." (1265-2) The reading then goes on to give the following mode of application of this principle: "... until each entity may see in the individual who is as his enemy, as that one he dislikes or whose ways he dislikes, such as is the image of that he would worship in the Father, he may not in deed and in truth know the way."

A few brief statements are made about the conversion of Zacchaeus, which also occurred in Jericho (cf. Luke 19:1-10). The fact that "... Zacchaeus was called from the tree ..." and that a "feast [was] made by Zacchaeus for the Master and His disciples" is duly noted (3377-1). "... the enthusiam of Zacchaeus" (254-54) is cited as if it were somewhat excessive and not accompanied by adequate understanding; yet, even though it exceeded proper bounds, with loving patience "that day the Lord supped with him." (254-54) Another reading gives in a few striking words something of the deeper meaning of the event: "... Zacchaeus climbed higher that he might have the broader vision, and that day dined with Truth." (307-4)

VIII
The Last Week

About the prelude to the events of the last week of Jesus' life on earth we read:

In those days preceding the entry into Jerusalem, we find those periods of much disturbance among the disciples who were of Galilee and those who were of the Judean ministry. These were in disputations as to what was to take place when He, Jesus, was to go to Jerusalem [cf. Mark 10:32-34, etc.].

Yet He chose to go, entering through the period of rest at Bethany with Mary, Martha, Lazarus; and *there* the triumphal entry and the message that was given to those throngs gathered there.

5749-10 (cf. Mark 11:1-11, etc.)

This decision of Jesus to go to Jerusalem is expressed in another reading which may constitute an extra-canonical saying of the Lord: "...when He gave, 'I must go up that I may be offered as the living sacrifice.'" (897-1) This statement, of course, is a very clear expression of the "intention" of Jesus (cf. Mark 10:45, etc.).

We read that at this time immediately preceding the Passover celebration "there were the gatherings of those from many lands..." (681-1) including "all the lands nigh unto the Galilean, the Phoenician or Syrophoenician, Tyre and Sidon [from which]... all the peoples had come as *one* for the days that were counted as holy." (1301-1)[77] Presumably these people were all Jews, proselytes or at least "worshipers of God"—to use the

---

77. We read elsewhere that people came from afar to Jerusalem not only for the purpose of worship but also "for the social and companionable activities during such feasts." (1456-1)

categories of the Acts of the Apostles; but, according to the readings, many had heard of Jesus—some from His visit to the territory of Tyre and Sidon—and there were differences of opinion as to whether "there was to be either the establishing of the material kingdom by that man, or there were to be the understandings of what those teachings were to bring into the experience of others." (681-1) Evidently this last quotation refers to a difference in interpretation and expectation as to whether the primary meaning of Jesus' ministry was political, "spiritual" or both.

One reading that uses the phrase "the triumphal entry into the city" comments, with regard to "the crowd of people..." welcoming Jesus, that "though man would have most believe that there were great throngs, they were mostly women and children..." (3615-1) Another reading notes that "the ass, upon which the Master rode, was...a physical manifestation of kingship, of lordship..." (5257-1) This reading, as does another, briefly refers to the singular effect of "the light of the eyes of the Master" (5257-1), "the eyes of the Master as He passed by on the road or the way to the city on that day of days..." (1301-1) This was the time "when He gave that if it were not for the cry of the peoples the very hills and mountains would cry out, 'Hosanna, Glory in the Highest—for the Prince of Peace comes to make those decisions whereunto man again has his closer, *closer* associations with his Maker'..." (1301-1)[78]

Another reading describes the scene as follows: "...even as He gave on that memorable day...if the people had not cried 'Hosanna!'—the very rocks, the very trees, the very nature about, would cry out *against* those opportunities lost by the children of men—to proclaim the great day of the Lord!...[For this was] He that brought hope and cheer to those that were ill in body, those that had lost hope through the holding to material things and to the old tenets of tradition..." (1468-1) The reading then speaks of "the great throng as they spread their garments—yea, those of high and low estate or position..."

---

78. This same reading gives a suggestive interpretation of a statement of Jesus recorded in the Gospel of John (John 10:34-36), in which Jesus, quoting Psalm 82:6, affirms the truth of the phrase "you are gods...to whom the word of God came." The reading states "that man as man may be far from God, but man as a god and acting godly may be close to the divine." (1301-1) This is, of course, to change the context of the discourse from primary concern with questions of ontology to the ethical and relational. We note elsewhere, as we have seen, the understanding of man as the *imago Dei*, created in the image of God (1265-2, A-1; cf. Gen. 1:27).

2

We have already taken some note of the Last Supper, which is specifically cited as "the passover—which He kept with His disciples" and as "the last supper with His beloved disciples." (2794-3) One reading in particular gives an astonishingly detailed picture of the event, a reading which was not asked for but was given voluntarily by Edgar Cayce at the end of another reading (1315-3), even though the suggestion to wake up had been given him three times:

The Lord's Supper—here with the Master—see what they had for supper—boiled fish, rice, with leeks, wine, and loaf.[79] One of the pitchers in which it was served was broken—the handle was broken, as was the lip to same.

The whole robe of the Master was not white, but pearl gray—all combined into one—the gift of Nicodemus to the Lord.

The better looking of the twelve, of course, was Judas, while the younger was John—oval face, dark hair, smooth face—only one with the short hair. Peter, the rough and ready—always that of very short beard, rough, and not altogether clean; while Andrew's is just the opposite—very sparse, but inclined to be long more on the side and under the chin—long on the upper lip—his robe was always near gray or black, while his clouts or breeches were striped; while those of Philip and Bartholomew were red and brown.

The Master's hair is 'most red, inclined to be curly in portions, yet not feminine or weak—*strong,* with heavy piercing eyes that are blue or steel-gray.

His weight would be at least a hundred and seventy pounds. Long tapering fingers, nails well kept. Long nail, though, on the left little finger.

Merry—even in the hour of trial. Joke—even in the moment of betrayal.

The sack is empty. Judas departs.

The last is given of the wine and loaf, with which He gives the emblems that should be so dear to every follower of Him. Lays aside His robe, which is all of one piece—girds the towel about His waist, which is dressed with linen that is blue and white. Rolls back the folds, kneels first before John, James, then to Peter—who refuses.

Then the dissertation as to "He that would be the greatest would be the servant of all."[80]

---

79. It is significant that, while the first day of unleavened bread is described as the time "when they sacrificed the passover lamb," (Mark 14:12, etc.) nowhere in the scriptural accounts is it stated that Jesus and the disciples actually ate lamb at the supper.
80. Here the Cayce readings agree with the Gospels of Luke and John, which, in contrast to Mark and Matthew, assign this teaching of Jesus to the occasion of the Last Supper (Luke 22:26-27; John 13:12-17; Mark 10: 43-44; Matthew 23:11-12). Another reading puts it as follows: "...that faith, that hope that brings into the present experience a *joy* in being of a

The basin is taken as without handle, and is made of wood. The water is from the gherkins, that are in the wide-mouth shibboleths, that stand in the house of John's father, Zebedee.[81]

And now comes, "It is finished."[82]

They sing the ninety-first Psalm—"He that dwelleth in the secret place of the Most High shall abide under the shadow of the Almighty. I will say of the Lord, He is my refuge and my fortress: my God; in Him will I trust."

He is the musician as well, for He uses the harp.

They leave for the garden.   5749-1 (cf. Mark 14:12-31, etc.)

In another reading we find a reference to the Last Supper that emphasizes the meaning of Jesus' washing His disciples' feet:

...in the upper chamber with the disciples, and the humbleness that was manifested.

Though He was their leader, their prophet, their Lord, their Master, He signified—through the humbleness of the act—the attitude to which each would come if he would know that true relationship with his God, his fellow man.   5749-10

Jesus' inauguration of the Lord's Supper as an abiding rite for His followers is briefly noted in the following words, which should be understood, to be sure, in conjunction with the explanations which were cited earlier: "...the establishing of the emblems as His body and blood, as a ritual for those who would honor and bring to remembrance those experiences through which each soul passes in putting on the whole armor of the Christ." (5749-10)[83] The last part of the sentence is simply another statement of the affirmation found frequently in the Cayce readings that though the scale and the "order" be different, the events and experiences of the life of Jesus the Christ constitute the true pattern for the life of every human being. Another reading, we should note, seems to affirm "the Real Presence" in the Lord's Supper: "And in the breaking of bread ye may know Him!" (1158-

service to others—from that lesson as gained then from the words He spoke at the Last Supper: 'He that would be the greatest among you will be the minister, the servant, serving others.'" (2778-2)

81. The word *gherkin* is evidently used here in the sense of gourd. The term *shibbleth* has the meaning in Hebrew of an ear of corn or a stream or river (cf. Judges 12:1-6); it would seem to mean here, as used in the plural, large water jars.

82. The scriptural record of this statement cites it as one of the words of Jesus from the cross (John 19:30; cf. John 4:34; 17:4).

83. Another reading describes this event thus: "...in the hour that there was set forth the emblem of the broken body and the shed blood, in order that man might ever be mindful of same..." (3615-1)

9)[84] Then again, as frequently found in the Cayce readings, the aspect of human cooperation in the process is emphasized: "He that would know his own way, his own relationships to Creative Forces or God, may seek through the promises in Him; as set in Jesus of Nazareth—He passeth by! Will ye have Him enter and sup with thee? *Open* then thy heart, thy consciousness, for He would tarry with thee!" (5755-1)

The picture of the Last Supper as given in the Edgar Cayce readings would not be complete without reference to the fact that there is frequent mention made in the readings, in a variety of contexts, to the fourteenth, fifteenth, sixteenth and seventeenth chapters of the Gospel of John as constituting the heart of the Christian Gospel, the essence of Jesus' teaching and the section of Scripture which those who wish to grow in faith, understanding and obedience should especially and frequently read. "Read then the fourteenth, fifteenth, sixteenth and seventeenth of John. And reading it, not as rote, ye will find that even He is speaking, even as to thee!" (1010-12)[85]

We find mention of the fact that the apostle John frequently related to Mary the mother of Jesus, "and the other Mary..." (2946-3) the events and words "...of the last hours of the Master." (2946-2) This last phrase refers not only to "those pronouncements made upon the cross...[and] the last hour in the garden, on the way to the garden..." (2946-3) but also to the Last Supper, for to these women "these [words] have a special meaning: 'Let not your heart be troubled—ye believe in God, believe also in me; for in my Father's house are many mansions— if it were not so I would have told you. I go to prepare a place for you, that where I am there ye may be also. The *way* ye know.' He, then, is indeed the Way, the Truth, the Light." (2946-3; cf. John 14:1-6)[86] Frequent mention is also made of the following: "...as He hath given, 'If ye love me ye will keep my commandments, and my commandments are not grievous—only that ye love one

---

84. The larger context of this reading affirms the presence of the Christ in various ways and modes in human experience: "Thou hast seen Him oft in the acts of others and the personality ye called by another name, yet ye may see Him. And when He speaks, 'Be not afraid, it is I,' know He is near. And in the breaking of bread ye may know Him!" (1158-9)
85. It is worthy of note that the well-known Indian Christian mystic of the earlier part of this century, Sadhu Sundar Singh, placed comparable emphasis upon the Gospel of John both for its intrinsic meaning and value and for its importance in his own devotional life. See B.H. Streeter and A.J. Appasamy, *The Message of Sadhu Sundar Singh* (New York: The Macmillan Co., 1921), pp. 153-156.
86. A significant rephrasing of these words is found elsewhere: "'Were it not so, I would have told you. I prepare a place for those that are faithful, are patient, that they—too— may be with me as from the foundations of the earth.'" (1158-5)

another.'" (2620-2; cf. John 14:15; I John 5:3) Very frequent reference is made in the Cayce readings to what is recorded in John 14:26 as to the role of "the Counselor, the Holy Spirit, whom the Father will send in my name, He will teach you all things, and bring to your remembrance all that I have said to you." This saying is found in various formulations but almost always with a wider perspective given, such as, "I will bring to thee remembrance of all that is necessary for thine understanding from the foundations of the earth, if ye will but keep my commandments." (518-1)

With regard to Judas' betrayal of Jesus, which in one sense comes to a focus at the time of the Last Supper, we read the following question and answer:

Q-27. Was Judas Iscariot's idea in betraying Jesus to force Him to assert Himself as a king and bring in His kingdom then?
A-27. Rather the desire of the man to force same, and the fulfilling of that as Jesus spoke of same at the supper.
2067-7 (cf. Mark 14:17-21, etc.)

The readings insist that Judas was a free agent in the process, "For did He not commit the keeping of the worldly goods to Judas? [cf. John 12:4-6; 13:29] Did He not give to him the power, the opportunity to meet himself?" (1265-2) In this same reading, which was given for a person who believed himself to have been Judas Iscariot in a former incarnation (a mistaken belief, according to the reading), the statement is made that there was a "cult" at the time which had foretold that Judas would betray his Lord and commit other crimes, and therefore it was noted with special interest by some that he had been "accepted by one that others proclaimed as a teacher, a master..." This reading goes on to emphasize, however, that no one is to despair, not even Judas! (cf. 137-125)

For know within that the Master, the Lord thy God, overlooks that thou hast done and has given, "Whosoever will may take the cup" ... Know, He hath willed that each soul should know the way, and hath prepared a way. Then look not back upon those associations, those environmental forces, nor thine own curiosity; but rather look up—to Him who may call thee that thou may know and see His face!
1265-2 (cf. John 14:4-6)

3

The Cayce readings lay singular weight upon Jesus' inner experience in the garden of Gethsemane as among the most painful of all, although the references to this event are few in number. "Those periods in the garden—these become that in which the great trial is shown, and the seeming indifference [of His disciples] and the feeling of the loss of one in whom trust and hope had been given; and the fulfilling of all that had been in the purpose and the desire in the entrance into the world." (5749-10; cf. Mark 14:32-52, etc.) "The real test was in the garden . . . in the realization that He had met every test and yet must know the pang of death." (5277-1) Another reading states that " . . . He sighed with the very blood of His body in Gethsemane. . . " (1158-5) In one sense the readings seem to include the whole of the last week, as indeed the whole life of Jesus, as part of His "passion."

Quite another dimension, however, is added to the experience by a reading in which the person addressed is told, "See the funny side—don't be too serious. Remember, He even made the joke as He walked to the garden to be betrayed. Remember, He looked with love upon His disciple that denied Him, even as He stood alone." (2448-2) Another reading states, "The smile is as that look which the Master gave Peter, and he went out and wept—for he found himself." (3578-1; cf. Luke 22:61; Matthew 10:39) This perception of the humor of Jesus, even at the most critical or perilous moments, is one of the most significant of the original contributions of the Cayce readings. It is even said of Jesus on the way to the cross, "remember—He laughed even on the way to Calvary; not as pictured so oft, but laughed even at those that tormented Him. This is what angered them the most." (3003-1)

Details given of the trial of Jesus either before the Sanhedrin or before Pontius Pilate are few. We have already noted that Jesus had healed Pilate's son (1207-1; 1151-10, A-1), and we read elsewhere that Pilate's wife suffered in her position as his wife (764-1).[87] It was she who had been persuaded by one in her own household "to seek help in those periods just before the time of the crucifixion." (2513-1) Her son had suffered from epilepsy (17541),

87. The readings relate that following the crucifixion of Jesus a report was made to the Roman emperor which was largely favorable to the Christians and that, as a result, Pilate was recalled to Rome "and one closer in association or in sympathy with the Christian movement . . . appointed in the stead—as is seen or recorded by profane history as well as by intimation in sacred history." (1151-10; see also 1158-4, 3006-1 and 2021-1) Pilate is said to have been personally questioned "by Caesar as related to those things which had come about." (877-27)

and in the company of a Roman soldier of Pilate's personal bodyguard she "brought their afflicted or epileptic son to the Master..." (1217-1)

We read that at the time of the trial before Pilate there could be perceived on the face of the Master "that tenderness with which He felt and experienced His aloneness when deserted by those who had been close to Him." (2620-2) It was at this time that Jesus is said to have told a sympathetic woman who had friends among the temple guards, "Be not afraid, for me nor for thyself. All is *well* with thee." (2620-2) Reference is made to "the unjustness of His trial, the persecutions of His body, that [yet] made the way for mankind, ye His brethren, ye thy own self, to *have* and know the way that leads to 'That peace I leave with thee; not as the world knoweth peace, but my peace I give'..." (1504-1; cf. John 14:27)

Not only Pilate, however, is held responsible for Jesus' death. We read also of the activities "of the high priest in the condemning..." (333-2) The "priest who first condemned the Master" is said to have been a son-in-law of Caiaphas (2934-1). The Cayce readings, however, while fully admitting the physical dimensions of Jesus' suffering in the garden of Gethsemane, at the trial, and on the cross, tend to focus on the meaning of the whole and at the same time to indicate certain qualifying or even compensatory factors at work. This is to say that the readings do not focus on the physical agony in the fashion of certain forms of Hispanic Christianity. Thus we read, "The trial—this was not with the pangs of pain as so oft indicated, but rather glorying in the opportunity of taking upon self that which would *right* man's relationship to the Father—in that man, through his free will, had brought sin into the activities of the children of God. Here *His Son* was bringing redemption through the shedding of blood that they might be free." (5749-10) This was "the activity of Him that is free indeed." That is, the passion of Jesus the Christ—above all, His suffering on the cross—is seen as cosmically redemptive in the deepest and widest sense of the word— "... He gave Himself as a ransom for all..." (5749-10)—but this is perceived as occurring in the mental and spiritual context of the statement in the Biblical Letter to the Hebrews: "Jesus the pioneer and perfecter of our faith, who for the joy that was set before him endured the cross, despising the shame, and is seated at the right hand of the throne of God." (Hebrews 12:2)

In this same reading we find another direct reiteration of the theme of Hebrews. In answer to a question asking for an explanation of the phrase in John 19:34, "forthwith came out blood and water," the reading says, "The fulfilling of 'Without the shedding of blood there is no remission of sins.' Hence His blood was shed as the sacrifice of the just for the unjust, that ye all may stand in the same light with the Father." (5749-10; Hebrews 9:22; cf. Romans 5:15-21) The Cayce readings, therefore, follow directly in the tradition of the New Testament, of both the gospels and the apostolic writings, in their perception of the vicarious or substitutionary meaning of the passion of Jesus the Christ (cf. Mark 10:45; Matthew 20:28; I Timothy 2:6). They are equally concerned, however, to stress, along with the cosmic meaning, also the aspects of personal and present application of Jesus' redemptive work in the everyday lives of human beings. Thus, precisely where we read " . . . He gave Himself as a ransom for all" (5749-10), we find that this is for the purpose of our "becoming indeed brethren with Him . . . that whoever will may take *their* cross and *through* Him know the joy of entering into that realm of replacing jealousy and hate and selfishness with love and with joy and with gladness." This statement is followed with the admonition, "Be ye glad. Be ye joyous when those things come to be thy lot that should or would disturb the material-minded. Like Him, look up, lift up thy heart, thy mind unto the Giver of all good and perfect gifts; and cry aloud even as He, 'My God, my God! Be Thou near unto me!' " (5749-10; cf. James 1:17)

This last quotation is not intended to mean that the readings do not take seriously the Biblical, "Eloi, Eloi, lama sabachthani?" (Mark 15:34, etc.) For we read of "that day when the sun was darkened and the cry went out to the world, 'My Lord, my God, why hast Thou forsaken me?' " (1929-1) Elsewhere we read of the death of Jesus, "Not only was He dead in body, but the soul was separated from that body. As all phases of man in the earth are made manifest, the physical body, the mental body, the soul body became as each dependent upon their own experience. Is it any wonder that the man cried, 'My God, my God, *why* hast Thou forsaken me?' " (5749-6)

But in the Cayce readings the victory involved in and wrought by the passion of Jesus the Christ is seen not only in its later effects on and in others, but on the spot, so to speak, and in the person of Jesus. This is the reason that the readings make a present application of the "finished work" of Jesus the Christ in saying, "In those periods of transition from 'It is finished,' comes that which is to each heart the determination that it, too, may know the blessed hope that comes in seeing, knowing, experiencing the cross in the heart, the body, the mind." (5749-10; cf. John 19:30)

That is, we ourselves may know a blessed hope in the very act of experiencing the multidimensional sufferings of our own crosses because He Himself did just that, and perfectly. The Cayce readings, in this context, quote what is given as an extra-canonical word of Jesus Himself, "Be ye joyous in the service of the Lord." (518-1)

We find, therefore, a continual alternation in the Cayce readings between Jesus' suffering and His hope and joy, between our crosses and our hope and joy. His victory on the spot—perfect and completed—made possible our present appropriation and application—even if imperfect and developing. It is in this context of understanding that we read, "His heart ached, yea His body was sore and weary; yea, His body bled not only from the nail prints in His hands and feet but from the spear thrust into the heart of hearts! For the blood as of the perfect man was shed, not by reason of Himself but that there might be made an offering once for all ... " (1504-1) In this same reading we find emphasis of the fact that herein we may see "the love the Father hath shown to the children of men, through the very gift of Him, thy brother, the Christ ... " Actually, all "life indeed is an eternal expression of the love of the Father ... " coming into expression "through the individuality of each and every soul ... " And in spite of our present weaknesses in material manifestation, "we find the strength in the Lord ... " to the end that we may experience "the glories [of] His beauteous purpose with each soul; that purpose that ye might be the companions, one with Him." "For we be joint heirs, as one with Him [the Christ]; not strangers, not aliens but joint heirs with the Christ to the kingdom of the Father—that is, that was, that ever shall be—even before the foundations of the earth were laid." (1504-1; cf. Romans 8:17; Matthew 25:34)

As we have seen previously, the perception that the final purpose of God the Father is that all souls may be reunited with Him while yet retaining each its own individuality is central to the Cayce readings. The goal of each entity is "to become one with, yet aware of its *own* identity *in*, the Creative Force." (261-15; see also 1456-1) For this reason we find in the readings an alternation between the use of the word atonement, in the sense of vicarious redemption, and at-onement, in the sense of spiritual unity. And both dimensions are seen as operative within the framework of divine or cosmic law. We see thus that "the activity of Him that is free indeed" is in accordance with "the law of love, of causation, of mercy, of justice, of all that makes for self becoming in the at-onement relationship, of filling the purposes for which one is called in materiality..." (5749-10) Or, as it has been put elsewhere, "Though He were in the world, He was not of the world; yet subject to the laws thereof, of materiality." (1504-1; cf. John 17:14-18)

It is in the context of this understanding of at-onement that we note an extra dimension of "the need of the Son to suffer the death on the cross, to offer Himself as a sacrifice..." That is, "He offered it not alone for thyself [the person addressed in the reading], for the world, for the souls of men, but for His *own* being!" (877-29) The context of this reading makes it clear that the good of salvation is relational; and therefore, while the redemptive work of Jesus the Christ constitutes a free gift in behalf of others, the unique relationship of the Son to the Father is in no wise intended to replace the relationship of the Father with each soul, but exists and works precisely to restore and enhance that relationship. For this reason, also, since the final goal is relational, the work of Jesus the Christ served to further His own relationship with the Father. Even though at this stage of His being Jesus had indeed become perfect—and therefore the sacrifice was perfect—yet the recapitulation of all as Jesus of Nazareth completed or fulfilled every aspect of His relationship with God the Father (cf. 5749-10). And that relationship is intended not to displace our own, but to make it possible: "That [of each soul] may *not* be supplied by another." (877-29) Each one of us is to know God and be personally related to Him primarily, although not exclusively, "within." "For thy body is indeed the temple of the living God. There He has promised to meet thee. There He has promised to make Himself known to thee—His will, His purpose with thee." (877-29; cf. I Cor. 3:16)

There are numerous references in the Cayce readings, as we have seen, to "the holy women," a term which came to be used as such only after the resurrection. These are the women who contributed of both their means and services to the public ministry of Jesus and His disciples (cf. Luke 8:1-3). They were the ones who brought spices to anoint Jesus' body for burial and served the disciples so well in the later days of persecution (5122-1; 2794-3).[88] And on that "day when the sun was darkened and not by an eclipse alone, and when the earth shook and the temple veil was rent..." (333-2) a number of these women "stood beneath

---

88. In a reading the question was asked, "Who were the women at the cross?" The answer given was, "Many were there. Those of his own household, Mary Magdalene, the mother of John and James, and those who were of that whole group were among the women at the cross." (5749-10)

the cross..." of "the teacher, the lowly one, yet the Great I AM..." (1463-2; see also 3006-1)

This day, "when the earth was darkened and the foundations of the deep were broken up; for the Son of man, the Son of God, was suspended between earth and the sky" (518-1), came also to have special meaning for some of the Roman soldiers present. There were those "of the Roman guard who were struck by the sincerity of the *man* and of the followers of the man, as man ..." (2365-2) Several references are made to these soldiers—they "*saw* the Prince of Peace die on the cross" (333-2)—and to members of their household who later gave direct or indirect aid to the early Christian movement in Rome and elsewhere. Some themselves aided in the spreading of the teachings. The name of one of the soldiers who "stood by the cross when the Son of man was put thereon ..." (405-1) is cited as Marcellus. Marcellus' wife is said later to have been "in that position as being able to give help both to those persecuted and strength to those whom duty demanded oft to act in the capacity of the persecutors." (405-1)

Scattered widely in the Cayce readings are various statements or expressions showing further the understanding held of the event and the meaning of the cross of "... Him that gave Himself as the ransom in the earth, despised of men yet without fault, showing forth His love..." (518-1) "... Him that blessed and cursed not; that gave to those though they bruised His body, though they sought to do away with those principles." (1058-1) In another reading we find what is, even if not a so-called "word from the cross," one expression of Jesus' intended communication "to those gathered at the cross: 'Peace I give; not as men count peace, but the purpose in the heart is sure in the Lord—I have shown thee the way.'" (649-1) Elsewhere we read, "... then as He hung upon the cross, He called to those that He loved and remembered not only their spiritual purposes but their material lives. For He indeed in suffering the death on the cross became the whole, the entire way; *the* way, *the* life, *the* understanding, that we who believe on Him may, too, have the everlasting life. For He committed unto those of His brethren not only the care of the spiritual life of the world but the material life of those that were of His own flesh, His own blood." (5749-6; cf. John 19:26-27)[89] This concern for the fact and details of physical

89. In one of the readings addressed to the woman who is said to have been Jesus' sister Ruth, we read, "... He looked upon thy mother and thy friends and gave, 'Behold the woman,' and to thy cousin and to thy friend gave, 'To you she is given. Be to her a son in my stead.'" (1158-5; cf. John 19:26-27)

and material human needs is typical of the Cayce perception of Jesus; but the phrase "the care of the spiritual life of the world," as indicative of the nature of the ongoing mission of "those of His brethren," is particularly significant.

In another reading the mission of Jesus' followers, "His brethren," is described as follows: "... He hath entrusted to thee—those that love Him—the redemption of the world, to make known His willingness, His care, His promises that may be the activity of each and every soul." (5749-13) "Rededication of self..." is appropriate for "being a true messenger of His in and among men." (5749-6) Elsewhere we read:

> ...those that honor, those that love Him even as He loved the world, would give, do give their own heart's blood that the world may know that He *lives* and is at the right hand of the Father; that ye—yea, thy brethren, thy friends, thy enemies—may have an advocate before that throne of mercy, pleading the cause of the wayward, hearing the cry of those persecuted, and saying, "Be patient—be patient, my child; for in patience know ye thine own soul and become aware that I am able to sustain thee, even though ye walk through the valleys and in the shadows of death." For death hath no sting, it hath no power over those that know the resurrection...   1158-5 (cf. I Cor. 15:55-57)

In another reading we find an admonition which gives further insight into Jesus' posture or manner on the cross: "Let that mind ever be in thee as was in Him as He offered Himself up: 'Father, forgive them—they know not what they do. Father, it is finished—I come to Thee. Give Thou Thy servant that glory which Thou has promised.'" (5749-13; cf. Luke 23:34; John 17:5; 19:30)

Something of the meaning of the whole is given in the following excerpt:

> For indeed He is the Creator, He indeed is the Maker of all that doth appear. For all power in heaven and earth has been given unto His keeping through the faith He kept with His fellow man; by His advent into the earth, by His doing good in all ways, at all times, under every circumstance. Yet not railing, on any—though they demanded His life in the material , though they cuffed and buffeted Him, though they swore and spit upon Him, though they crowned Him with thorns, though they abased Him in every manner, yet opened He not His mouth—though He were their Lord, their Master.
>
> 1499-1 (cf. Is. 53:1-12)

The centrality of the cross, both in its cosmic as well as its individual or personal meaning, is indicated in the advice given in the following reading: "...*do not* attempt to shed or to surpass or go around the cross. *This* is that upon which each and every soul *must* look and know it is to be borne in self *with* Him." (5749-14) Here again we find expression of the oft repeated emphasis in the Cayce readings that the work of Jesus the Christ has an objective, vicarious efficacy for others *and* at the same time constitutes the pattern for each and every person's own life, a pattern, however, which is to be followed not in isolation nor in a self-help manner, but "*with* Him." (cf. Matthew 10:38-39; 16:24-26)

As has already been intimated, the central meaning of the cross of Jesus the Christ in the Cayce readings is not in the heroism of the physical suffering, although this dimension is, of course, not to be disregarded. The readings, rather, lay emphasis upon Jesus' making His will one with the Father, upon the perfection of His obedience, in spite of all that the power of evil could do, physically or mentally or spiritually. Thus we read:

...Jesus, became the ensample of the flesh, manifest in the world, and the will one with the Father, He became the first to manifest same in the material world. Thus, from man's viewpoint, becoming the only, the first, the begotten of the Father, and the ensample to the world, whether Jew, Gentile or of any other religious forces. In this we find the true advocate with the Father, in that He, as man, manifested in the flesh the ability of flesh to make fleshly desires one with the will of the spirit. For God is spirit, and they who worship Him must worship in spirit and in truth...   **900-17 (cf. John 4:23-24)**

This same reading goes on to make more explicit the relationship of Jesus the Christ with the other religious traditions of world history; i.e., it affirms their positive significance in the larger economy of God in the world, even their progressive movement in the direction of serving unto the fulfillment of God's final purposes, and at the same time insists upon the uniqueness and specific supremacy of the role of Jesus. "As we see in all the religions of the world, we find all approaching those conditions where man may become as the law in his connection with the divine, the supreme, the oneness, of the world's manifestation. In Jesus we find the answer." (900-17) "...*Jesus*, the *man*, WAS the Son, *was* the Savior, *is* the manifestation of the God Consciousness in materiality!" (1527-1)[90]

---

90. This reading goes on to say, "Yet it must needs be that *He*, too, suffer through the trials

4

The Cayce readings emphasize, as we have seen, that it was the so-called holy women who brought spices and other materials to anoint the body of Jesus after His death. In one case mention is made of a woman who "was not able to bring spices because of the value, so brought flowers of the field which were just as acceptable as was the widow's mite, she of whom the Lord said, 'She hath given more than them all.'" (5122-1; cf. Luke 21:1-4) The statement is also made that the preparation was made "hurriedly—as it were; for the day was at an end when it [Jesus' body] was delivered to Joseph of Arimathea, and those that took care of same." (897-1; cf. John 19:38) The readings follow the Johannine tradition in observing that Nicodemus was among those who "cared for the body when the burial time came..." (1402-1) In this very context the comment is added, "Know that Nicodemus *was* right; He [Jesus] had, He *has*, He *is* the words of life; He is the Word that maketh all things anew!" (1402-1; cf. John 19:39; 3:1-21) Mention is also made of "the preparations of the linens about the head of the Master when entombed by Josephus and the friends..." (1801-1; cf. John 19:38)

In one of the readings that refer to the activities of this time we find a passage of moving power which refers to Jesus as "the Law of One," an expression frequently used in the Cayce readings to denote the basic ontological principle characteristic of the Godhead:

> ...He the man represented in that taught was the Law of One; that each soul is a portion—its own portion of that Creative Force that we may make manifest by the manner in which we minister to those whom we contact in every way, in every manner; whether they be those in high estate or those that are struggling along the road of fear and doubt, or those that have fallen by the wayside. For each soul is precious in His sight, and He hath not willed that any should perish but that all— through that *will* as was manifested in the man that the entity...saw hung upon the tree upon the hill—might have eternal life in Him.
>
> 897-1 (cf. II Peter 3:9)

Another reading describes the basic issue with reference to Jesus the Christ as it was perceived by many at the time. There

of being buffeted, being tried by those who under the *law* (of man) were in authority but who under the spiritual law were His inferiors, His subjects; and die even the death on the cross!" (1527-1)

were "questionings as to whether that proclaimed by the fisherfolk, or that proclaimed by those in power or in authority, was to become the rule of the peoples. . ." (1402-1) These were the "two influences, two forces" between which many were set and by which they felt drawn.[91]

---

91. It may be well to note that this reading contains the observation, "He without an ideal is sorry indeed; he with an ideal and lacking courage to live it is sorrier still." (1402-1)

IX
The Resurrection
and the Ascension

The Cayce readings are indeed rich in materials relating to the resurrection of Jesus and include insights that have not heretofore been widely known. "The period of resurrection—here we find that in which ye *all* may glory. For without the fact of His overcoming death, the whole of the experience would have been as naught." (5749-10) Like the Biblical book of Hebrews, the readings portray Jesus the Christ, even though He was "the Maker of the earth, the Giver of life..." (518-1) as "the man Jesus—who became the Christ through the things which He suffered, and through demonstrating in the earth the abilities to overcome *death*, the law of death." (1877-2; cf. Hebrews 1:1-2; 2:10, 18)

> **Then, though He were the first of man, the first of the sons of God in spirit, in flesh, it became necessary that He fulfill *all* those associations, those connections that were to wipe away in the experience of man that which separates him from his Maker...**
>
> **...Yea, as He gave His physical blood that doubt and fear might be banished, so He overcame death; not only in the physical body but in the *spirit* body—that it may become as *one* with Him [God the Father], even as on that resurrection morn—that ye call thy Eastertide.   5749-6**

This perception of the need to overcome death in the spirit as well as in the physical is, as we have seen, in keeping with the Cayce tripartite view of the nature of man: body, mind, and soul, or spirit. Also, this experience of Jesus is said to be akin to the experience of every person in the following way: "Each soul comes to stand as He before that throne of his Maker, with the deeds that have been done in the body, in the mind, presenting the

173

body-spiritual before that throne of mercy, before that throne of the Maker, the Creator, the God." (5749-6)

We find in the Cayce readings several intimations of the nature of the event or process involved in the resurrection of Jesus. "The passing of the material life into the spiritual life brought the *glorified* body; thus enabling the *perfect* body to be materialized in material life—a *glorified* body made perfect!" (5749-10) On the one hand, we find the following kind of symbolic language: "It is that... breaking forth from the sleep that it may rise as He with healing in its very life, to bring all phases of man's experience to His consciousness—that indeed became then the fulfilling of the law." (5749-6)

On the other hand, we find attempts to describe the phenomenon in more technical language. In answer to a question asking whether the real mystery of the resurrection involved "transmutation of human flesh to flesh divine..." (2533-8) the sleeping Cayce denied that this was so. "Not transmutation of flesh but creation..."

There is no mystery to the transmutation of the body of the Christ. For having attained in the physical consciousness the at-onement with the Father-Mother-God, the completeness was such that with the disintegration of the body—as indicated in the manner in which the shroud, the robe, the napkin lay—there was then the taking of the body-physical form. This was the manner. It was not a transmutation, as of changing from one to another.

Just as indicated in the manner in which the body-physical entered the upper room with the doors closed, not by being a part of the wood through which the body passed but by forming from the ether waves that were within the room, because of a meeting prepared by faith. For as had been given, "Tarry ye in Jerusalem—in the upper chamber—until *ye* be endued with power from on high." **2533-8 (cf. Luke 24:49)**

Another suggestive reading gives the following: "... when the Prince of Peace came into the earth for the completing of His *own* development in the earth, *He* overcame the flesh *and* temptation. So He became the first of those that overcame death in the body, enabling Him to so illuminate, to so revivify that body as to take it up again, even when those fluids of the body had been drained away by the nail holes in His hands and by the spear piercing His side." (1152-1)

That there was a certain process involved, with even temporal dimensions included, is suggested as the reading quoted earlier continues:

As indicated in the spoken word to Mary in the garden, "Touch me not, for I have not yet ascended to my Father." The body (flesh) that formed that seen by the normal or carnal eye of Mary was such that it could not be handled until there had been the conscious union with the sources of all power, of all force [cf. John 20:17].

But afterward—when there had been the first, second, third, fourth and even the sixth meeting—He *then* said, "Put forth thy hand and touch the nail prints in my hands, in my feet. Thrust thy hand into my side and *believe*." This indicated the transformation.

2533-8 (cf. John 20:27)

This point is further developed as follows:

Just as it was with the Christ-body: "Children, have ye anything here to eat?" This indicated to the disciples and the apostles present that this was not transmutation but a regeneration, recreation of the atoms and cells of body that might, through desire, masticate material things—fish and honey (in the honeycomb) were given [cf. Luke 24:41-43].

As also indicated later, when He stood by the sea and the disciples and apostles who saw Him from the distance could not, in the early morning light, discern—but when He spoke, the voice made the impression upon the mind of the beloved disciple such that he spoke, "It is the Lord!" [cf. John 21:7] The body had prepared fire upon the earth—fire, water, the elements that make for creation [cf. Luke 12:49; Gen. 1:2]. For as the spirit is the beginning, water combined of elements is the mother of creation.

Not transmutation of flesh but creation, in the pattern indicated.

2533-8

Further details are given in the following passage:

Hence when those of His loved ones and those of His brethren came on that glad morning when the tidings had come to them, those that stood guard heard a fearful noise and saw a light, and—"the stone has been rolled away!" Then they entered into the garden, and there Mary first saw her *risen* Lord. Then came they of His brethren with the faithful women, those that loved His mother, those that were her companions in sorrow, those that were making preparations that the law might be kept that even there might be no desecration of the ground about His tomb. They, too, of His friends, His loved ones, His brethren, saw the angels.

How, why, took they on form? That there might be implanted into their [the disciples'] hearts and souls that *fulfillment* of those promises.

5749-6 (cf. Mark 16:9-11; John 20:11-18)[92]

---

92. Another reading speaks of one who "beheld those visions and knew of the quaking of the earth, knew of those that arose from the tomb." (3615-1; cf. Matt. 27:52-53)

In one of the readings a question was specifically asked about the first meeting in the upper room after Jesus' resurrection (cf. John 20:19-23):

Q-4. Please explain: "He breathed on them, and saith unto them, Receive ye the Holy Ghost."

A-4. That change of doubt and fear which arose in the minds and hearts of those gathered in that room. For [their] fear of the interpreting of the phenomenon being experienced, He breathed. As the breath of life was breathed into the body of the man, see, so breathed He that of love and hope into the experience of those who were to become witnesses of Him in the material world. 5749-10

Elsewhere we find a reference to one who "saw Him bless those about Him, after the resurrection." (2620-2) Here once again we find reference to the necessary spiritual equipping of those who were and are to serve in His ongoing mission and work in the world.

Another reading makes mention of one who "was with that group when there came the proclamation by Peter, John and James that 'the Master goeth before thee into Galilee.'" (3615-1; cf. Matthew 26:32; 28:7, 10, 16) This same reading describes the ascension of Jesus in speaking of one who "was among the five hundred who beheld Him as He entered into glory and saw the angels, heard their announcement of the event that must one day come to pass—and will only be to those who believe, who have faith, who look for and who expect to see Him as He is." (cf. Luke 24:44-53; Acts 1:6-11; Mark 16:15-20) This quotation, we note, also relates to the "second coming" of Jesus, a theme which we shall consider later.

The Cayce readings endeavor to explain in various ways the meaning of the resurrection as well as its appropriate modes of present application in human life. One recurrent theme of understanding is the worthiness of Jesus. "... when to man's estate alone upon the cross, yea into the grave, all hope seemed abandoned; yet even as the inn could not contain His birth, neither could the grave contain His body; because of IT *being purified*, in love, in service, in harmony with God's will." (1152-4) Perhaps neither Shakespeare nor Bunyan could surpass the rough-hewn beauty and power of this passage.

The same theme is further expressed in the following:

There should be the reminding that—though He bowed under the burden of the cross, though His blood was shed, though He entered into

the tomb—through that power, that ability, that love as manifested in Himself among His fellow men He broke the bonds of death; proclaiming in that act *there is no death* when the individual, the soul, has and does put its trust in Him...[93]

Through that ability to make Himself one with the Father, He has gained that right, that honor to declare Himself unto as many as will hearken.   5749-13

Perhaps the single theme most universally characteristic of the Edgar Cayce readings is their emphasis upon the need for personal as well as corporate appropriation and application of truth. Theology, theory, even faith, are never allowed to exist for their own sake, but must serve to the enhancement of the relational quality, both interior and exterior, of everyday human life. Thus we read, "The resurrection of Jesus, the Christ, is a significant fact to each individual only according to how he applies same (as it is significant to him) in his daily life, experience and conversation with his fellow man." (5749-12)

In this context of understanding, various admonitions and exhortations are given. Thus the question is put to the persons addressed in a particular reading:

Then, in a material world—a world of hate, of divided opinions— what is the course that you each will pursue, in relationships to your fellow men?

Is it the course outlined by the tenets, the principles which He, the Teacher of teachers, gave as respecting the manner of life, of activity, that you each would give in your dealings and relationships with your fellow men?[94]

---

93. Immediately following this passage we find these words of contemporary (March 12, 1941) validity: "Thus in this hour of despair throughout the world, when those activities are such as to indicate hate, injustice, tyranny, desire to enslave or to impel others to submit to the dictates of this or that power—let all take heart and know that this, too, as the hour upon Calvary, must pass away; and that as upon the wings of the morning there comes that new hope, that new desire, to the hearts and minds of all who seek to know His face." Then, in characteristic fashion, the sleeping Cayce turned in direct address to the person who had requested the reading, and said, "This must begin within thine own heart. Then, let all so examine their hearts and minds as to put away doubt and fear; putting away hate and malice, jealousy and those things that cause man to err. Replace these with the desire to help, with hope, with the willingness to divide self and self's surroundings with those who are less fortunate; putting on the whole armor of God—in righteousness." (5749-13; cf. Eph. 6:11-17)

94. This reference to "the course outlined by the tenets, the principles" taught by Jesus is an expression of the consistent Cayce understanding of Jesus' mode of teaching. That is, the emphasis is upon larger principles of conduct, the application of which in concrete situations must be made by each individual as he, to the extent of his attunement with the Spirit of God, perceives the will of God and His guidance. Since, however, the Cayce readings do not proclaim any form of unbridled individualism, ethical decisions made by

We know, and only need to be reminded, that the whole law is in Him. For, as He gave that which is the basis, the principle, of the intent and desire and purpose which should prompt our activity, so we in the world—as we live, as we speak, as we pray—are to let it be in that tempo, in that way and manner which was prompted by Him, as He taught His disciples how to pray.

Then, as we analyze this prayer in our experience, we see what the life, the death, the resurrection of Jesus, the Christ—who is the Way, the Truth, the Light—must mean in this period in the experience of man.

5749-12 (cf. Luke 11:1-13)[95]

Further insight is given into the cosmic meaning of the resurrection of Jesus, together with aspects of its proper application, in the following: "Then, as ye meditate upon the meaning of the resurrection of this man of God—know that the way is open to thee to approach the throne of God; not as an excuse, not as a justification, but rather in love, in harmony, in that which brings hope for a sin-sick world." (5749-12) The persons addressed were reminded that this way of life meant also "such a manner as to bring peace and harmony, even among those who *appear* to be at variance to the cause of the Christ in the material world."

Persons close to Edgar Cayce were told in a reading given on April 5, 1936:

Open thine eyes and behold the glory, even of thy Christ present here, now, in thy midst! even as He appeared to them on that day!...

Ye, too, oft doubt; ye, too, oft fear. Yet He is surely with thee. And when ye at this glad season rededicate thy life, thy body, thy mind to His service, ye—too—may know, as they, that He *lives*—and is at the right

---

this means are understood to emerge in the context of participation in the fellowship of concerned others, especially those of the "household of faith." (518-1) The subsequent reference to His "tempo...way and manner" (5749-12) makes it clear that the process involved is one which lays stress upon spiritual sensitivity in the larger and deeper sense, rather than upon mere rationality. The delicacy, the artistry, involved in this activity is suggested by the following quotation: "...magnify, glorify Him in every word, every activity, in all thy dealings with thy fellow man. By thy very step, by thy very look, by thy word, create *hope* in the hearts, minds and lives of others." (5749-13)

95. The Cayce readings frequently emphasize that meditation is an integral element of the larger category of prayer, that one must listen to God as well as speak to Him (262-127; 5265-1; 2051-5; 987-2; 282-4; 262-89). One reading gives the following version of what is called the Lord's Prayer: "Our Father who art in heaven, hallowed be Thy name. Thy kingdom come. Thy will be done; as in heaven, so in earth. Give us for tomorrow the needs of the body. Forget those trespasses as we forgive those that have trespassed and do trespass against us. Be Thou the guide in the time of trouble, turmoil and temptation. Lead us in paths of righteousness for Thy name's sake." (378-44) This prayer was introduced with the words, "Let not the material things so blind thee that they become a stumbling block in thine experience. Give praise to thy Maker in the name of Him that taught thee to pray..."

hand of God to make intercession for *you*—if ye will believe; if ye will believe that He is, ye may experience.   5749-6

...[He is] thy Brother, thy Savior, thy Jesus, thy Christ; that would come and dwell in the hearts and lives of you all—if you will but let Him, if you will but invite Him, if you will but open thy own heart, each of you, that He may enter and abide with you...

Crucify Him not in thy mind nor in thy bodily activities. Be not overcome by these things that are of the earth-earthy. Rather clothe thy body, thy mind, with the thoughts, the deeds, the privileges that His suffering as a man brought to thee...

5749-6 (cf. Phil. 2:1-11)

Elsewhere in this same reading Cayce posed a larger question:

...why did He put on flesh and come into the earth in the form of man, but to be one with the Father; to show to man *his* (man's) [derivative] divinity, man's relationship to the Maker; to show man that indeed the Father meant it when He said, "If ye call I will hear. Even though ye be far away, even though ye be covered with sin, if ye be washed in the blood of the lamb ye may come back."

5749-6 (cf. Is. 1:18; 65:24; Rev. 7:33; 11:11)[96]

At every possible point the Cayce readings emphasize the present significance, effects and reality of the resurrection, or rather of Him who is the risen Lord and is present with those who will receive Him. "...I *am* the resurrection, the life..." (1747-3; cf. John 11:25-26)[97] "...to the heart and the soul He brought a light that faileth not, a water that is living, a home that is eternal, a bread that is *indeed* a staff of life! For He IS that life—that LIFE!" (1152-4) He is "...Life, Light and Immortality to the world today—ever. For He changeth not." (1290-1; cf. II Timothy 1:10)

Another mode of present application is given in the following: "For death hath no sting, it hath no power over those that know the resurrection...[which] brought to the consciousness of man that power that God hath given to man, that may reconstruct, resuscitate, even every atom of a physically sick body, that may resurrect even every atom of a sin-sick soul, may resurrect the soul

96. It may be appropriate to remind the reader that in the Cayce readings the "divinity" of man is more a moral and spiritual issue than an ontological one. "...man as a *godly* man may be close to the divine." (1301-1; cf. John 10:34-36)

97. This same reading continues with a statement, spoken as the word of Jesus, referring, however, to past events: "...'I *told* thee to destroy the body and in three days I would raise it again.'" (1747-3; cf. John 2:19)

that it lives on and on in the glory of a resurrected, a regenerated Christ in the souls and hearts of men!" (1158-5; cf. I Cor. 15:55-57)

A very suggestive passage speaks of the experience of Jesus—and properly of us as well—in terms of a kind of universal principle of reciprocity:

For it has ever been and is, even in materiality, a reciprocal world. "If ye will be my people, I will be thy God." [cf. Jer. 7:23, etc.] If ye would know *good*, do good. If ye would have life, give life. If ye would know Jesus, the Christ, then be like Him; who died for a cause, without shame, without fault yet dying; and through that able to make what this season [reading given on March 28, 1937] represents—*resurrection*!

Resurrection means what? It is reciprocal of that which has been expressed. How hath it been put again by him whom ye knew but disliked (for ye loved Peter the better)?[98] "There is no life without death, there is no *renewal* without the dying of the old." [cf. II Cor. 4:10-11; 6:9] Dying is not blotting out, it is transition—and ye may know transition by that as comes into the experience by those very activities, that "With what measure ye mete it shall be measured to thee again." [cf. Matthew 7:2] That was His life, that is thy life, that is each one's life...

He put away self, letting it be nailed to the cross; that the *new*, the renewing, the fulfilling, the BEING the law, becomes the law!

For it is the law to BE the law, and the LAW is love! Even as He showed in all of His manifestations, in the material experiences in the earth...

...Is it not a reciprocal world? What ye sow, ye reap.

                                                    1158-9 (cf. Gal. 6:7)

We note a few references in the readings to the walk to Emmaus (1158-2). Details, however, are not given. We read elsewhere that "there were about five thousand who saw and heard the words of the Master after the resurrection..." (1877-2; cf. I Cor. 15:1-8)

---

98. The Cayce readings, in their extensive references to the period of the early church, especially that of its first or apostolic generation, are quite clear and specific in their recounting of contemporary criticisms of the person and life style of the apostle Paul (1151-10; 1541-11, A-1).

X
His Abiding Presence

In this essay I do not intend to consider the coming of the Holy Spirit at Pentecost, as that would take us into the period of the early church, an era which I hope to treat separately at another time. This event, of course, is neither historically nor theologically unrelated to the abiding presence of Jesus the Christ. But because of the limitations of space, I must make what may appear to be an arbitrary exclusion.

We have already seen that many of the readings cited in connection with other events in the life of Jesus have much to say also about His abiding presence as the Christ. This is, of course, to be expected in light of the strong concern of the Cayce readings for present appropriation and application. In connection with a quotation of the Great Commission, we read, "positions or power or wealth or fame may be set at naught compared to the peace that came and *is* the understanding of those who have seen and known and become aware of His presence abiding—even as. . . promised, 'Lo, I am with you always, even unto the end of the world.'" (1602-4; cf. Matthew 28:20) "'I will abide with thee always!' Know that this means thy own self! For He hath not left thee comfortless, but the spirit of truth abides ever with thee." (1904-2; cf. John 14:18) ". . . to those of the earth hath He given the message, 'Lo, I am with thee always—*always*!' To *you*, to *all* who have named and do name His Name is given that charge, 'Feed my sheep, care for my lambs.'" (1158-5; cf. John 21:15-17) Here, in typical Cayce fashion, the promise of the Lord's abiding presence is conjoined with a statement of the human responsibilities appropriate to the believing, accepting awareness of that presence.

In the following, at points astonishing, reading we note that the abiding presence of the Christ is in no way to be divorced from the human Jesus. Jesus and the Christ are now one! "...though He wept bodily over Jerusalem, though He sighed with the very blood of His body in Gethsemane, He smiled upon the cross—as He smiles upon thee and gives, '*I* am with thee; be not afraid, it is I—even I who AM the Life, who *am* the Way, who *am* the Word!'" (1158-5; cf. Mark 6:50, etc.; John 14:6) This affirmation of Jesus' smiling even while upon the cross, surprising as it is at first sight, is in fact quite in keeping with other Cayce perceptions of the manner of Jesus on the way to or upon the cross.

As we have seen, the Cayce readings emphasize the importance of a proper human response to these promises of the Lord's abiding presence. This response is to be not only that of external obedience and doing, as when we are told, "they that would know Him [God the Father] must *believe* that He is; and most of all ACT that way!" (1158-9; cf. Hebrews 11:6) The inner, personal and relational dimensions of the response are equally, if not surpassingly, stressed:

> How personal is thy God? Just as personal as ye will let Him be! How close is the Christ as was manifested in the physical body, Jesus? Just as near, just as dear as ye will let Him be!...
> In the love of thine own children, is it those who ask or those who do not ask that make a response? Not that ye love one more than the other; not for impunity, but a reciprocal reaction!   **1158-9**

This is to say that God desires our response in affectionate love and that faith is not a means primarily to gain exemption from punishment or harm (impunity), but the way to the deepest and noblest of personal relationships. To bring this kind of relationship into effect, "...He hath promised to stand in the places of those who are discouraged, disconsolate, who have lost a vision, lost hope..." (2156-1)

The ongoing significance and effects—and reality in personal relationships—of the work of Jesus the Christ is indicated in the following reading: "...the lowly Nazarene was that fulfilling of that priesthood [the priesthood of Israel] in His offering of Himself as the lamb that was not to roll back but to take away the sins of the people. Not as an escape but as an atonement in which each soul does find, would find, the lamb standing *ever* as that offering in its relationships as an individual to its fellow man." (1000-14; cf. Hebrews 4:14-16) "...if the heart is open, He will come and abide with thee." (1770-2) Not only was Jesus resurrected, "...He *is* indeed the resurrection. He is indeed mindful of the sorrows as well as the joys of mankind." (993-5; cf. John 11:25-26)

The Cayce readings make it abundantly clear that in this context we are dealing with universal realities, "For He indeed stands at the door of every consciousness of man that seeks to know; and will enter if man will but open." (1842-1) This is in order that "individuals become aware of the Christ Consciousness and become one with the operative forces of the Christ Spirit abroad in the earth..." (262-29) "Christ is the ruling force in the world...all power in heaven, in earth, is given to Him who overcame." (5749-4; cf. Matthew 28:18) This affirmation, however, of the present lordship of the Christ is seen in the Cayce readings as indeed in structured potentiality effective in relation to all, but inwardly effective only for those who will let it be. "...He hath given His angels charge concerning those that seek to be a channel of blessing to their fellow man; that purge their hearts, their bodies, of every selfish motive and give the Christ— *crucified, glorified*—a place in its stead." (696-3) "...He is of Himself in space, in the force that impels through faith, through belief, in the individual entity. As a spirit entity. Hence not in a body in the earth...[He] may come at will to him who *wills* to be one with [Him], and acts in love to make same possible." (5749-4) "...in the spirit world He seeks to make manifest that sought by those who do His biddings." (5749-4) "Is He abroad today in the earth? Yea, in those that cry unto Him from every corner..." (5749-5; cf. Luke 18:7-8)

Before we proceed further a few words are in order to explain what the Cayce readings mean by the term Christ Consciousness. We read that "The Christ Consciousness is a universal consciousness of the Father Spirit." (5749-4) This is contrasted with "the Jesus Consciousness," which is the application of the Christ Consciousness in the physical body, perfect in Jesus of Nazareth, as yet imperfect in all others (5749-4). At the same time, however, we read that the Christ Consciousness is in every human being in embryonic form, so to speak; this is another way in which Cayce expresses the concept of man's creation in the image of God. The Christ Consciousness is described as "the awareness within each soul, imprinted in pattern on the mind and waiting to be awakened by the will, of the soul's oneness with God..." (5749-14; cf. Gen. 1:27; Rom. 2:15)

Thus we read, "Not so much self-development, but rather developing the Christ Consciousness in self, being selfless, that

He may have *His* way with thee, that He—the Christ—may direct thy ways, that He will guide thee in the things thou doest, thou sayest." (281-20) The application of the Christ Consciousness is elsewhere described as manifesting the fruits of the Spirit; to do this, one is to "Practice, then, brotherly love, kindness, patience, long-suffering gentleness." (3580-1; cf. Gal. 5:22-23) A point of very great significance for everyday living is given in the following statement of the possible and proper protective role of the Christ manifest as Christ Consciousness: "... no influence without or within may be of a detrimental force to self; so long as self will surround self with the thought and ability of the Christ Consciousness, and then practice same in its dealings with its fellow man." (2081-2) Another reading, we should note, specifically identifies the Christ Consciousness with the Master Jesus (3459-1).

If we ask how we may receive or participate in this Reality, how we may open ourselves aright, the answer is, "Through searching, seeking, humbling thyself before the throne of grace and mercy, as was manifested in Him; acknowledging Him as thy Lord, thy Master, yea thy elder brother. He has given also, 'If ye open I will come and abide with thee.'" (2845-1; cf. Rev. 3:20) "... He may be approached by those who in sincerity and earnestness seek to know Him—and to be guided by Him. As He has given, by faith all things are made possible through belief in His name." (5749-4; cf. Mark 10:27, etc.)

In several instances the readings give answers to specific questions of this kind, like, for example, "... how may I contact Him so that I see Him and hear Him speak?" (5749-4) The answer given in this reading is, "The making of the will of self one with His will makes a whole attunement with Him. He *will*, with the making of self in accord and desiring same, speak with thee, 'Be not afraid, it is I.'" (cf. Mark 6:50, etc.) Elsewhere we are told: "Making the will, the desire of the heart, one with His, believing in faith, in patience, all becomes possible in Him, through Him to the Father; for He gave it as it is." (5749-4) "... He comes again in the hearts and souls and minds of those that seek to know His ways... those that call on Him will not go empty-handed... Yet *here* ye may hear the golden sceptre ring—ring—in the hearts of those that seek His face." (5749-5) "... thy brother, thy Savior, thy Jesus, thy Christ... would come and dwell in the hearts and lives of you all—if you will but let Him, if you will but invite Him, if you will but open thy own heart, each of you, that He may enter and abide with you." (5749-6)

In another reading this theme is expressed succinctly in the following way: "Invite Him, by name, by purpose, by desire, to be thy companion in all that ye do, all that ye say. He rejecteth not those who willingly, honestly, sincerely, invite Him to be with them. As He never rejected an invitation by any as He walked in the earth as an individual, neither does He reject the invitation of a soul that *seeks*—in sincerity—His companionship." (622-6)

Another person was told, "let the theme of the mental body ever be *Jesus*, the Savior, the merciful companion to those who seek to know God's way with men. For He *is* that friend that would ever guide, direct and *accompany* thee, in trials, temptations, in thy joys as well as sorrows." (1173-10)

XI
The Second Coming

As we have noted, the Cayce readings forthrightly affirm the second coming of Jesus the Christ: "... how hath the angel given? 'As ye have seen Him go, so will ye see Him come.' Were those just as words? No." (1158-9; cf. Acts 1:10-11) This manifestation, as we have seen, is to be literally like that of Jesus' ascension; but we also find the statement that it "will only be to those... who look for and expect to see Him as He is." (3615-1; cf. I Thess. 4:16-17) This language seems to imply a mode of manifestation that is not necessarily public or perceptible to all. Yet the manifestation is not to be understood as merely a vague influence; "... He shall come as ye have seen Him go, in the *body* He occupied in Galilee. The body that He formed, that was crucified on the cross, that rose from the tomb, that walked by the sea, that appeared to Simon, that appeared to Philip, that appeared to 'I, even John.'" (5749-4; cf. I Cor. 15:3-8)[99]

In several readings it is stated that "the day of the Lord is indeed at hand." (2156-1) In one reading this statement is explained in the following exchange:

Q-3. What is meant by "the day of the Lord is near at hand"?
A-3. That as has been promised through the prophets and the sages of

---

99. The first-person reference to the apostle John in this quotation is one of the few instances in the readings in which the "source" is willing to reveal its identity. Other sources so identified are the archangel Michael (254-42; 254-66; 294-100), the angel Halaliel (4976-15) and possibly Jesus Himself (993-3; 137-125). It should be emphasized, however, that this kind of phenomenon is extremely rare in the whole corpus of Cayce materials, and that which is ordinarily called "mediumship" is almost totally nonexistent. The only example of the latter of which I know is reading 5756-5, and this experience was not intended nor requested by Cayce.

old, the time—and half time [cf. Dan. 7:25]—has been and is being fulfilled in this day and generation, and that soon there will again appear in the earth that one through whom many will be called to meet those that are preparing the way for His day in the earth. The Lord, then, will come, "even as ye have seen Him go."

Q-4. How soon?

A-4. When those that are His have made the way clear, *passable*, for Him to come. 262-49

The reference in the above reading to the "one" apparently means the same person described elsewhere as the "one who is to be a forerunner of that influence in the earth known as the Christ Consciousness, the coming of that force or power into the earth that has been spoken of through the ages." (5749-5) The name of this "forerunner" is not revealed in the readings, but it is possible to interpret at least this one reading as identifying him with Edgar Cayce himself. The same reading, however, goes on to use more conventional language concerning the second coming, speaking of "those days when He will come in the flesh, in the earth, to call His own by name." In reference to the return, another reading says, "*Then* shall the Christ Spirit be manifest in the world . . . " (262-29)

To return to the issue of the time, we note the following: "The time no one knows. Even as He gave, not even the Son Himself. *Only* the Father [cf. Mark 13:22, etc.]. Not until His enemies— and the earth—are wholly in subjection to His will, His powers." (5749-2) But then in answer to the further question, "Are we entering the period of preparation for His coming?" the same reading says, "Entering the test period, rather." Another reading, given in the context of discussion of changes in the earth predicted for the second half of the twentieth century, states, "these will begin in those periods in '58 to '98, when these will be proclaimed as the periods when His light will be seen again in the clouds." (3976-15; cf. Mark 13:26, etc.) Beyond this the Cayce readings give us no further details as to time.

We find in one of the Cayce readings a kind of millenarian view. The question was asked, "When Jesus the Christ comes the second time, will He set up His kingdom on earth and will it be an everlasting kingdom?" The answer was as follows: "Read His promises in that ye have written of His words, even as I gave. He shall rule for a thousand years. Then shall Satan be loosed again for a season." (5749-4; cf. Rev. 20:7-10) This, again (see footnote 99), is one of the very few cases in the Cayce readings in which the speaker is revealed to be other than Edgar Cayce's own subconscious self. Here the speaker would seem to be the John who wrote the book of the Revelation. With regard, however, to the millennial phenomena, no further information is given.

The general posture of the Cayce readings is to combine hopeful anticipation of the future with positive emphasis upon present possibilities. Thus we read:

> ... if ye will believe that He is, ye may experience. For as many as have named the name, and that do unto their brethren the deeds that bring to them (to you) that closeness, oneness of purpose with Him, may know—ye, too—in body, in mind, that He *lives* TODAY, and will come and receive you unto Himself, that where He is there ye may be also...
> For thy Christ, thy Lord, thy Jesus, is nigh unto thee—just now!
> 5749-6 (cf. Hebrews 11:6; Matthew 25:31-46; John 14:3)

This dual emphasis is revealed in yet another reading:

> Then again He may come in body to claim His own. Is He abroad today in the earth? Yea, in those that cry unto Him from every corner; for He, the Father, hath not suffered His soul to see corruption; neither hath it taken hold on those things that make the soul afraid. For, He *is* the Son of Light, of God, and is holy before Him. And He comes again in the hearts and souls and minds of those that seek to know His ways.
> These be hard to be understood by those in the flesh, where prejudice, avarice, vice of all natures holds sway in the flesh; yet those that call on Him will not go empty-handed...
> 5749-5 (cf. Gal. 5:19-21; Rom. 10:12-13)

XII
Theological Interpretations

The Cayce readings do not hesitate to make larger or comprehensive theological interpretations and statements when necessary. Thus, "remember that the whole Gospel of Jesus Christ is: 'Thou shalt love the Lord thy God with all thy mind, thy heart and thy body; and thy neighbor as thyself.' Do this and thou shalt have eternal life." (2072-14) We also find the following: " ... the whole duty of man in any experience is to show forth the love the Father has shown, in the manner and in the way as to bring hope to those that—from the material things—have lost sight of the promises to the children of men." (1469-1)

In the course of this essay many readings have been quoted which contain theological interpretations of the meaning of the person and work of Jesus the Christ. In this section I shall attempt to bring these into a more specific focus, especially by bringing together readings or statements from readings which purpose to do this very thing.

One reading combines in a few words the cosmic range of that meaning and its effects in the personal lives of individuals. The reference is to "that activity [of Jesus the Christ] that *changed*—as it were—the course of the stars in their movement about the earth, and that becomes in the hearts and souls of men that hope which *quickens* as the water of life, that heals as does the touch of His hand upon the brow, that awakens as does the kind word spoken to those that are in doubt and fear." (587-6)[100] We read that the birth of the Christ Child was "for *all* the peoples!" (1152-3)

---

100. As we have seen to be so common in the Cayce readings, this statement regarding Jesus the Christ is immediately followed by an interpretation of its meaning that calls for comparable action from His followers and at the same time involves personal fellowship with Him. "For this is His teaching, 'As ye do it unto the least of my brethren ye do it unto me.'" (587-6; cf. Matt. 25:40)

In another reading we have the statement that "in Him is indeed the light that lightens the world..." (1010-12; cf. John 1:9) This statement, however, is immediately followed, in typical Cayce fashion, by its corollary, "...only in just living His way may we indeed be like Him. Only may the awareness come in being that character of individual, with that purpose, that attitude which He manifested ever." Then we are given in brief vignette form a summary of the character of Jesus: "Though He came to His own and His own received Him not, never—*never*—did He rail at them! Never did He manifest any other than just gentleness, kindness, brotherly love, patience, with those who were the most unkind." (1010-12; cf. John 1:11) As a Canadian missionary friend of mine, Ian MacLeod, has said more than once in my hearing, Jesus warned people, He never threatened them. Incidentally, the last words of the above quotation would normally, and properly, be referred to Galatians 5:22-23. The Cayce readings, however, affirm that Jesus Himself, and His loved ones, also taught specifically what the fruits of the Spirit are: "...they bring hope where none has been, they bring cheer where confusion has existed, they bring the longings for peace where turmoil or misunderstanding has existed; and the result becomes more and more...the peace that makes the heart glad, that brings the renewing of hope, that brings the understanding of joy unabated in the lives and the hearts of all that *will* come and take of the water of life freely. For the spirit and the bride say 'Come, and whosoever *will* let him take of the water of life freely.'" (1158-10; cf. Rev. 22:17)

We have seen in the section on the cross and resurrection of Jesus the Christ that the central significance of Jesus' work was its redemptive character for others. That is, although certain aspects of this work were for the benefit of Jesus Himself, the primary significance lay in its value as a vicarious substitutionary atonement for others. And we have seen that the effect of that work of "...Christ, who took upon Himself the burden of the world" (262-3), was and is universal in its scope. For this and other reasons the Cayce readings also specifically refer to Jesus as God, "For Jesus, the Christ, as God, is the same yesterday, today and forever!" (1152-3; cf. Hebrews 13:8)[101]

At the same time, the readings affirm that Jesus "became

---

101. The perceptive reader may already have noticed that the theological understanding manifested in the Edgar Cayce readings is especially close to much of the thought of the author of the Biblical book of Hebrews, as it is to that of the author of the Johannine literature.

indeed the Son—through the things which He experienced in the varied planes [in the earth and in supernal realms] as the development came to the oneness with the position in that which man terms the Triune." (5749-3) This was the result of "the development of that first entity of flesh and blood through the earth... " (5749-3) This is to say that we are dealing with a process of moral and spiritual development to the end that He "became... the Son" and thus a part of the Trinity. "He, through all, grew to where [it could be said of Him], 'This is my beloved son; hear ye him,' for He hath the words of life." (262-82; cf. Mark 1:11; John 6:68)[102] This emphasis upon Jesus' worthiness to be called the Son because He "developed" or "grew" to the point of manifesting fully the fruits of that status is to some extent reminiscent of the emphasis of the writer of Hebrews, who wrote, "Although he was a Son, he learned obedience through what he suffered, and being made perfect he became the source of eternal salvation to all who obey him, being designated by God a high priest after the order of Melchizedek." (Hebrews 5:8) The apostle Paul also seems to have something of the same thought in mind, as indicated in his use of the language of "designation": "the gospel concerning his Son, who was descended from David according to the flesh and designated Son of God in power according to the Spirit of holiness by his resurrection from the dead, Jesus Christ our Lord." (Rom. 1:3-4) We may properly recall that Paul elsewhere speaks of Jesus as "the image of the invisible God, the first-born of all creation." (Col. 1:15) These last phrases seem to correspond precisely with the Christology of the Cayce readings.

This then is the background for the series of statements in the readings which emphasize the uniqueness of Jesus' person, status and role. "... He is the Way, He is the Truth, the Light, and no other name is given under heaven whereby man may be made whole, or whereby man may know his true relationships to God." (1152-3; cf. John 14:6; Acts 4:12) As we have already seen, this kind of statement in the Cayce readings is not to be understood in a mechanical or exclusivistic way, as if verbal repetition of a name or any other external performance constitutes an authentic and effective religious posture. In its main thrust the Bible itself, with its Hebraic perception of the "name" as designative of the whole person, forthrightly rejects such an interpretation; and we note

---

102. We read elsewhere, "The soul is an individual, individuality, that may grow to be one with, or separate from, the Whole." (5749-3) Jesus of Nazareth had grown to be "one with... the Whole."

later in the Biblical Acts of the Apostles that the author—and probably Peter also—took steps to insure that Acts 4:12 not be understood in any narrowly exclusivistic sense (cf. Acts 10:34-35; 14:15-17). Furthermore, the Cayce readings insist that "God calls on man everywhere to seek His face, through that channel that may be blessed by the Spirit of the Son—in whatsoever sphere this may take its form." (364-9) This language, of course, means that to every human being some spiritual channel is available that may be blessed by the Son—and therefore be consonant with His name—even though that channel may not bear the name of Christian. It is in this context of understanding that we are to read that "There's only one Master" (3545-1) and "there *is* a light in Israel..." (774-5)

Therefore we also read, "know today there is no other than that found in the admonition given by Jesus of Nazareth, Jesus the Christ—'If ye believe in God, believe also in me.'" (2629-1; cf. John 14:1) He is "*the* only one; for, as He gave, 'He that climbs up any other way is a thief and a robber.'... there *is only* one..." (364-9; cf. John 10:1) The Cayce readings have a further distinction to make: "CHRIST is not a man! *Jesus* was the man; Christ the messenger; Christ in all ages, Jesus in one, Joshua in another, Melchizedek in another..." (991-1) But the readings do not put Jesus, Joshua and Melchizedek all on precisely the same level. The spiritual or soul entity is the same; yet, on the basis of the moral and spiritual development noted above, there is a perfection of union of Jesus and the Christ which does not obtain comparably in the other cases. And, given the high view of man— even more, the view of the entity who became Adam and then Jesus of Nazareth—expressed in the Cayce readings, ontological discontinuity between the man Jesus and the universal Christ Consciousness is not as sharply perceived as in some traditional or contemporary Christological formulations. In any case, the union which issued in Jesus the Christ made possible cosmically effective activity for the redemption and salvation of all mankind which had not been possible in any other way or through any other historical or supernal persons.

This view of the cosmic uniqueness of the person and work of Jesus the Christ is affirmed, however, in such a way as to assign to personages and movements outside the Judeo-Christian tradition some, and in certain cases not a little, value and meaning in the larger saving work of God in the world (which theologians, often with much narrower scope of meaning, have called the history of salvation). Even though the work of Jesus Himself in His previous incarnations is not to be considered as precisely the same in kind or degree as that in His role as Jesus of Nazareth, we note that He "influenced either directly or indirectly all those forms of philosophy or religious thought that taught God was One." (364-9) We read that this entity who became Jesus "associated with—in the meditation or spirit of . . . " (364-9) Gautama the Buddha.[103] These words should be interpreted, I believe, so as to affirm that the Buddha's perception of the Dharma was such as to include him in the category of those who taught that God is One.

Furthermore, the point is made that in subsequent historical developments in Judaism, Hinduism, Buddhism, Confucianism, Platonism and Islam, there has "been added . . . much from that as was given by Jesus in His walk in Galilee and Judea." (364-9) The Cayce readings give no blanket approval to all that has been said and done in these historical movements. They simply affirm that as an accessible Reality "In all of these, then, there is that same impelling Spirit." Their historical founders or subsequent leaders "are as teachers or representatives . . . " to be duly respected but not to be considered comparable, in either person or role, with the Master, Jesus the Christ, even though "the Spirit of the Master, the Spirit of the Son, was manifest—as was given—to each in their respective sphere . . . for, as has been given, there *is only* one—the others are as those acting in the capacity of the thought that was given to them through that same power, that 'In the last days has He spoken unto us through the Son, as one born out of due season.'" (364-9; cf. Hebrews 1:1; I Cor. 15:8) The other great figures of man's religious pilgrimage have been but as "stepping-stones" to the higher knowledge of the Son of God in the lives of men. In Jesus the Christ is found the supreme Advocate with the Father (262-14). Thus we are told, "Pray rather to the Son, the Father through the Son, that He walks with thee—and He *will* walk and talk with thee. Be *not* satisfied with ANY other . . . *He* is the Way; there is no other." (5749-4) " . . . Jesus, the Christ . . . to whom all honor and all glory are due . . . " (1158-5) " . . . Jesus *is* the one who was promised from that day [when the Lord God said to Eve], '—and her seed shall bruise his head.'" (2067-1; cf. Gen. 3:15) That is, Jesus who became the Christ is the central figure in the history of universal salvation.

---

103. For my own views on this theme the reader is invited to consult my *Gautama the Buddha, an Essay in Religious Understanding* (Grand Rapids, Michigan: Wm. B. Eerdmans Publishing Co., 1974), pp. 153-208.

2

With the above as general background, let us attempt a survey of the theological interpretations of Jesus the Christ found in the Edgar Cayce readings; it is hoped that this survey will constitute at least a partial recapitulation of the whole. As we have seen, "in the beginning God moved and mind, knowledge, came into being—and the earth and the fulness thereof became the result of same." (5000-1) "... God moved and said, 'Let there be light,' and there was light, not the light of the sun, but rather that of which, through which, in which every soul had, has, and ever has its being. For in truth ye live and move and have thy being in Him." (5246-1; see also 3508-1; cf. Gen. 1:1, 3; Acts 17:28)

God is described as Universal Consciousness (2823-1); He is "that which is everlasting; which is and can be only constructive..." (1493-1) God is also perceived as "good," (1580-1; cf. Mark 10:18, etc.) as "all-inclusive love," (2110-1) which in a uniquely pure way was manifested by Jesus the Christ, He "who took upon Himself the burdens of the world..." (2110-1; see also 1497-1; cf. I John 4:16) This manifestation of divine love by Jesus, however, lies not only in Jesus' expression of the same quality of love as the Father's, but in the fact that the entire event constituted by Jesus the Christ is the consequence of activity of the Father, for "... God so loved the world as to give—give—His only begotten Son, who took on the form of flesh that He might know the manner of man's experience in the earth..." (276-2; cf. John 3:16) He is "the very gift" of the Father (1504-1). The Father's love is infinite (1158-14; cf. Matthew 5:45); Jesus the Christ is, was, and "EVER WILL BE the expression, the concrete expression..." of that love (696-3). He is "the manifested love of an All-Wise, All-Merciful Father..." (823-1) and for this reason "no soul has been left without that access to the throne of mercy and grace through which each soul—as the promise has been given—may be at-one with those Creative Forces that are found in Him who has given, 'If ye love me ye will keep my commandments, and I will come and abide with thee,' and ye shall have peace in thine inner self that passeth understanding to those that know Him not." (823-1; cf. John 14:15, 18, 27; Phil. 4:7)

In the Edgar Cayce readings the Godhead is frequently described as triune; "the Godhead is the Father, the Son, the Holy Spirit." (1348-1) We are informed of the interrelationship of the "Members" of the Trinity in the statement that the ideal mode of human cooperation is "just as in Father, Son and Holy Spirit."

(2396-2) Indeed, "the Father, the Son and the Holy Spirit are One..." (1597-1); as we have seen, the basic oneness of God is a central thesis of the readings. This, however, is a oneness capable of bearing distinctions within it, "capable of manifestation in the varied planes of development" (5749-3), with the word "individual entity" even being used of each "Member" of the Trinity. The relationship of the human body, mind, and soul is frequently used to indicate this combination of oneness and distinction within the Trinity (1597-1; 1348-1; 2559-1).

We find, however, the further assertion that we are dealing here with human concepts, that "man's concept of the Godhead is three-dimensional—Father, Son and Holy Spirit." (4035-1) This is not to say that the concept has no relationship to reality; it is rather the human perception of the Godhead as this is knowable in a three-dimensional world, "three-dimensional activity in a three-dimensional world" (2283-1), the components of which world are frequently cited in the readings as "time, space and patience." (4035-1) Thus, it is asserted that since man—the soul of man—"may think in an eight-dimensional consciousness... the universal consciousness manifested or expressed in the three-dimensional as Father, Son, Holy Spirit... might be manifested or indicated in many more..." dimensions in other realms than the earth (3037-1; see also 3188-1). This is, of course, to say no more than sensitive theologians have long been saying, viz., God is more than our human theologies are able adequately to state (cf. Rom. 11:33-36). The Cayce readings, incidentally, occasionally make references to the vastness of the universe, to "the other chambers of God's universe..." to the fact that "we pass from one room to another, from one consciousness to another" and these are "but stepping-stones to the greater consciousness which He would have each soul attain in its relationships with and usage of its fellow men." (2282-1) "... the earth is that speck, that part in creation where souls [previously created] projected themselves into matter..." (5755-2) "... *the earth is only an atom in the universe of worlds!*" (5749-3)

The primary theological issue, however, is, of course, the nature of the relationship of Jesus of Nazareth to the Divine Trinity, for "in the beginning was the Word, and that Spirit, that Christ Spirit *was* the Word." (524-2; cf. John 1:1) As we have seen, the emphasis of the Cayce readings is that Jesus "became the Son" and therefore can be called God. The further question is then whether there was a time when the entity who became Jesus of Nazareth and came, rightly, to be called the Christ was not a part of the Trinity. The answer is both yes and no. Yes, in the sense that He was created, both in the primal sense of creation as a soul and in the sense of creation as the first man (1158-5; 2072-4; 5749-3). Yet even at this point the Cayce readings consistently affirm a uniqueness. "...that entity, that *soul* called Jesus...is...the only begotten, the first-born, the first to know flesh, the first to purify it." (1158-5; cf. Col. 1:15) Not only is He "the elder brother to all who are *born* in the earth..." but He is also known "as the maker, as the creator, as the first, as the last; as the beginning, as the end of man's soul's experience through the earth and throughout the spheres of consciousness in and about the earth." (1158-5; cf. Rev. 22:13) He is the Son of man *par excellence* and therefore is also "the Son of God, the Son of the First Cause, making manifest in a material body." (5749-3)

For this reason the answer is also no; that is, the entity who became Jesus was also "a part of the Creator..." (2072-4) from the beginning. He was "the portion of God that manifests." (1158-5) This is at least in part possible because of the high view of man in the Cayce readings, that "each soul is a son of God..." (5252-1)[104] But this statement is immediately followed in this particular reading by the addition: "...but He was the first; the light, the way, the truth, the high priest of the soul of men, the brother in mind and body; that we as individuals might know the Father-God." The readings thus in effect tell us that Jesus was both God and man from the beginning, but that as man He became the perfect man and, as such, the perfect instrument of the Father for the redemption of mankind.

3

The reasons for Jesus' becoming the Christ are given in considerable abundance, but it is necessary to recall that in the Cayce readings the pre-existence of not only the Christ is affirmed. *All* souls have pre-existed from the beginning of creation; "all souls in the beginning were one with the Father. The separation, or turning away, brought evil." (262-56) In the Cayce readings, of course, this "separation" denotes not an ontological phenomenon—as though the fact of distinct consciousness, or

---

104. We read elsewhere that "each soul—not the body but the soul—is the image of the Maker..." (2246-1; cf. Gen. 1:27) We are "the offspring of the Creative Forces..." created to be companions therewith (2428-1). "The soul of each individual is a portion then of the Whole, *with* the birthright of Creative Forces to become a co-creator with the Father, a co-laborer with Him" (1549-1) and thus "a channel of blessing to others..." (3161-1)

creation itself, constituted evil—but a primarily ethical phenomenon, therefore a "turning away." And the Father has willed from the beginning that no soul should perish. In order that every individual entity should be "in peace, in harmony, build those purposes whereunto it hath been called, or whereunto the spirit of truth has purposed in an entity's consciousness" (2812-1; cf. II Peter 3:9), God has prepared the way, of which we find the culmination in Jesus the Christ.

According to the Cayce readings, there are various aspects and a variety of meanings to the whole of the Christ event. On the one hand, we read, "As man found himself out of touch with that complete consciousness of the oneness of God, it became necessary that the will of God, the Father, be made manifested, that a pattern be introduced into man's consciousness. Thus the Son of man came into the earth, made in the form, the likeness of man; with body, mind, soul. Yet the soul was the Son, the soul was the Light." (3357-2) This is to affirm the role of Jesus in providing the perfect pattern of God's will and also to say that the soul of Jesus was indeed one with the Second Person of the Divine Trinity, the primal Light. In the same passage, on the other hand, we read of the specifically redemptive aspect of Jesus' work: "For, all men (and He was a man) have fallen short of the glory of God. Only in Him, through Him, by Him may one attain to that true sonship, that true fellowship, that true relationship to the Creative Forces or God." He is "that One that has been given into the world to become the Savior, the Redeemer of the world." (413-3) One might say that the person and work of Jesus the Christ represent the will and action both of the Father and of Jesus Himself. Thus we read, "the Christ Consciousness in the earth was manifested through the lowly Nazarene; that came in order that man—through His example, His love, His patience, His hope manifested, through the attributes of the Spirit that He exemplified in His activity both as to word and as to precept—might choose, as He, to do that which is right, that which is just, that which is sincere, that which is honest in the activities one with another." (272-9)

"...the Christ Child was born into the earth as man; one born in due season, in due time, in man's spiritual evolution, that man might have a pattern of the personality and individuality of God Himself." (5758-1; cf. Col. 1:15; Hebrews 1:3) This same reading affirms that "ye have been justified once for all, through the Christ Consciousness that ye seek." But that there be no misunderstanding, that we may then take up our own responsibility, we read, "each individual must do unto others as he would have his brother, the Christ, his God, the Father, do unto him; and indeed, then, apply first, last and always His 'Forgive, O God, as I forgive others. Find fault in me, O God, as I find fault in my brother.'" (5758-1; cf. Matthew 6:14-15) However, He "came into the earth that we through Him might have eternal life." (1747-5; cf. John 3:16) Elsewhere we read that He put on flesh "that He might become the *way* through which man might find his way home—*home!*" (849-18)[105] We see "...God as manifested in the Christ Child..." (849-18) Another passage, in addressing a thirty-year-old woman, says, "Did not the Son of man descend even from the presence of the Father into the earth, and then into hell itself, that...all might know He walks and talks with thee, my child, if ye will but listen to the voice from within!" (295-9; cf. Eph. 4:8; I Peter 3:18-19) We find frequent references to, or paraphrases of, a famous Pauline passage: "Jesus, the Christ...who made His life of *no* estate, that others might *know* the love and the Fatherhood of God, that He, the Christ, might become the Living Way, the Approach to the Father..." (294-71) He "thought it not robbery to make Himself equal with God, yet put on flesh..." (849-18; cf. Phil. 2:5-7)

We read that "...He manifested in flesh that the evil forces, as manifest in the relationships of individuals as one to another, may be eradicated from the experience of man." (1293-1) There are frequent references to Jesus' having overcome all the obstacles of man; the Cayce readings consistently reveal Jesus as Christus Victor, victor over the forces of evil of every kind, in every form. "...He overcame the flesh, the death, and evil—the devil...He passed through the garden, the cross, the grave, hell, and rose in the *newness* of all being put *under* submission; for having overcome He *became* the Way, the Light, the *Savior.*" (288-30) And because He overcame, we, too, by abiding in Him, "may overcome the world also." (3051-2; see also 3508-1; cf. John 16:33; 17:15; 15:5) Elsewhere we read that He "overcame sin, error, dis-ease, disease and even death itself in the material plane ... " (479-1)

It is specifically said that "In the *cross* He *became* the Savior...In the *cross* He overcame..." (793-2) But the background of the event of the cross and the basis of His overcoming was His "surrendering all power unto Power itself, surrendering all will unto the will of the Father; making of self

---

105. We also note reference to "the way of the cross that leads home." (3347-1)

then a channel..." (1152-1)[106] "...though He were the Son, yet learned He obedience through the things which He suffered. He used, then, that which was necessary in the experience in the earth as periods of suffering, as periods of rejection, even by His own that He had called, that were His friends; not as stumbling stones but as stepping-stones to make for thee, for the world, that access for each soul, for the closer relationship of the Father, through the Son, to the children of men." (2600-2; cf. Hebrews 5:8) This means, as we have seen, that the cross of Jesus the Christ is the focus of His whole life, and the resurrection its fruit. We read elsewhere, "He has attained the Christ Consciousnes in giving of Himself. Though able in mental and physical to lay aside the cross, He accepted same, offering self as the sacrifice; that ye might have an advocate in the Father. Thus are ye saved, by grace." (3459-1; cf. Eph. 2:8) "For the blood as of the perfect man was shed... that there might be made an offering once for all..." (1504-1; cf. Hebrews 7:27) "...His sacrifice was in faith, that it may be counted to thee as righteousness." (683-2; cf. Phil. 3:9) "...He, the Christ, stands in self's stead..." (288-36)

The New Testament word "ransom" is also used to describe the nature of the work of Jesus the Christ. The reference is to the effective power of "the love He showed in *giving* Himself as the ransom for many." (347-2; cf. Mark 10:45, etc.) "...He Himself paid..." (3213-2) The relationship of the person and work of Jesus the Christ to the "older dispensation" and, again, their proper effect in the life of believers is beautifully revealed in the following reading.

...as the law of sacrifice as committed unto men bespoke the coming of the law of mercy that was and is demonstrated in the life of the man Jesus, thy Christ, who offered Himself as the sacrifice once for all, entering into the Holy of Holies where He may meet thee day by day, thou art then indeed—as many as have named the Name—come under the law of mercy, *not* of sacrifice. That is not in the term that no man offers sacrifice, for the life of every soul that seeks in the material world to demonstrate the spiritual life is a life of sacrifice *from* the material angle; but to such that have passed from death unto life, in that law of mercy in naming Him as thine God, thine brother, thine Savior, who has paid, who has offered Himself, thou art passed from death unto life—

106. This reading goes on to suggest that frequent use of the prayer, "Thy will, O God; not mine, but Thine, be done in me, through me," (1152-1) can facilitate a proper application by human beings of this spirit of self-surrender to the Father. This prayer is cited as the prayer of Jesus and of all who would know "a cleansing of the body, of the flesh, of the blood, in such measures that it may become illumined with power from on high..." (1152-1)

and the sacrifice is as *mercy* from thy God to thy brother. Hence he that would despitefully use thee, a kind word is as mercy. As ye would have mercy, show mercy. 262-72 (cf. Matthew 9:13; Hos. 6:6)

The "spirit of Him who gave Himself as the ransom for many" is described as "making self of low estate, as is called in man's realm. All-powerful—yet never using that power, save to help, to assist, to give aid, to give succor to someone who is not in that position to help or aid self..." (900-147) Because He gave Himself as a ransom, "each soul... might know that it has an advocate *with* the Father..." (524-2; cf. I John 2:1) Through Jesus the Christ we are also reconciled with God the Father; "in the day that ye accept Him as thy sacrifice and *live* thyself according to His precepts, *ye* become reconciled—through Him—to the Father, and He—too—walketh and talketh with thee." (2879-1; cf. II Cor. 5:18-19)[107] Thus, in typical Cayce fashion, the work of reconciliation is affirmed to be the work of Jesus the Christ, but it is not seen as being automatic or mechanical in its operation in human life. Without human cooperation it is not truly effective.

4

We are now in a position to move, so to speak, from the cosmic to the contemporary and the "practical." For Jesus the Christ as our Mediator (357-13; 2796-1; cf. I Timothy 2:5; Hebrews 8:6; 9:15) and Advocate is also "the answer to every problem in material existence." (1981-1) "...with every disturbing factor, with every ill, with every way, there has been prepared a manner, a means, a way of escape *in* Him!" (540-3; cf. I Cor. 10:13) "For this experience of every soul in the material plane is not mere chance..." (1786-1) "For to each soul is given that which if applied in the daily life will make that soul one with the Infinite. But keep humble, keep patient, keep in the manner in which the pattern has been given. For it is even as that one manifested in the flesh, even Jesus who became the Christ, who offered Himself that ye through belief, through faith, through the pattern of His life, might find thy way... might find thy true relationship to the Creator, God. And He will not withhold any good thing from thee." (3660-1)

These sentences give some indication of the extensive material

---

107. We also find the expression, He "gave Himself; that the Creative Forces, God, might be reconciled... And thus mercy, through the shedding of blood, came into man's experience." (357-13; cf. Heb. 9:22)

in the Cayce readings descriptive of the Providence of God, a theme which is treated more fully elsewhere in this collection of essays. The point to be emphasized, however, is the total sufficiency of that Providence, made effective through Jesus the Christ, for *all* human situations or predicaments. The affirmation is that "all problems may be met in Him." (288-36) His promise is, "If ye will love me, believing I am able, I will deliver thee from that which so easily besets thee at *any* experience." (987-4; cf. II Thess. 3:3; Phil. 4:7; Rom. 8:28) "Be not afraid, for He will be thy Guide, if ye seek His face." (2851-1; cf. John 14:1) The promise is also made that this guidance reaches into all the details of human life: "I will not leave thee comfortless but my presence, my consciousness, will abide with thee, giving thee the thought, the word, that thou shouldst think at all times." (282-6; cf. John 14:18) We read of "the harbor of safety that is only in Him" (26501); "... He is able to keep thee through any experience." (2116-2)

These promises lead naturally in the Cayce readings to a new focus upon prayer. Rather than having a supine or passive approach to life's problems and challenges, one should be "constant in prayer—knowing and taking, knowing and understanding that he that is faithful is not given a burden beyond that he is able to bear, if he will put the burden upon Him that has given the promise, 'I will be *with* thee; there shall not come that which shall harm thee, if thou will but put thy trust, thy faith, in me.'" (290-1; cf. I Peter 5:7; Mark 16:18) In language reminiscent of the older Protestant evangelicalism, we are told, "Take it to Jesus! He *is* thy answer. He is Life, Light and Immortality. He is Truth and is thy elder brother." (1326-1; cf. II Timothy 1:10)[108] "... His grace, is sufficient—and has been the stay. Hold fast to that, for *that* is good!" (513-2; cf. II Cor. 12:9)

We are told that the Lord "is mindful of the prayers of the children of men." (845-6; cf. Ps. 102:17) Therefore the promise is, "... 'What thou asketh in *my name, believing*, ye shall have. If ye love me, keep my commandments, and I will come and dwell in thine own heart.' That is: 'I will so *fill* your mind, your *mental forces with the good*, until all else shall be driven away.'" (294-71; cf. John 14:13-14; 14:15-16) "... 'I will be with thee *always*, ' if ye

---

108. In this same reading we find approval of the phrase well known to readers of the best seller *In His Steps*, by Charles Monroe Sheldon: "What would Jesus have me do?" The reading insists that this question, rather than "What shall I do?" should be asked regarding all matters "in thy relationships with thy fellow man, in thy home, in thy problems day by day." (1326-1; see also 288-36, A-4)

seek!" (1877-1; cf. Matthew 28:20) In this context we may understand the following injunction: "Meditate, pray, read the Scriptures—these particularly: The 30th of Deuteronomy, the first seven verses of the 6th of Joshua, the 23rd Psalm, the 1st Psalm, the 24th Psalm, the 150th Psalm; and know John 14, 15, 16, 17, not merely by heart—as rote—but as the *spirit* of the law, the love, the grace, the mercy, the truth that is expressed there. For as He hath given, 'The earth, the heavens will pass away, but my words shall *not* pass away!'" (1376-1; cf. Mark 13:31, etc.)[109] As a guide to the best method of prayer, the readings advise, "Enter into the holy of holies with thy God..." who meets us within, in our body (body-physical, body-mental, bodyspiritual), as we are assured in a frequent affirmation of the Cayce readings (1376-1; cf. I Cor. 6:19).

The earthly prayer life of Jesus continues on the cosmic plane: "He makes intercession for man. They that will call upon Him shall not be left empty-handed." (3213-1; see also 938-1; cf. Hebrews 7:25) "And His promise *is*, has been (for He changeth not): 'Though ye may be afar off, if ye call I will hear—and answer speedily.'" (2524-3; see also 3902-2 and 2900-2; cf. Acts 2:39; Luke 18:8; Jer. 33:3)

With reference to this matter of the divine-human relationship, we note the perhaps surprising affirmation that "... He, thy God, thy Christ, is conscious of and hath need of thee..." (5064-1) "First be conscious of this—that the Lord hath need of thee with thy faults, with thy virtues." (3685-1) This thesis, however, becomes comprehensible in the light of the insistence of the Cayce readings that the original purpose in creation was God's desire for companionship (1567-2). Therefore the message of the following passage is in order.

How beautiful the face of those whom the Lord, the Christ, smiles upon! He would walk and talk with thee, my children, if ye will but put away from thy mind those things and conditions that ye feel are in the

---

109. With regard to the essence of the content of the Bible, we note the following reading. Quoting Jesus' teaching, "To love the Lord with all thy heart, thy mind, thy body, and thy neighbor as thyself!" (cf. Mark 12:29-31, etc.) the reading goes on to say, "This is the whole will of the Father to His children. The rest of that recorded in Holy Writ—as may be said by man in his relationships, in meeting the problems every day, every age, every experience—is merely the attempt to explain, to analyze, to justify or to meet that saying, that truth..." (2524-3) In this context of emphasis upon the great ethical principles which are said to express the divine will, we note the statement, "He set no rules of ethics, other than 'As ye would that men should do to you, do ye even so to them,' and to know 'Inasmuch as ye do it unto the least of these, thy brethren, ye do it unto thy Maker.'" (357-13; cf. Matthew 7:12, 25:40)

way. For, they are as naught compared to the great love that He has bestowed upon His brethren.

How beautiful the face, how lovely the clouds! In His presence abide; ye *every one* of you are before Him just now. His face is turned toward thee, His heart and hand is offered you. Will ye not accept Him just now? How glorious the knowledge of His presence should awaken in the hearts of you, for He is *lonely* without thee; for He has called each of you by name. Will ye fail Him now?   254-76

5

In a real sense, anything that might be said after the last excerpt is but an appendage or afterthought. A few more words, however, are in order as a brief explanation. Our God, and our Christ, has need of us to "be a witness for [our] Maker" in the specific "material activities in which [we] might enter into..." (5064-1) This means, in other words, we are to participate in the work of God in the world, even in His vast program and activity of universal redemption and restoration.

In the Edgar Cayce readings, however, perception of and participation in this vision and activity of vast cosmic scope do not necessarily imply what the world in common parlance might call some "big deal." We are told to "be a channel of blessing to others..." for this "is that purpose for which each soul has come into conscious activity in a material world." (3161-1) The reading continues, giving a more detailed picture of what being a "channel of blessing" entails:

Self in the physical grows weary, because you are only human, because you are finite; you have a beginning, you have an end of your patience, your love, your hope, your fear, your desire. These are to be considered also; not as unto self, but when these problems arise know, as He has given, you cannot walk the whole way alone, but He has promised in the Christ Consciousness to give you strength, to give you life and that more abundant [cf. John 10:10]. What, then, is life? God; in power, in might, in the awareness of the strength needed to meet every problem day by day.

Know it is in the little things, not by thunderous applause, not by the ringing of bells, nor the blowing of whistles, that the Son of man comes—humble, gently, kind, meek, lowly—for "He that is the greatest among you serveth all."   3161-1 (cf. Matthew 23:11, etc.)

"And He will come again and again in the hearts, in the minds, in the experiences of those that *love* His coming." (1152-1; cf. II

Peter 3:12) The Christ "offers His hand to those who are disturbed in any way, in any manner in any problem; and He promises to give that peace. Not as the world knows peace, but that peace of assurity that you are one with Him." (3165-1; cf. John 14:27)

XIII
Epilogue

We must conclude this study essentially at this point. The Cayce readings affirm, as we have seen, that Jesus the Christ, in the Holy Spirit, continues to be present and to work in the world, especially with and within those who will let Him and invite Him. There is an abundance of materials available about the activities of Jesus' disciples after His resurrection and ascension and after the experience of the coming of the Holy Spirit with power on the day of Pentecost. There seems also to be discernible in the Cayce readings a special concern of Jesus the Christ for His church, even though His activity is definitely not limited to the institutional organizations thereof. Indeed, He who "was set as the Head of the church is the church." (262-87) That is, as "An *individual* soul becomes aware that it has taken that Head, that Son, that Man even, to be the intermediator. That [association of such individuals in communion with the Head] is the church; that is what is spoken of as the Holy Church." (262-87)

Elsewhere we read, "the true church is within you, as the Master, as the Christ gave... 'I to *you* am the bridegroom—I to *you* am the church. The kingdom is within *you!*'" (452-7; cf. Luke 17:21; Mark 2:19; John 3:29) The Cayce readings, therefore, refuse to give any *ultimate* spiritual significance or value to ecclesiastical organizations, structures or personages, but they did advise several people that it is well and wise to become associated with such. "A particular church organization is well. For it centers the mind." (3350-1) "As to the organization, choose that—not as a convenience for thee but where ye may serve the better, whatever its name..." (3342-1) "Render unto the church that which is the church, whether in creed or in organization, but render unto God, unto Christ, the *service* that is His in whatever field of activity thou goest." (556-1) "As He has given, it will ever be found that Truth—whether in this or that schism or ism or cult—is of the one source. Are there not trees of oak, of ash, of pine? There are the needs of these for meeting this or that experience. Hast thou chosen any one of these to be the *all* in thine usages in thine own life? Then, all will fill their place. Find not fault with *any*, but rather show forth as to just how good a pine, or ash, or oak, or *vine* thou art!" (254-87)[110]

---

110. In one reading, an individual asked whether she should become affiliated with the Association for Research and Enlightenment, Inc., the organization primarily engaged in the work of doing research in and disseminating information about the Edgar Cayce readings; she was told, "This is identified with the Christian forces. Hold fast to the basic principles in that phase of same." (1152-11)

THE EDGAR CAYCE LEGACIES

Among the vast resources which have grown out of the late Edgar Cayce's work are:

The Readings: Available for examination and study at the Association for Research and Enlightenment, Inc.,(A.R.E.®) at Virginia Beach, Va., are 14,256 readings consisting of 49,135 pages of verbatim psychic material plus related correspondence. The readings are the clairvoyant discourses given by Cayce while he was in a self-induced hypnotic sleep-state. These discourses were recorded in shorthand and then typed. Copious indexing and cross-indexing make the readings readily accessible for study.

Research and Information: Medical information which flowed through Cayce is being researched and applied by the research divisions of the Edgar Cayce Foundation. Work is also being done with dreams and other aspects of ESP. Much information is disseminated through the A.R.E. Press publications, *A.R.E. News* and *The A.R.E. Journal.* Coordination of a nationwide program of lectures and conferences is in the hands of the Department of Education. A library specializing in psychic literature is available to the public with books on loan to members. An extensive tape library has A.R.E. lectures available for purchase. Resource material has been made available for authors, resulting in the publication of scores of books, booklets and other material.

A.R.E. Study Groups: The Edgar Cayce material is most valuable when worked with in an A.R.E. Study Group, the text for which is *A Search for God,* Books I and II. These books are the outcome of eleven years of work by Edgar Cayce with the first A.R.E. group and represent the distillation of wisdom which flowed through him in the trance condition. Hundreds of A.R.E. groups flourish throughout the United States and other countries. Their primary purpose is to assist the members to know their relationship to their Creator and to become channels of love and service to others. The groups are nondenominational and avoid ritual and dogma. There are no dues or fees required to join a group although contributions may be accepted.

Membership: A.R.E. has an open-membership policy which offers attractive benefits.

For more information write A.R.E., Box 595, Virginia Beach, Va. 23451. To obtain information about publications, please direct your query to A.R.E. Press. To obtain information about joining or perhaps starting an A.R.E. Study Group, please direct your letter to the Study Group Department.